THE PHILOSOPHY OF SYMBOLIC FORMS

Volume 2

Published on the Louis Stern Memorial Fund

By the same author

THE PHILOSOPHY

OF SYMBOLIC FORMS

VOLUME TWO: MYTHICAL THOUGHT

BY ERNST CASSIRER

translated by Ralph Manheim

introductory note by Charles W. Hendel

NEW HAVEN AND LONDON: YALE UNIVERSITY PRESS

Published in Great Britain, Europe, and Africa by
Yale University Press, Ltd., London.
Distributed in Latin America by Kaiman & Polon,
Inc., New York City; in Australasia by Book & Film
Services, Artarmon, N.S.W., Australia; in India by
UBS Publishers' Distributors Pvt., Ltd., Delhi;
in Japan by John Weatherhill, Inc., Tokyo.

Contents

Introductory Note by Charles W. Hendel

Das Mythische Denken, the second of three books comprising *Die Philosophie der Symbolischen Formen,* was originally published in 1925. A reprinting in German has recently (1953) been issued by *Die Wissenschaftliche Buchgemeinschaft,* Darmstadt, and Bruno Cassirer, Oxford.

The translation of the first volume, *Language,* is prefaced with a factual account of the publication of the series on Symbolic Forms, showing its relation to other writings and its central importance in the whole corpus of Cassirer's philosophical works. Our Introduction in that book is also intended to serve for all three volumes of the translation. It is an essay in interpretation, an attempt, first of all, to see the creative advance of Cassirer's mind. The "rich sources of inspiration" which he acknowledged are examined in relation to the attainment of his own distinctive conception of symbolic form. His other writings, early and late, are drawn upon, too, for the light they shed on "the making of Cassirer's 'image-world.'" Having thus undertaken to interpret Cassirer's consummate masterwork in terms of his own thinking, we then ventured to indicate its significance in a section entitled "Consequences for Philosophy." The whole introductory essay, however, claims to be no more than "one symbolic rendering," and the reader is advised to consult the various interpretations in *The Philosophy of Ernst Cassirer* (1949), the Library of Living Philosophers, edited by Paul Arthur Schilpp.

In the present Preface it is appropriate to recall the observation made in the Preface to the first volume that the possibilities of Cassirer's theory "were not yet completely realised" (p. xi). For as *An Essay on Man* (1944) reveals, Cassirer was still en route toward a goal which he called the "phenomenology of human culture" (p. 52). His philosophy was not a finished system, even though his use of the term "phenomenology" and the expressed appreciation in the present book of Hegel's purpose in the famous *Phenomenology of the Spirit* may mislead a reader into supposing that Cassirer had pretensions similar to those of the full-fledged Hegelian system. This was certainly not the case, and it is important to draw particular attention to the fact. In each of his three books Cassirer investigates the function and meaning of symbolic form in some special context, that is, with reference to the phenomena of language, myth, and science. While each work is thoroughgoing, systematic, and comprehensive in the treatment of its subject matter, taken together they still do not constitute an exhaustive and definitive rationale of the whole of culture. Hence Cassirer's own explanatory comment in *Theoria* should be kept in mind: "The 'Philosophy of Symbolic Forms' cannot and does not try to be a philosophical system. . . . All it attempted to furnish were the 'Prolegomena' to a future philosophy of culture." [1] The word "prolegomena" directs our thought away from Hegel to Kant, the author of *A Prolegomena to Every Future Metaphysic*.

But with that statement in *Theoria* Cassirer went on to use language which has still other historical associations. "Only from a continued collaboration between philosophy and the special disciplines of the 'humanities' (*Geisteswissenschaften*) may one hope for a solution of the task." [2] This recalls the Descartes of the *Discourse on Method* announcing his new method in a volume that included his scientific studies in dioptric, meteorology, and geometry, presented simultaneously as first samples of results achieved. Descartes held forth the prospect there of further applications of his method, to medicine for instance, and he invited the collaboration of the learned toward a fuller achievement of his ideal of the unity of knowledge. In like manner Cassirer presented his own general theory of symbolic form in conjunction with three particular scientific studies which were also initial samples of new knowledge achieved in the fields under investigation, and other thinkers were being invited to try out the theory in different universes of discourse. He might have gone on to do so himself, as was previously suggested in our Preface to the first volume (p. xi).

We should consider more particularly now Cassirer's concern with mythical thought and how he came to write this book on it. There seems to have been a certain element of chance as well as logic in his choosing of myth to be the second subject of his investigation. For instance, he could have embarked at that time on an elaboration of the symbolic forms involved in art, since he was richly dowered with artistic appreciation and especially a love of poetry and music. But the fact was that his appointment

1. *Theoria* (1938), p. 173, cited and translated by Carl H. Hamburg in *The Philosophy of Ernst Cassirer*, p. 119.
2. *Ibid.*

as professor at the new University of Hamburg in 1919 put an unexpected, and possibly diverting, opportunity in his way. Dr. F. Saxl, in a memorial address, has described an occasion in the year 1920 when he first showed Cassirer the materials of the Warburg Institute:

> He was a gracious visitor, who listened attentively as I explained to him Warburg's intentions in placing books on philosophy next to books on astrology, magic, and folklore, and in linking the sections on art with those on literature, religion, and philosophy. The study of philosophy was for Warburg inseparable from that of the so-called primitive mind: neither could be isolated from the study of imagery in religion, literature, and art. These ideas had found expression in the unorthodox arrangement of the books on the shelves.
>
> Cassirer understood at once. Yet, when he was ready to leave, he said, in the kind and clear manner so typical of him: "This library is dangerous. I shall either have to avoid it altogether or imprison myself here for years. The philosophical problems involved are close to my own, but the concrete historical material which Warburg has collected is overwhelming." [3]

One can readily appreciate why Cassirer spoke as he did, for he was then preoccupied with other projects, as is clear from the fact that during the following year two books appeared, *Zur Einsteinschen Relativitätstheorie* and *Idee und Gestalt,* the latter consisting of essays on the poets Goethe, Schiller, Hölderlin, and Kleist. Moreover, the first volume on symbolic forms, *Language,* was still in preparation. Yet Cassirer's confession that he feared the dangerous temptation of the Warburg Library reveals that he was primed within to be tempted, and in due course he did yield—"when the time was ripe for him, Cassirer became our most assiduous reader." [4] Out of those studies came this book on mythical thought, which was a second demonstration of the fruitfulness of his theory of symbolic form.

Here Cassirer became a pioneer—there was no "partially blazed trail" as in language, he tells us in his own Preface. For linguistic theory had already undergone a long development, and in thinking his way through it Cassirer had had a congenial guide in Wilhelm von Humboldt, who like himself had been steeped in the philosophy of Kant. There was, however,

3. *The Philosophy of Ernst Cassirer,* pp. 47–8.
4. *Ibid.,* p. 49.

one philosopher of the Kantian tradition of special help to him, namely Schelling, who had recognized myth as an essential modality of human thought. Schelling imparted to his reader an appreciative attitude toward mythical thinking. But all the rest had to be done by Cassirer himself, the defining of the categories, so to speak, the delineating of the forms involved in mythical construction. Yet when he ended his work he simply expressed the modest hope that he had really "started on a road leading to insight."

While Cassirer was still engaged in writing this book he also gave expression to his abundance of ideas in collateral studies, *Die Begriffsform im Mythischen Denken* (1922) and *Der Begriff der Symbolischen Form im Aufbau der Geisteswissenschaften* (1923), both published by the Warburg Institute. Here he was venturing to advance beyond myth to the "humanities." In the following year, moreover, he contributed an essay to the *Festschrift für Paul Natorp* entitled "Zur Philosophie der Mythologie," which then became part of his general introduction to *Das Mythische Denken* in 1925. And in the same year *Sprache und Mythos* appeared.[5] Clearly Cassirer had done well with the resources of the Warburg Library: the phenomenology of myth had now become an integral and indispensable part of his whole philosophy.

The subject remained, indeed, ever vital to Cassirer. Nineteen years after the publication of *Das Mythische Denken*, when Cassirer was living in the United States, he composed in English his *Essay on Man*, in which the discussion of myth and religion (ch. 7) was actually made to precede that of language (ch. 8), thus reversing the sequence in the *Philosophy of Symbolic Forms*. In the *Essay*, too, one sees the other forms of culture ranged in order—after the chapter on language come those on art, history, and science. Close upon the *Essay* came the *Myth of the State*, issued posthumously in 1946, a fragment of which had been published in *Fortune*, Vol. 29 (June, 1944). Part I of that book contains a series of chapters, "The Structure of Mythical Thought," "Myth and Language," "Myth and the Psychology of Emotions," "The Function of Myth in Man's Social Life"— all of which may profitably be read after the present volume, for they represent in summary Cassirer's latest reflections. It would not be amiss if the reader should proceed to the concluding portion of the *Myth* to see what Cassirer has to say about "The Myth of the Twentieth Century."

Finally, attention may be drawn to the essays of the above-mentioned volume, *The Philosophy of Ernst Cassirer*. The contributors were scholars

5. Translated by Susanne K. Langer, *Language and Myth* (1946).

who had already found Cassirer's philosophy very rewarding. Their essays illuminate by their criticism—their differences as well as agreement—both Cassirer's treatment of myth as a form of culture and his theory of symbolic form in general. The following essays are especially pertinent:

Robert S. Hartman, "Philosophy of Symbolic Forms."

Folke Leander, "Further Problems of Symbolic Forms."

M. F. Ashley Montague, "Cassirer on Mythological Thinking."

Susanne K. Langer, "On Cassirer's Theory of Language and Myth."

Wilbur M. Urban, "Cassirer's Philosophy of Language."

James Gutmann, "Cassirer's Humanism."

David Bidney, "On the Philosophical Anthropology of Ernst Cassirer . . ." (secs. 8–15).

Helmut Kuhn, "Cassirer's Philosophy of Culture."

Fritz Kaufmann, "Cassirer's Neo-Kantianism and Phenomenology, VI" (containing a brief résumé, pp. 833–4, of Martin Heidegger's review of *Das Mythische Denken* in *Deutsche Literaturzeitung,* 1928, pp. 1000–12).

CHARLES W. HENDEL

September 23, 1954

Preface

A CRITIQUE OF THE MYTHICAL CONSCIOUSNESS, as attempted in this second volume of the *Philosophy of Symbolic Forms,* cannot but seem hazardous and even paradoxical in the present state of critical, scientific philosophy, for since Kant the term *critique* has presupposed the reality of a fact toward which the philosophical question is directed. Philosophy does not create this fact with its intrinsic significance but, having found it to be present, investigates it for the "conditions of its possibility." But is the world of myth a fact of this kind, in any way comparable to the worlds of theoretical cognition, art, or ethical consciousness? Or does this world not belong from the very outset to the sphere of illusion—from which philosophy as a doctrine of essences ought to remain aloof, in which it should not lose itself but from which, on the contrary, it should ever more clearly free itself? Indeed, the history of philosophy as a scientific discipline may be regarded as a single continuous struggle to effect a separation and liberation from myth. The forms of this struggle vary according to the stage of theoretical self-consciousness, but the general trend stands out plainly.

However, it was above all in philosophical idealism that a sharp distinction between philosophy and myth was first fully achieved. Once philosophical idealism arrived at its own concept, once it saw the idea of "being" as its original and fundamental problem, the world of myth was relegated to the realm of nonbeing. And ever since ancient times Parmenides' dictum forbidding pure thought to concern itself with nonbeing, ἀλλὰ σὺ τῆσδ' ἀφ' ὁδοῦ διζήσιος εἶργε νόημα, has stood as a warning at the gates of this realm. While philosophy has long seemed to view such a warning as obsolete insofar as perception is concerned, it is still resolutely on its guard against this danger in the case of the world of myth. Ever since pure thought conquered its own province and its own autonomous laws, the world of myth seems to have been transcended and forgotten. It is true that a change seemed to set in after the Romantics rediscovered this vanished world at the beginning of the last century and Schelling attempted to give it a definite status within the system of philosophy. But the newly awakened interest in myth and the basic problems of comparative mythology was of greater benefit to material research than to a philosophical analysis of the *form* of myth. Thanks to the work done in this field by systematic religious science, ethnology, and the history of religions, we have abundant material at our disposal. But today the systematic problem of the *unity* of this manifold and heterogeneous material is seldom raised, and where a solution is attempted, it is only by the methods of developmental psychology and general ethnic psychology. Myth is held to be "explained" if its origin in certain basic predispositions of "human nature" can be made plausible and if light can be thrown on the psychological rules in accordance with which it develops out of this original germ. If logic, ethics, and aesthetics have been able to assert their own systematic independence against all attempts to explain and derive them in this way, it is because they could evoke an independent principle of objective validity which resisted reduction to psychology. Myth, on the other hand, seems to lack any such support and therefore to be forever at the mercy of psychology and psychologism. Insight into the conditions of its origin has seemed to be synonymous with the negation of its independent reality. To understand it was seemingly to demonstrate simply its objective nullity, to see through the universal but wholly "subjective" illusion to which it owes its existence.

And yet in this "illusionism" that keeps cropping up—both in the theory of mythical representations and in attempts to establish a theory of aesthetics and art—there lurks a grave problem and a grave danger, as soon as we consider the matter from the point of view of a system of cultural forms. For if these forms as a whole really do constitute a systematic unity, the fate of any one of them is closely bound up with that of all the others. Every negation applying to the one must therefore, directly or indirectly, extend to the others—any destruction of a single member of the system endangers the whole if this whole is regarded not as a mere aggregate but as an organic, spiritual unity. And that myth has so crucial a significance in and for this whole becomes evident the moment we consider the genesis of the basic forms of cultural life from the mythical consciousness. None of these forms started out with an independent existence and clearly defined outlines of its own; in its beginnings, rather, every one of them was shrouded and disguised in some form of myth. There is scarcely any realm of "objective spirit" which cannot be shown to have entered at one time into this fusion, this concrete unity, with myth. The productions of art and knowledge—the contents of ethics, law, language, and technology—all point to the same basic relationship. The question of the origin of language is indissolubly interwoven with that of the origin of myth: the one can be raised only in relation to the other. Similarly, the problem of the beginnings of art, writing, law, or science leads back to a stage in which they all resided in the immediate and undifferentiated unity of the mythical consciousness. Only very gradually do the basic theoretical concepts of knowledge (space, time, and number) or of law and social life (the concept of property, for example) or the various notions of economics, art, and technology free themselves from this involvement. And this genetic relationship is not understood in its true significance and depth so long as it is regarded as merely genetic. As everywhere in the life of the human spirit "becoming" points back to a "being" without which it cannot be understood, without which it cannot be recognized in its peculiar "truth." And in its modern scientific form, psychology itself discloses this relationship, for here it has become increasingly evident that genetic problems can never be solved solely by themselves but only in thoroughgoing correlation with structural problems. The emergence of the specific cultural forms from the universality and indifference of the mythical consciousness can never be truly understood if this primal source itself remains an unsolved riddle—if instead of being recognized as an independent mode of spiritual *formation* it is taken as a formless chaos.

Seen in this way the problem of myth bursts the bonds of psychology and psychologism and takes its place in that universal domain of problems which Hegel designated as "phenomenology of the spirit." That myth stands in an inner and necessary relation to the universal task of this phenomenology follows indirectly from Hegel's own formulation and definition of the concept. "The spirit which . . . knows itself as developed spirit," he writes in the preface to the *Phänomenologie des Geistes,*

is science. It is its reality and the realm that it builds itself in its own element. . . . The beginning of philosophy presupposes or postulates that consciousness shall realize itself in this element. But this element itself gains its completion and intelligibility only through the movement of its unfolding. It is pure spirituality as the universal that has the mode of simple immediacy. . . . Science for its part demands that self-consciousness raise itself into this ether, in order that it may live with and for science. Conversely, the individual has the right to demand that science provide him with a ladder at least to this level, that it show him this level in himself. . . . When the general point of view of consciousness—that of knowing objective things as standing opposed to itself and itself likewise in opposition to them—is taken as applicable to science, then the element of science is a thing of the remote distance where consciousness is no longer in possession of itself. Each of these two parts seems to the other a perversion of the truth . . . whatever science may be in its own nature, it seems quite absurd in its relation to immediate self-consciousness; self-consciousness has the principle of its reality in the immediate certainty of itself, but the certainty of science lies outside itself and consequently seems to wear the aspect of unreality. For that reason science must unite such an element of the unreal with itself, or rather show that there is such an element and how it pertains to science. For in default of such reality science is a mere content as such, a purpose which for the present is only an inner something, not spirit but only spiritual substance. This thing in itself must manifest itself and become "for itself," which means simply that self-consciousness must equate it with itself. . . . Knowledge as it is at first or *spirit* in its immediacy is the spiritless, the *sensory consciousness*. To become true knowledge, or to produce the element of science that is its pure concept, it must struggle a long way.

These sentences in which Hegel characterizes the relation of science to the sensory consciousness apply fully and precisely to the relation of knowledge to the mythical consciousness. For the actual point of departure for all science, the immediacy from which it starts, lies not so much in the sensory sphere as in the sphere of mythical intuition. What is commonly called the sensory consciousness, the content of the "world of perception"—which is further subdivided into distinct spheres of perception, into the sensory elements of color, tone, etc.—this is itself a product of abstraction, a theoretical elaboration of the "given." Before self-consciousness rises to this abstraction, it lives in the world of the mythical consciousness, a world not of "things" and their "attributes" but of mythical potencies and powers, of demons and gods. If then, in accordance with Hegel's demand, science is to provide the natural consciousness with a ladder leading to itself, it must first set this ladder a step lower. Our insight into the development of science—taken in the ideal, not temporal sense—is complete only if it shows how science arose in and worked itself out of the sphere of mythical immediacy and explains the direction and law of this movement.

And this is no mere requirement of philosophical systems but a need of knowledge and cognition. For knowledge does not master myth by banishing it from its confines. Rather, knowledge can truly conquer only what it has previously understood in its own specific meaning and essence. Until this task has been completed, the battle which theoretical knowledge thinks it has won for good will keep breaking out afresh. The foe which knowledge has seemingly defeated forever crops up again in its own midst. The positivistic theory of knowledge provides a striking example of this. Here the true goal of thought consists in separating the pure, given fact from any subjective admixture of the mythical or metaphysical spirit. Science arrives at its own form only by rejecting all mythical and metaphysical ingredients. And yet, precisely those factors and motifs which Comte thought he had surpassed at the very start remain alive and active in his doctrine. Comte's system, which began by banishing all mythology to the prescientific period or the earliest beginnings of science, itself culminates in a mythical-religious superstructure. And thus it develops that there is no hiatus, no sharp *temporal* dividing line, as asserted in Comte's "law of the three phases," between the theoretical and the mythical consciousness. Science long preserves a primordial mythical heritage, to which it merely gives another form. For the natural sciences it suffices here to recall the centuries-long and still inconclusive struggle to free the concept of force from all mythical components, to transform it into a pure concept of function. And here we are speaking not merely of the continuous struggle attending our efforts to define the *content* of certain basic concepts but of a conflict that reaches deep down into the very form of theoretical knowledge. That no sharp boundary has been drawn between myth and logos is best shown by the recent reappearance of myth in the realm of pure methodology. Today it is openly asserted that no clear logical division can be made between myth and history and that all historical understanding is and must be permeated with mythical elements. If this thesis were sound, history itself and the entire system of the cultural sciences grounded in it would be withdrawn from the sphere of science and relegated to that of myth. Such infringements of myth on the province of science can only be prevented if we can know myth in its own realm, can know its essence and what it can accomplish spiritually. We can truly overcome it only by recognizing it for what it is: only by an analysis of its spiritual structure can its proper meaning and limits be determined.

The clearer this general task became to me in the course of my investigation, the more plainly I perceived the difficulties in the way of carrying it out. Here even less than in connection with the problems of linguistic philosophy treated in the first volume could one speak of any sure path ahead or even of a partially blazed trail. While in the case of language a systematic inquiry could—from the standpoint of method if not of content—start from Wilhelm von Humboldt's fundamental inquiries, there was no such methodological guide in the field of mythical thinking. The plethora of material which the research of the last decades has brought to light offered no compensation; on the contrary, it made the lack of systematic insight into the "inner form" of mythology all the more evident. It is hoped that the present study has started on a road leading to such an insight—but I am far from supposing that it has reached the end of it. It by no means claims to be conclusive and is at most a beginning. Only if the formulation of the problem here attempted is taken up and carried further, not only by systematic philosophy but also by the various scientific disciplines—in particular ethnology and the history of religions—is it to be hoped that the aim which this inquiry originally set itself will progressively be achieved.

The first drafts and other preliminary work for this volume were already far advanced when through my call to Hamburg I came into close contact with the Warburg Library. Here I found abundant and almost incomparable material in the field of mythology and general history of religion, and in its arrangement and selection, in the special stamp which Warburg gave it, it revolved around a unitary, central problem closely related to the basic problem of my own work. This circumstance gave me fresh encouragement to continue along the road on which I had started, for it suggested that the systematic task undertaken by my book is intimately related to tendencies and demands which are the outgrowth of concrete work in the cultural sciences themselves and of an endeavor to deepen and reinforce their historical foundations.

In my use of the Warburg Library Fritz Saxl provided me with helpful and expert guidance. I am convinced that without his active aid and the lively personal interest which he showed in my work from the very start many difficulties in obtaining and penetrating the material could scarcely have been overcome. I should not wish this book to appear without this expression of my heartfelt gratitude.

ERNST CASSIRER

Hamburg, December, 1924

Introduction: The Problem of a Philosophy of Mythology

PHILOSOPHICAL inquiry into the contents of mythological consciousness and attempts at a theoretical interpretation of these contents go back to the very beginnings of scientific philosophy. Philosophy turned its attention to myth and its configurations earlier than to the other spheres of culture. This is understandable from both a historical and a systematic point of view, for it was only by coming to grips with mythical thinking that philosophy could arrive at the first clear formulation of its own concept and its own task. Wherever philosophy sought to establish a theoretical view of the world, it was confronted not so much by immediate phenomenal reality as by the mythical transformation of this reality. It did not find "nature" in the form which it acquired (not without the decisive contribution of philosophical reflection) in a later period characterized by a highly developed consciousness of experience; on the contrary, the whole material world appeared shrouded in mythical thinking and mythical fantasy. It was these which gave its objects their form, color, and specific character. Long before the world appeared to consciousness as a totality of empirical things and a complex of empirical attributes it was manifested as an aggregate of mythical powers and effects. And when the specific philosophical trend emerged, it could not immediately detach its concept of the world from this view, which was its source and native spiritual soil. For a long time afterward philosophical thought preserved a middle position, as though undecided between a mythical and a truly philosophical approach to the problem of origins. This twofold relation is clearly and pregnantly expressed in the concept which early Greek philosophy created for this problem, the concept of the ἀρχή. It designates the zone between myth and philosophy—but a boundary which as such partakes of both the spheres it divides, representing the point of indifference between the mythical concept of the beginning and the philosophical concept of the "principle." As philosophy advanced in methodological self-awareness and beginning with the Eleatic school pressed toward a "critique," a κρίσις within the concept of being itself, the new world of the logos which now arose and asserted its autonomy was increasingly differentiated from the world of mythical forces and mythical gods. But though the two worlds could no longer *coexist,* an attempt was made to justify the one as at least a preparatory stage of the other. Here lies the germ of that allegorical interpretation of myths which is present in all ancient science. If myth was to retain any essential significance at all, if, in the face of the new philosophical concept of being and the world, it was to embody even a mediate truth, it would apparently have to be recognized as foreshadowing and preparing the way for this very concept of the world. The images of mythology, it was held, must conceal a rational cognitive content which it is the task of reflection to discover. Especially after the fifth century, the century of the Greek "enlightenment," this method of interpreting myths was persistently practiced. It was in this interpretation of myths that the Sophists particularly liked to practice and test the force of their newly founded "doctrine of wisdom." They "explained" myths by transposing them into the conceptual language of popular philosophy, by interpreting them as a cloak for a speculative, scientific, or ethical truth.

It is no accident that the very Greek thinker in whom the characteristic figurative power of mythology was still alive was foremost in opposing this view, which leads to a total leveling of the mythical world. Plato maintained an attitude of ironical superiority toward the interpretation of myths attempted by the Sophists; he regarded them as a mere exercise of the wit, a gross and labored wisdom (ἄγροικος σοφία, *Phaedrus* 229D). Goethe once praised the simplicity of Plato's view of nature, compared with the boundless multiplicity, fragmentation, and complexity of modern theories; and in Plato's view of myth we find the same characteristic trait. For in his contemplation of the mythical world Plato never dwells on the endless details; this world seems to him a self-contained whole which he juxtaposes to the whole of pure knowledge in order to measure one by the other. His philosophical manner of "rescuing" myth, which at the same time meant its philosophical annulment, was to view it as a form and stage of knowledge itself—a form necessarily pertaining to a specific realm of objects, of which it is the adequate expression. Thus for Plato, too, myth harbors a certain conceptual content: it is the conceptual language in which alone the world of becoming can be expressed. What never is but always becomes, what does not, like the structures of logical and mathematical knowledge, remain identically determinate but from moment to moment manifests itself as something different, can be given only a mythical representation. Thus, sharply as the mere *probability* of myth is distinguished from the *truth* of strict science, this very distinction creates a close methodological tie between the world of myth and that world which we call the empirical reality of phenomena, the reality of nature. Here the meaning of myth is quite beyond anything merely material; it is conceived as a specific *function*—necessary in its place—of man's way of knowing the world. Thus understood, it could become a truly creative and formative force in the development of Plato's philosophy. This profound view, to be sure, was not always sustained in the subsequent course of Greek thought. The Stoics and Neoplatonists went back to the old speculative-allegorical interpretation of myths, and through them this method was handed down to the Middle Ages and Renaissance. The very thinker who first communicated the philosophy of Plato to the Renaissance may be regarded as a typical example of this trend: Georgios Gemistos Phethon's exposition of the theory of ideas is so intermingled with his own mythical-allegorical theory of the gods that the two are fused into an inseparable whole.

As opposed to this objectivizing hypostasis of mythical figures in Neoplatonic speculation, modern philosophy has in this point turned more and more to man's subjectivity. Myth became a problem of philosophy insofar as it expresses an original direction of the human spirit, an independent configuration of man's *consciousness*. Anyone aiming at a comprehensive system of human culture has, of necessity, turned back to myth. In this sense, Giambattista Vico, founder of the modern philosophy of language, also founded a completely new philosophy of mythology. For Vico the true unity of human culture is represented in the triad of language, art, and myth.[1] But this idea of Vico achieved full systematic definition and clarity only with the foundation of cultural science by the philosophy of romanticism. Here, as in other spheres, romantic poetry and philosophy opened up roads to each other; it was perhaps in response to an idea of Hölderlin that Schelling, in the first sketch of his system of the objective spirit composed at the age of twenty, called for a union of the "monotheism of reason" and the "polytheism of the imagination," that is, a mythology of rea-

1. Cf. *1*, 149 f.

son.[2] In realizing this aim the philosophy of absolute idealism found itself once again depending on conceptual means created by Kant's critical teaching. The question of origins which Kant had raised for the theoretical, ethical, and aesthetic judgments was applied by Schelling to the realm of myth and the mythical consciousness. As in Kant the question was concerned not with psychological genesis but with pure being and value. Like knowledge, morality, and art, myth now becomes an independent, self-contained world, which may not be measured by outside criteria of value and reality but must be grasped according to its own immanent, structural law. All attempts to explain this world as a mere mediation, a cloak for something else, are forthrightly rejected once and for all. Like Herder in the philosophy of language, Schelling in his philosophy of mythology discards the principle of allegory and turns to the fundamental problem of symbolic expression. He replaces the allegorical interpretation of the world of myths by a tautegorical interpretation, i.e. he looks upon mythical figures as autonomous configurations of the human spirit, which one must understand from within by knowing the way in which they take on meaning and form. This principle, as Schelling's introductory lectures in the *Philosophie der Mythologie* show, is overlooked both by the euhemeristic interpretation which transforms myth into history and by the physical interpretation which makes it a kind of primitive explanation of nature. They do not explain but rather subtilize and deny the distinctive reality which myth possesses for the human consciousness. True speculation takes an exactly opposite road, aiming not at analytical disintegration but at synthetic understanding, and striving back toward the ultimate positive basis of the spirit and of life itself. And myth must be taken as such a positive basis. The philosophical understanding of myth begins with the insight that it does not move in a purely invented or made-up world but has its own mode of *necessity* and therefore, in accordance with the idealist concept of the object, its own mode of *reality*. Only where such necessity is demonstrable is reason, and hence philosophy, in place. The purely arbitrary and accidental cannot provide it even with an object of *inquiry;* for philosophy, the study of essence, cannot establish a foothold in the void, in a sphere which is itself without essential truth. At first sight, to be sure, nothing seems more disparate than truth and mythology; and accordingly no two spheres seem more opposed to each other than philosophy and mythology.

2. Cf. "Hölderlin und der deutsche Idealismus," in my *Idee und Gestalt* (2d ed. Berlin, 1924), pp. 115 ff.

But in this very opposition lies a challenge and a specific task, to discover reason in this seeming unreason, meaning in this apparent meaninglessness, and not as has hitherto been done, by making an arbitrary distinction; that is, by declaring something which one believes to be rational and meaningful to be the essential, and everything else to be mere accident, cloak, or perversion. Our intention must rather be to make the form itself appear necessary, hence rational.[3]

In line with the general conception of Schelling's philosophy this basic purpose must be realized in a twofold direction, toward the subject and toward the object, in regard to the self-consciousness and the absolute. As for the self-consciousness and the form in which it experiences mythology, this form in itself suffices to exclude any theory attributing myth to pure "invention," for such a theory passes over the purely *objective* existence of the phenomenon it is supposed to explain. The phenomenon which is here to be considered is not the mythical content as such but the significance it possesses for human consciousness and the power it exerts on consciousness. The problem is not the material content of mythology, but the intensity with which it is experienced, with which it is *believed*—as only something endowed with objective reality can be believed. This basic fact of mythical consciousness suffices to frustrate any attempt to seek its ultimate source in an invention—whether poetic or philosophical. For even if we admit that the purely theoretical, intellectual content of mythology might in this way be made intelligible, the dynamic, as it were, of the mythical consciousness—the incomparable force it has demonstrated over and over again in the history of the human spirit—would remain completely unaccounted for. In the relation between myth and history myth proves to be the primary, history the secondary and derived, factor. It is not by its history that the mythology of a nation is determined but, conversely, its history is determined by its mythology—or rather, the mythology of a people does not *determine* but *is* its fate, its destiny as decreed from the very beginning. The whole history of the Hindus, Greeks, etc. was implicit in their gods. Hence, for an individual people as for mankind as a whole there is no free choice, *no liberum arbitrium indifferentiae,* by which it can accept or reject given mythical conceptions; on the contrary, a strict necessity prevails. It is a real force that seizes upon consciousness in myth, i.e. a force that is not within its control. True mythology arises out of something independent of

3. F. W. Schelling, *Einleitung in die Philosophie der Mythologie,* in *Sämmtliche Werke* (2 pts. Stuttgart and Augsburg, J. Verlag, 1856), Pt. II, *1,* 220 ff. Cf. pp. 194 ff.

all invention, something indeed which is opposed to invention both in form and substance; it arises out of a process necessary from the standpoint of a consciousness the origins of which are lost in a suprahistorical sphere, a process which consciousness can perhaps resist at certain moments but which as a whole it cannot impede, much less annul. We see ourselves carried back to a region where there is no time for invention, either by individuals or by a people, no time for artificial disguises or misunderstanding. No one who understands what its mythology means to a people, what inner power it possesses over that people and what reality is manifested therein, will say that mythology, any more than language, was invented by individuals. With this realization, Schelling held, philosophical speculation had hit upon the actual vital source of mythology, but it can barely discover this source and cannot explain it further. Schelling expressly claimed it as his special achievement to have replaced inventors, poets, and individuals in general by the human consciousness as the source, the *subjectum agens* of mythology. True, he says, mythology has no objective existence *outside* of consciousness; but even though the mythological process consists solely in determinations of consciousness—that is, in ideas—this process, this succession of representations, cannot have been merely *represented* as such but must *really* have taken place, must really have occurred in consciousness. Thus mythology is not merely a successive series of mythological representations: the successive polytheism which is its empirical content can be explained only if we assume that the human consciousness actually lingered successively on every moment of it. "The gods which followed upon one another really seized successively upon the human consciousness. Mythology as a history of gods could only be produced in life; it had to be experienced and lived." [4]

But if myth is thus shown to be a specific and original *form* of life, it thereby loses all semblance of mere one-sided subjectivity. For "life," in Schelling's view, is neither merely subjective nor merely objective but stands on the exact borderline between the two; it is a realm of indifference between the subjective and objective. The movement and development of mythical representations in human consciousness must correspond to an objective process, a necessary development in the absolute, if this movement is to possess inner truth. The mythological process is a theogonic process: one in which God himself *becomes,* by creating himself step by step as the true God. Each particular stage in this creation, insofar as it can be appre-

4. Schelling, pp. 124 ff.; cf. pp. 56 ff., 192 ff.

hended as a necessary stage of development, has its own significance; but only in the whole, only in the unbroken context of the mythical movement passing through all moments, are its complete meaning and true goal disclosed. Then each particular and contingent phase appears necessary, and hence justified. The mythological process is the process of the truth re-creating and so realizing itself. "Thus, to be sure, it is not truth in the particular moment, for if it were it would require no progression to a successive moment, no process; but the *truth* which is the end of the process, which consequently the process as a *whole* contains complete, generates itself in it and therefore lies—self-creating—in the process."

More closely examined, what determines this development for Schelling is a progress from the unity of God as a merely existing but not conscious unity to a multiplicity from which, through opposition to multiplicity, the true existing and recognized unity of God is gained. The earliest human consciousness to which we can go back must be conceived as a divine consciousness, a consciousness of God: in its true and specific meaning the human consciousness is a consciousness which does not have God outside it but which—though not with knowledge and will, not by a free act of the fancy but rather by its very nature—contains within it a relation to God. "The original man postulates God not *actu* but *natura sua* . . . the original consciousness is nothing other than the consciousness which postulates God in His truth and absolute unity." But if this is monotheism it is only a *relative* monotheism: the God who is here postulated is *one* only in the abstract sense that he is as yet undifferentiated, that there is still nothing with which he can be compared or to which he can be opposed. Only in the progress to polytheism is this "other" achieved: the religious consciousness undergoes a split, a differentiation, an inner alteration, for which the multiplicity of the gods is only a figurative expression. But on the other hand, it is this development which enables man to rise from the relative One to the absolute One which is really worshiped in Him. Man's consciousness had to pass through the cleavage, the "crisis" of polytheism before it could differentiate the true God as such, i.e. Him who remains one and eternal, from the original God whom it now regards as the relative One and only temporarily eternal. Without the second God, without the solicitation to polytheism, there would have been no advance to true monotheism. No doctrine, no knowledge taught man of the original period what God was—"the relation was a real one and could therefore only be a relation to God *in his actuality,* not to God in his essence, hence not to the *true*

God; for the actual God is not *ipso facto* the true one. . . . The God of prehistory is an actual, objective God, in whom the true God *is* but is not known *as such*. Mankind thus worshiped *what it did not know,* a God to which it had no ideal (free), relation, but only an empirical one." To create this ideal and free relation, to transform existing unity into known unity—such is the meaning and content of the whole mythical, or strictly speaking, theogonic process. Herein we see once again a *real objective* relation of the human consciousness to God, whereas all previous philosophy had spoken only of a "religion of reason," i.e. a rational relation to God, and had seen all religious development only as a development of the *idea,* i.e. of representations and thoughts. And with this, according to Schelling, the cycle of enlightenment is complete—subjectivity and objectivity are placed in their proper relationship within myth.

> It is not with things that man has to do in the mythological process, it is *powers arising within consciousness itself that move him*. The theogonic process by which mythology arises is a *subjective* one insofar as it takes place in consciousness and manifests itself by the production of representations: but the causes and therefore the objects of these representations are the *truly* and *essentially* theogonic powers, those powers by virtue of which consciousness originally postulates God. The process consists not merely of *represented* potencies but of those very *potencies* which create consciousness and which, since consciousness is only the end of nature, create nature as well and are therefore actual powers. The mythological process deals not only with natural *objects* but with the pure creative potencies whose original product is consciousness itself. So it is here that our explanation breaks through into objectivity and becomes wholly objective.[5]

This is indeed the highest form of objectivity known to Schelling. Myth has attained its essential truth when it is conceived as a necessary factor in the self-development of the absolute. It has no relation to the "things" of naive realism and represents solely a reality, a potency of the *spirit;* but this does not argue against its objectivity, essentiality, and truth, for *nature* itself has no other or higher truth than this. Nature itself is nothing other than a stage in the development and self-unfolding of the spirit—and the task of a philosophy of nature consists precisely in understanding it and elucidating it as such. What we call nature—and this is already stated in

5. Schelling, pp. 207 ff.; cf. pp. 175 ff., 185 ff.

the system of transcendental idealism—is a poem hidden behind a wonderful secret writing; if we could decipher the puzzle, we should recognize in it the odyssey of the human spirit, which in astonishing delusion flees from itself while seeking itself. This secret writing of nature is now explained from a new angle by the study of myth and its necessary phases of development. The "odyssey of the spirit" has here reached a stage in which we no longer, as in the world of the senses, perceive its ultimate goal through a semi-transparent mist, but see it before us in configurations familiar to the spirit though not yet fully permeated by it. Myth is the odyssey of the pure consciousness of God, whose unfolding is determined and mediated in equal measure by our consciousness of nature and the world and by our consciousness of the I. It discloses an inner law which is fully analogous to the law prevailing in nature but of a higher mode of necessity. Precisely because the cosmos can be understood and interpreted only through the human spirit, hence through subjectivity, what would seem to be the purely subjective content of mythology has at the same time a cosmic significance.

> Not that mythology arose under an influence of nature, for it is rather a withdrawing of the inner life of man from such an influence, but that *in accordance with the same law,* the mythological process passes through the very stages through which nature originally passed. . . . Thus it has not merely a religious but also a *universal* significance, for it is the universal process that is repeated in it; accordingly, the truth contained in the mythological process is a universal truth, excluding nothing. We cannot, as is commonly done, deny the historical truth of mythology, for the process through which it arises is itself a true history, an actual occurrence. Nor can we exclude physical truth from it, for nature is as necessary a period of transition in the mythological as in the universal process.[6]

The characteristic merit and limitations of Schelling's idealism appear clearly in this passage. It is the concept of the unity of the absolute which truly and definitively guarantees the absolute unity of the human consciousness by deriving every particular achievement and trend of spiritual activity from a common ultimate origin. The danger of this concept of unity is however that it will ultimately absorb all concrete, particular differentiations and make them unrecognizable. Thus for Schelling myth becomes a second "nature," because previously nature has been transformed into a

6. Schelling, p. 216.

kind of myth, and its purely *empirical* significance and truth have been absorbed into its spiritual significance, into its function, the self-revelation of the absolute. If we hesitate to take this first step, it would seem that we must abandon the second as well; there seems to be no remaining road to a specific essence and truth, a distinctive objectivity of the mythical. Or is there, perhaps, a means of retaining the question put forward by Schelling's *Philosophie der Mythologie* but of transferring it from the sphere of a philosophy of the absolute to that of critical philosophy? Does it embody both a problem of metaphysics and a purely transcendental problem, which as such is susceptible of a critical-transcendental solution? True, if we take the concept of the "transcendental" in a strictly Kantian sense, it seems paradoxical even to suggest such a question. For Kant's transcendental formulation of the problem limits itself expressly to the conditions under which *experience* is possible. And what manner of experience can be demonstrated through which the world of mythology can be accredited and claim some form of objective truth and validity? If such an objective truth is demonstrable for myth, it would seem to reside in its *psychological* truth and psychological necessity. The necessity with which myth arises in relatively similar forms at specific stages of cultural development seems to constitute its only objective and tangible content. And indeed, since the epoch of German speculative idealism, the problem of myth has been formulated only in this light. Inquiry into the ultimate and absolute foundations of myth has been replaced by inquiry into the natural causes of its genesis: the methodology of metaphysics has been replaced by the methodology of ethnic psychology. True access to the world of mythology seemed to have been opened only after the Schellingian and Hegelian dialectical concept of development had been replaced once and for all by the empirical concept of development. It was now taken for granted that the mythical world was merely an aggregate of "representations"; and it was held that these representations could be explained by the general rules governing all production of representations, namely the elementary laws of association and reproduction. Here myth appeared in an entirely different sense, as a "natural form" of the human spirit, which could be understood simply by the methods of empirical natural science and empirical psychology.

And yet, can we not conceive of a third approach to the mythological "form" which neither seeks to explain the mythical world through the essence of the absolute nor merely reduces it to a play of empirical-psychological forces? If this approach agrees both with Schelling and the psychologists in seeking the *subjectum agens* of mythology solely in the human consciousness, does this compel us to accept either the empirical-psychological or the metaphysical concept of consciousness? Or is there not a critical analysis of the consciousness, distinct from these two views? Modern critical epistemology, the analysis of the laws and principles of knowledge, has detached itself more and more resolutely from the assumptions both of metaphysics and of psychologism. The struggle between psychologism and pure logic in this field seems today to have been finally decided, and we may venture to predict that it will never recur in the same form. But what is true of logic is no less true of all independent forms and all original functions of the human spirit. The determination of their pure content, of what they signify and are, is independent of the question of their empirical genesis and its psychological conditions. We can and must inquire in a purely objective sense into the substance of science, into the content and principles of its truth, without reflecting upon the temporal order in which the particular truths and insights are manifested to the empirical consciousness, and the same problem recurs for all forms of cultural life. We can never do away with the question of their essence by transforming it into an empirical, genetic question. For art and myth as well as cognition the assumption of such a unity of essence implies the assumption of general laws of consciousness which determine all particular formation. In the critical view we obtain the unity of nature only by injecting it into the phenomena; we do not deduce the unity of logical form from the particular phenomena, but rather represent and create it through them. And the same is true of the unity of culture and of each of its original forms. It is not enough to demonstrate it empirically through the phenomena; we must explain it through the unity of a specific "structural form" of the spirit. Here again, as in its approach to knowledge, critical analysis stands between metaphysical deduction and psychological induction. Like the latter, it must always start from the given, from the empirically established facts of the cultural consciousness; but it cannot stop at these mere data. From the reality of the fact it must inquire back into the conditions of its possibility. In these conditions critical philosophy seeks to disclose a certain hierarchical structure, a superordination and subordination of the structural laws of the sphere in question, a reciprocal determination of particular formative factors. To seek a "form" of mythical consciousness in this sense, means to inquire neither after its ultimate metaphysical causes nor after its psychological, historical or social causes: it is solely to seek the unity of the spiritual *principle* by which all its particular configurations, with all their vast empirical diversity, appear to be governed.[7]

And with this the question of the *subject* of myth takes a new turn. Metaphysics and psychology have answered it in opposite senses, metaphysics from the standpoint of theogony, psychology from the standpoint of "anthropogeny." In metaphysics the mythological process is explained as a particular instance, a specific and necessary phase, of the "absolute process"; in psychology mythical apperception is deduced from the general factors and rules governing the production of representations. But is this not fundamentally a recurrence of that allegorical view of mythology which in principle had already been discredited by Schelling's *Philosophie der Mythologie*? Do we not in both cases explain myth by referring it and reducing it to something other than what it immediately is and signifies? "Mythology," writes Schelling,

> is recognized in its truth and hence truly recognized only if it is recognized in its process; and the process which is repeated in it, though in a particular way, is the universal, *absolute* process. The true science of mythology is accordingly that science which represents the absolute process in it. But to represent this process is the affair of philosophy; the true science of mythology is therefore the philosophy of mythology.[8]

Ethnic psychology only replaces this identity of the absolute with the identity of human nature, which always and necessarily brings forth the same elementary mythical ideas. But in thus starting from the constancy and unity of human nature and making it the basis for all its attempted explanations it ultimately falls into a *petitio principii*. For instead of dem-

---

7. It is one of the fundamental achievements of Edmund Husserl's phenomenology to have sharpened once again our perception of the diversity of cultural "structural forms" and to have pointed out a new approach to them, departing from the psychological method. Particularly, the sharp distinction between psychological "acts" and the "objects" intended in them is crucial. Husserl's own development from the *Logische Untersuchungen* (2 vols. Halle, 1913–22) to the *Ideen zu einer reinen Phänomenologie und phänomenologischen Philosophie* (Halle, 1928) makes it increasingly clear that the task of phenomenology, as Husserl sees it, is not exhausted in the analysis of cognition but calls for an investigation of the structures of entirely different objective spheres, according to what they "signify" and without concern for the "reality" of their objects. Such an investigation should include the mythical "world," not in order to derive its specific actuality by induction from the manifold of ethnological and ethnic-psychological experience, but in order to apprehend it in a purely ideational analysis. As far as I can see, however, no attempt of this sort has been undertaken either in phenomenology or in mythological research, where the genetic-psychological approach still holds almost uncontested sway.

8. Pp. 216 ff.

onstrating the unity of the human spirit through analysis it treats this unity as a pre-existing and self-evident datum. But here as in cognition the certainty of systematic unity stands at the end rather than at the beginning; it is not a point of departure but a goal of inquiry. In a critical approach we cannot conclude the unity of the function from a pre-existing or pre-supposed unity of the metaphysical or psychological substrate; we must start from the function as such. If, despite differences in particular factors, we find in the function a relatively constant inner form, we shall not from this form go back to infer the substantial unity of the human spirit; on the contrary, the constancy of inner form seems to constitute this unity. Unity, in other words, appears not as the *foundation* but as another *expression* of this same determination of form, which it must be possible to apprehend as purely immanent, in its immanent significance, without inquiring into its foundations, whether transcendent or empirical. Thus we may inquire into the pure essential character of the mythical function—its τί ἔστι in the Socratic sense—and set this pure form in contrast with that of the linguistic, aesthetic, and logical functions. For Schelling mythology has philosophical truth because in it is expressed not only a thought but a real relation of the human consciousness to God, because it is the absolute, because it is God himself, who here passes from the first potency of "being-in-himself" to the potency of "being-outside-himself" and through it to perfect "being-with-himself." For the opposite view, for anthropogeny as championed by Feuerbach and his successors, it is the empirical unity of *human nature* that is taken as a starting point—as an original causal factor of the mythological process, which explains why under the most diverse conditions and starting at the most diverse points in space and time it develops in essentially the same way. As opposed to these approaches a critical phenomenology of the mythical consciousness will start neither from the godhead as an original metaphysical fact nor from mankind as an original empirical fact but will seek to apprehend the subject of the cultural process, the human spirit, solely in its pure actuality and diverse configurations, whose immanent norms it will strive to ascertain. It is only in these activities as a whole that mankind constitutes itself in accordance with its ideal concept and concrete historical existence; it is only in these activities as a whole that is effected that progressive differentiation of "subject" and "object," "I" and "world," through which consciousness issues from its stupor, its captivity in mere material existence, in sensory impression and affectivity, and becomes a spiritual consciousness.

From this point of view the relative truth of myth is no longer in question. We shall no longer seek to explain it as the expression and reflection of a transcendent process or of certain constant psychological forces. Its objectivity—and from the critical standpoint this is true of all cultural objectivity—must be defined not thing-wise but functionally: this objectivity lies neither in a metaphysical nor in an empirical-psychological "reality" which stands *behind* it, but in what myth itself is and achieves, in the manner and form of *objectivization* which it accomplishes. It is objective insofar as it is recognized as one of the determining factors by which consciousness frees itself from passive captivity in sensory impression and creates a world of its own in accordance with a spiritual principle. If we formulate the question in this sense, the "unreality" of the mythical world can no longer be said to argue against its significance and truth. The mythical world is and remains a world of mere representations—but in its content, its mere *material*, the world of knowledge is nothing else. We arrive at the scientific concept of nature not by apprehending its absolute archetype, the transcendent object behind our representations, but by discovering in them and through them the rule determining their order and sequence. The representation gains objective character for us when we divest it of its accidents and demonstrate in it a universal, objectively necessary law. Likewise, in connection with myth, we can only raise the question of objectivity in the sense of inquiring whether it discloses an immanent rule, a characteristic "necessity." True, we seem limited to an objectivity of low degree, for is this rule not destined to vanish in the face of scientific truth, the concept of nature and of the object gained in pure cognition? With the first dawn of scientific insight the mythical world of dream and enchantment seems to sink into nothingness. And yet, even this circumstance appears in a different light when, instead of comparing the content of myth with the content of scientific cognition, we compare the *process* of the mythical world's growth with the logical *genesis* of the scientific concept of nature. Here we find stages and phases in which the different spheres of objectivization are not yet sharply divided. Indeed, even the world of our immediate experience—that world in which all of us constantly live and are when not engaged in conscious, critical-scientific reflection—contains any number of traits which, from the standpoint of this same reflection, can only be designated as mythical—most particularly, the concept of causality, the general concept of force, which must pass through the mythical intuition of efficacy before dissolving in the mathematical-logical concept of the function. Thus everywhere, down to the configuration of our perceptive world, down to that sphere which from the naive standpoint we designate as actual "reality," we find this characteristic survival of original mythical traits. Little as they correspond immediately to objects, they are nevertheless on the way to objectivity as such, insofar as they represent a concrete and necessary (not accidental) mode of spiritual formation. Thus the objectivity of myth consists primarily in that wherein it seems farthest removed from the reality of things—from the reality of naive realism and dogmatism—this objectivity is not the reproduction of a material datum but is a specific and typical mode of formation, in which consciousness disengages itself from and confronts the mere receptivity of the sensory impression.

Proof of this relationship cannot, to be sure, be attempted from above, by pure construction but presupposes the facts of the mythical consciousness, the empirical material of comparative mythology and comparative religion. The problem of a philosophy of mythology has been vastly broadened by this material, particularly by the increasing mass of data that have come to light since the middle of the nineteenth century. For Schelling, who depended principally on Georg Creuzer's *Symbolik und Mythologie der alten Völker* (1810-23), all mythology was essentially the theory and history of the gods. For him the concept of God and the knowledge of God constituted the *beginning* of all mythological thinking—a *notitia insita* which he takes as his actual starting point. He violently attacked those who made the religious development of mankind begin not with the unity of the concept of God but with the multiplicity of partial, or even initially local, representations, with so-called fetishism or deification of nature, in which the object of worship was not even concepts or kinds, but a particular natural object, e.g. this tree or this river. "No, mankind did not start from such wretchedness, the majestic course of history had quite a different beginning, the dominant tone in the consciousness of mankind was always that great One, who did yet know his likeness, who truly filled heaven and earth, i.e. the universe." [9] Certain modern ethnologists—e.g. Andrew Lang and Wilhelm Schmidt—have attempted to revive Schelling's thesis of a primary "original monothesim" and to support it by abundant material.[10] But the farther they went the more evident became the im-

9. Schelling, p. 178.

10. A summary of this material and an examination of the arguments that have been raised against the theory of Lang is to be found in Wilhelm Schmidt, *Der Ursprung der Gottesidee* (6 vols. Münster, 1926-35). Eng. trans. by H. J. Rose, *The Origin and Growth of Religion* (London, Methuen, 1931). See also Schmidt, *Die Stellung der Pygmäenvölker in der Entwicklungsgeschichte des Menschen* (Stuttgart, 1910).

possibility of reducing the configurations of the mythical consciousness to a unity and deriving them from it genetically as from a common root. Animism, which was the dominant trend among mythologists for a considerable time after the appearance of Tylor's basic work, found this root not in the primary intuition of God but in the nature of the primitive psyche; but today this interpretation seems to have been increasingly discredited. More and more clearly we see the beginnings of a mythological view which assumes a distinct concept neither of God nor of the psyche and personality, but starts from a still entirely undifferentiated intuition of magical efficacy, of a magical force inherent in things. Here we encounter a characteristic stratification within mythical thinking—a superordination and subordination of its structural elements, which is significant in a purely phenomenological sense, even for those who do not venture to identify the temporally first elements, the empirical *beginnings* of myth on the strength of it.[11] Thus a new direction of inquiry leads us to an insight which Schelling looked upon as the basic postulate of his philosophy of mythology, the insight that no factor in the development of mythical thinking, no matter how unimportant, fantastic, or arbitrary it may seem, may be regarded as insignificant, that each factor must be assigned to that specific place within mythology as a *whole,* where it takes on its ideal meaning. This whole contains an inner truth of its own, for it designates one of the paths by which mankind has advanced both to its specific self-consciousness and to its specific objective consciousness.

2

Even among purely empirical investigators of myth and comparative mythology a tendency has been evident for some time not merely to survey the field of mythical thinking but to describe it as a unitary form of consciousness with its specific and characteristic features. This is in keeping with the return from positivism to idealism that has been manifested in other fields, such as natural science and linguistics. The striving for a unitary physical view of the world has given new depth to the general principles of physics, and in ethnology the notion of a universal mythology

11. On the theory of so-called pre-animism cf. Konrad T. Preuss, "Der Ursprung der Religion und Kunst," *Globus, 86* (1904); and Vierkandt, "Die Anfänge der Religion und Zauberei," *Globus, 92* (1907). Cf. particularly Robert R. Marett, "Pre-Animistic Religion," *Folk Lore, 46* (1900), 162–182; and "From Spell to Prayer," *Folk Lore, 54* (1904), 132–165, reprinted in Marett's *The Threshold of Religion* (London, 1909).

has been particularly fruitful among those engaged in specialized research. The only possible issue from the maze of conflicting views seemed to lie in the discovery of unitary trends and fixed points of orientation. But as long as students of mythology thought they could simply derive these trends from the *objects* of mythology, as long as they started from a classification of mythical objects, it soon became evident that the fundamental conflicts could not be resolved. Inquiry revealed basic mythical motifs, a clear kinship of myths found all over the world, even where considerations of time and space seemed to preclude any direct borrowing. But as soon as attempts were made to differentiate these motifs, to characterize some as original and others as derived, the controversy again became acute. It was agreed that ethnology in conjunction with ethnic psychology must strive to determine the universal principles underlying the particular manifestations of myth.[12] But no sooner did the unity of these principles seem assured than it was lost amid the diversity of concrete objects. There was psychological mythology and nature mythology—and nature mythology in turn included different trends, each of which strove stubbornly to prove that some particular object in nature was the heart and source of myth formation. The basic principle of these views was that each particular myth—insofar as it was susceptible of scientific "explanation"—must be linked with some specific natural being or occurrence, because this was the only way of controlling the production of arbitrary fantasies and guiding research into strictly objective channels.[13] But the hypotheses resulting from this supposedly objective method proved in the end no less arbitrary than the hypotheses of the fantasy. The older form of storm and tempest mythology now shared the field with astral mythology, which soon disintegrated into the various forms of sun, moon, and planet mythology. As each of these forms strove, to the exclusion of the others, to assert itself as the sole principle of explanation, it became increasingly clear that association with specific spheres of empirical objects could by no means guarantee an objective unity of explanation.

Another path to a unitary source of myth seemed to open when this unity was defined as spiritual rather than natural, as implying the unity of a cultural sphere rather than a sphere of objects. If it were possible to

12. Cf. Paul M. A. Ehrenreich, *Die allgemeine Mythologie und ihre ethnologischen Grundlagen* (Leipzig, 1919); Heinrich Lessmann, *Aufgaben und Ziele der vergleichenden Mythenforschung* (Leipzig, 1908).

13. Ehrenreich—e.g., pp. 41, 192 ff., 213—makes this the postulate of every explanation of myth.

show that a particular cultural sphere was the common source of all the
basic mythical motifs, the center from which they gradually spread over
the whole earth, the inner relationship and systematic order of these motifs
would seem to be explained. However obscured this relationship might
be in the derived and mediate forms, it would be evident as soon as we
returned to the relatively simple conditions of the ultimate historical
sources. Older theories—such as Benfey's theory of folk legends—sought
the home of the most important mythical motifs in India. But a conclusive
proof of the historical relationships and historical unity of myth formation
seemed possible only when Babylonian culture was gradually opened up to
research. Now the question of the original, unitary structure of mythology
seemed answered along with the question of the original home of human
culture. According to the "Pan-Babylonian" theory, myth could never have
developed an inherently consistent *weltanschauung* if it had issued solely
from primitive magical conceptions or dream lore, from animistic beliefs or
other superstitions. Such a weltanschauung could develop only from a
specific concept, an *idea* of the world as an ordered whole—and this condition was fulfilled only in Babylonian astronomy and cosmogony. This
historical orientation seemed for the first time to open up the possibility
of viewing myth no longer as a pure product of fantasy but as a self-
contained *system*, intelligible in itself. Here we need not go into detail
regarding the empirical foundations of this theory; [14] but what makes it
noteworthy in a purely methodological sense is that on closer examination
it proves by no means to be a merely empirical statement concerning the
historical origins of *myth* but is a kind of a priori assertion about the
direction and aim of mythological *research*. The assumption that all myths
are of astral origin, that they are ultimately "calendar myths," was the
very cornerstone of the Pan-Babylonian method; its supporters made this
assumption the "Ariadne's thread" which alone could lead us through the
labyrinth of mythology. Repeatedly this general postulate was called upon
to fill gaps in empirical documentation and proof—but what it actually

14. For the arguments in support of Pan-Babylonianism cf. Hugo Winkler, *Himmelsbild
und Weltenbild der Babylonier als Grundlage der Weltanschauung und Mythologie aller Völker*, Der alte Orient und die Bibel, Vol. 3 (Leipzig, 1901); idem, *Die Weltanschauung des
alten Orients* (Leipzig, 1905); idem, *Die babylonische Geisteskultur* (Leipzig, 1907). See also,
Alfred Jeremias, *Handbuch der altorientalischen Geisteskultur* (Leipzig, 1913). For a critique
of Pan-Babylonianism see Morris Jastrow, *Religious Belief and Practice in Babylonia and
Assyria* (London and New York, 1911), pp. 413 ff.; Carl Bezold, *Astronomie, Himmelsschau
und Astrallehre bei den Babyloniern* (Heidelberg, 1911).

showed more and more clearly was that no definitive solution to the basic question of the unity of the mythological consciousness could be arrived at by the methods of purely empirical and historically objective inquiry.

More and more firmly the insight established itself that even if a merely factual unity of the basic mythical configurations could be demonstrated beyond any doubt, this unity would still represent a puzzle unless it could be referred back to an underlying *structural* form of the mythical fantasy and mythical thinking. But for those students of myth who did not wish to depart from the sphere of mere descriptive study, the only available concept by which to characterize this structural form lay in Bastian's theory of "folk ideas." From the standpoint of principle this theory possesses one important advantage over all purely objective hypotheses: it is concerned no longer merely with the contents and objects of mythology but also with the *function* of myth itself. Bastian sets out to show that the basic direction of this function is always the same, regardless of the diverse conditions under which it is exercised and the variety of the objects it draws into its sphere. Thus, from the very outset, the desired unity is transposed from the outside in, from the reality of things to the reality of the human spirit. But even this ideality is not unequivocal as long as it is determined solely by the categories of psychology. When mythology is spoken of as an integral spiritual possession of mankind and its unity imputed to the unity of the human psyche and its activity, the unity of the psyche immediately disintegrates into a multiplicity of different potencies and "faculties." When it is asked which of these potencies plays the decisive role in the building of the mythical world, a number of conflicting views arise. Does myth result from the play of the subjective *fantasy,* or does it, in each particular case, go back to an empirical intuition in which it is rooted? Does it represent a primitive form of *cognition* and is it therefore a product of the *intellect,* or does it fundamentally belong to the sphere of *affectivity* and will? The varying answers to this question seem to assign entirely different paths to scientific mythology. Just as the natural theories differed according to the class of objects viewed as crucial for myth formation, the psychological theories differ according to the basic psychological energy to which they are reduced. And again the explanations seem to multiply without end and succeed one another in a kind of cycle. Even the form of pure "intellectual mythology," which for a long time seemed superseded —the view that the core of myth was to be sought in an intellectual interpretation of phenomena—has recently been revived. In opposition to

Schelling's demand for a tautegorical interpretation of mythical figures an attempt has been made to rehabilitate allegory and allegoresis.[15]

All this shows that the unity of myth is in constant danger of losing itself in some *particular,* which is then accepted as a satisfactory solution. Whether this particular turns out to be a class of natural objects, a specific cultural sphere, or a psychological force is essentially indifferent. For in all these cases the desired unity is transposed into elements when it should be sought in the characteristic form which produces from these elements a new spiritual whole, a world of symbolic meaning. Critical epistemology, looks on knowledge—with all the infinite diversity of the objects toward which it is directed and of the psychological forces with which it operates— as an ideal whole, the universal constitutive conditions of which it seeks, and the same approach applies to every spiritual unity of meaning. In the last analysis this unity must be established not in a genetic and causal but in a *teleological* sense—as a direction followed by consciousness in constructing spiritual reality. Regardless of whether we gain an understanding of its genesis and regardless of what view we take of this genesis, the reality that is produced in the end stands before us as a self-contained configuration with a being and meaning of its own. And myth, although it is limited to no particular class of things or events but encompasses the whole of existence, and although it employs the most diverse spiritual potencies as its organs, represents a unitary perspective of consciousness from which both nature and soul, both "outward" and "inward" being, appear in a new form. It is this modality and its conditions which we must seek to understand.[16] The empirical data of comparative mythology and comparative religion merely present the problem, for the more extensive they become, the more evident becomes the parallelism of myth formation.[17] But behind

15. Cf. Fritz Langer, *Intellektualmythologie. Betrachtungen über das Wesen des Mythos und der mythischen Methode* (Leipzig, 1916), especially chs. 10–12.

16. On the concept of modality see *1,* 96.

17. It seems to me that the problem contained in this parallelism has been most sharply defined from the standpoint of pure positivism by Tito Vignoli, *Mito e scienza* (1879). German trans., *Mythus und Wissenschaft* (Leipzig, 1880). Eng. trans., *Myth and Science* (New York, 1882). Despite his strictly empiricist attitude Vignoli sees myth as a "spontaneous and necessary form of the understanding," an "innate" activity of the spirit, whose roots he tries to follow back to the thinking of animals, in which, according to Vignoli, we already find that tendency toward the objectivization, entification, and personification of sensory impressions from which, as this tendency is transformed from the particular to the universal—the singular to the typical—the world of mythical figures develops. A "transcendental principle" of its own is imputed to myth—a characteristic law of formation which does not simply disappear as the mind advances to empirical exact science but asserts itself side by side with the forms of

this empirical regularity we must once again seek the original spiritual necessity from which it derives. Just as, in cognition, we seek to ascertain the formal laws of thought which make a mere rhapsody of perceptions into a system of knowledge, so in mythology we must inquire into the nature of that formal unity through which the infinitely multiform world of myth ceases to be a mere conglomerate of arbitrary representations and unrelated notions and constitutes a characteristic spiritual *whole*. Here again the mere enrichment of our factual knowledge is fruitless until it serves to deepen our knowledge of principles, until a mere aggregate of particular factors is replaced by a specific articulation, a superordination and subordination of formative elements.

But though a subordination of myth to a general system of symbolic forms seems imperative, it presents a certain danger. For if a comparison of the mythical form with other cultural forms is taken in a purely objective sense, i.e. based on purely objective parallels and connections, it may well lead to a leveling of the intrinsic form of myth. And indeed there has been no lack of attempts to explain myth by reducing it to another form of cultural life, whether knowledge, art, or language. Schelling defined the relation between language and myth by calling language a "faded myth-ology" [18]—and a later school of comparative mythology set out conversely to show that language is the primary form, myth the secondary. Max Müller, for example, made verbal ambivalence the basis of myth. In his theory the connecting link between word and myth is the *metaphor* which is rooted in the very essence and function of language and gives to the *imagination* that direction which leads to the configurations of myth:

> Mythology is inevitable; it is an inherent necessity of language, if we recognize language as the outward form of thought; it is . . . the dark shadow which language casts on thought and which will never vanish as long as speech and thought do not fully coincide, and this can never happen. Mythology in the highest sense of the word is the power which language exerts on thought in every possible sphere of cultural activity."

The phenomenon of "paronymy," the use of one and the same word to convey entirely different imagery, becomes here the key to the interpreta-

---

strict science: "for the share of pure thought in the progressive development of myth is pre-cisely that activity of the understanding which creates science and makes it possible" (Vignoli, pp. 99 ff.).

18. Cf. *Philosophie der Mythologie*, p. 52.

tion of myths. The source and origin of all mythology is linguistic ambivalence, and myth itself is a kind of disease of the mind, having its ultimate root in a "disease of language." Because the Greek word δαφνή, signifying laurel, goes back to a Sanskrit root *ahana,* signifying the dawn, the myth of Daphne, who in her flight from Apollo is transformed into a laurel tree, is essentially an image of the sun god pursuing his bride, the dawn, who ultimately takes refuge in the bosom of her mother, the earth; because in Greek the words for men and stones (λαοί and λᾶας) resemble one another, men grow from stones in the familiar myth of Deucalion and Pyrrha.[19] The linguistic "explanation" of mythological motifs no longer takes this naive form, but it still seems tempting to seek the vehicle of myth formation in language.[20] Indeed, comparative mythology and comparative religion constantly reveal facts which seem to confirm from the most diverse angles the equation: *numina = nomina.* Usener has lent new depth and fertility to the idea at the base of this equation; in his work, analysis and critique of the names of the gods are shown to be an instrument which, if correctly used, can open up an understanding of the process by which religious concepts are formed. In this way he arrives at a universal theory of *signification* in which linguistic and mythical elements become inseparable correlates. Usener's theory represents a significant philosophical advance for both philosophy and religious history, for once again the emphasis is shifted from the naked content of particular myths to myth and language as a whole, as cultural forms subject to laws of their own. For Usener mythology is nothing more than the theory (λόγος) of myth, or the "morphology of religious representations," and its purpose is nothing less than "to demonstrate the necessity and lawfulness of the mythical imagination and thus to explain both the mythological configurations of the folk religions and the imaginative forms of the monotheistic religions." The possibilities inherent in this method of reading the essence of the gods in their names and the history of their names, and the light it can cast on the structure of the mythical world, are admirably shown by Usener's *Götternamen.* It brings the findings of philosophy and linguistics to bear on the meaning and development of the Greek gods and attempts to demonstrate a general and typical sequence—hence a correspondence—in

19. Cf. Friedrich Max Müller, "Über die Philosophie der Mythologie," append. to his *Einleitung in die vergleichende Religionswissenschaften* (2d ed. Strassburg, 1876).

20. Müller's basic thesis has recently been revived in somewhat modified form by Daniel G. Brinton, e.g.; cf. *Religions of Primitive Peoples* (London and New York, G. P. Putnam's Sons, 1899), pp. 115 ff.

mythical and linguistic representations.[21] And moreover, since myth embraces the first attempt at a knowledge of the world, since it perhaps also represents the earliest and most universal product of the *aesthetic fantasy,* Usener finds in it an immediate cultural unity, of which all the particular forms are mere fragments, mere partial manifestations. But once again our task as a whole will be to seek, not a unity of origin in which oppositions dissolve and seem to merge with one another, but a critical-transcendental unity in which the particular forms are preserved and clearly delimited. The principle of this differentiation becomes clear when we link the problem of signification with the problem of designation, i.e. when we consider how in the diverse cultural forms the "object" is bound up with the "image," the "content" with the "sign," and how at the same time they remain distinct from one another.

An essential element of the correspondence between the diverse cultural forms is that the sign exerts an active, creative force in all of them—myth and language, artistic configuration, and the formation of theoretical concepts of the world and its relationships. Humboldt says that man puts language *between* himself and the nature which inwardly and outwardly acts upon him, that he surrounds himself with a world of words in order to assimilate and elaborate the world of objects, and this is equally true of the configurations of the mythical and aesthetic fantasy. They are not reactions and impressions that act upon the spirit from outside, but true spiritual actions. In the very first, one might say the most primitive, manifestations of myth it becomes clear that we have to do not with a mere reflection of reality but with a characteristic creative elaboration. Here again we can see how an initial tension between subject and object, between "inside" and "outside" is gradually resolved, as a new intermediary realm, growing constantly more rich and varied, is placed between the two worlds. To the factual world which surrounds and dominates it the spirit opposes an independent image world of its own—more and more clearly and consciously it confronts the force of the "impression" with an active force of "expression." However, this creation does not yet bear the character of a free spiritual act; it has a character of natural necessity, of psychological "mechanism." Precisely because at this stage there is not yet an independent self-conscious I, free in its productions, precisely because we stand here at

---

21. See Hermann K. Usener, *Götternamen. Versuch einer Lehre von der religiösen Begriffs-bildung* (Bonn, F. Cohen, 1896). Cf. also my book *Sprache und Mythos. Ein Beitrag zum Problem der Götternamen* (Leipzig and Berlin, 1925).

the threshold of the spiritual process which is destined to delimit the "I" and the "world," the new world of signs must appear to the consciousness as a fully objective reality. Every beginning of myth, particularly every magical view of the world, is permeated by this belief in the objective character and objective force of the sign. Word magic, image magic, and writing magic are the basic elements of magical activity and the magical view of the world. And here, considering the general structure of the mythical consciousness, we may find a strange paradox. For if, according to a widely prevalent view, the basic mythical drive is a drive to endow with life, i.e. to apprehend and represent all the elements of material existence in a concrete, *intuitive* manner; how then does it come about that this drive is directed with particular intensity toward what is most unreal and lifeless, that the shadow realm of words, images, and signs exerts so substantial a power over the mythical consciousness? How can we account for this belief in the abstract, this cult of the symbol in a world where the universal concept seems to be nothing, where feeling, immediate instinct, sense perception, and intuition seem to be everything? An answer to this question can be found only if we recognize that the question is here falsely formulated, insofar as a distinction which we make, and must make, in intellectual reflection and scientific knowledge is introduced into a sphere of spiritual life which precedes this distinction and remains indifferent to it. The mythical world is concrete not because it has to do with sensuous, objective contents, not because it excludes and repels all merely abstract factors—all that is merely signification and sign; it is concrete because in it the two factors, thing and signification, are undifferentiated, because they merge, grow together, concresce in an immediate unity. From the very start myth, as an original mode of *configuration,* raises a certain barrier against the world of passive sense impression; it, too, like art and cognition, arises in a process of separation from immediate reality, i.e. that which is simply given. But though in this sense it signifies one of the first steps beyond the given, its product at once resumes the form of the given. Thus myth rises spiritually above the world of things, but in the figures and images with which it replaces this world it merely substitutes for things another form of materiality and of bondage to things. What seemed to free the spirit from the fetters of things becomes a new fetter which is all the stronger since it is not a mere physical force but a spiritual one. However, a force of *this* sort already contains within it the immanent condition for its own future dissolution; it contains the potentiality of a spiritual process of liberation which is indeed effected in the progress from the *magical-mythical* world view to the truly *religious* view. The condition for this development—as our investigation will show in detail—is that the spirit place itself in a new relation to the world of images and signs—that while still living in them and making use of them it achieve a greater understanding of them and thus rise above them.

This same dialectic of bondage and liberation, which the human spirit experiences with its own self-made image worlds, is still more evident when we compare myth with the other spheres of symbolic expression. For language there is at first no sharp dividing line between the word and its signification, between the content of the representation and the content of the mere sign: the two merge immediately with each other. The nominalistic view, in which words are mere conventional signs, mere *flatus vocis*, is a product of late reflection, not an expression of the "natural," immediate linguistic consciousness, for which the essence of the thing is mediately designated in the word and at the same time in some way contained and present in it. This concrescence of name and thing in the linguistic consciousness of primitives and children might be illustrated by a number of striking examples (we need only think of the various forms of name taboo). But as language develops, the differentiation becomes sharper and more conscious. At first the world of language, like that of myth in which it seems as it were embedded, preserves a complete equivalence of word and thing, of "signifier" and "signified." It grows away from this equivalence as its independent spiritual form, the characteristic force of the logos, comes to the fore. Distinct from all merely physical existence and all physical efficacy the word emerges in its own specificity, in its purely ideal, significatory function. And art leads us to still another stage of detachment. Here again there is at first no sharp differentiation between the ideal and the real; here again the configuration is not initially regarded as the outcome of a creative process, as a pure product of the productive imagination. The beginnings of creative art seem rather to partake of a sphere in which creative activity is still embedded in magical representations and directed toward specific magical *aims,* in which consequently the image itself still has no independent, purely aesthetic significance. And yet in the development of spiritual expression the very first stirrings of artistic activity provide an entirely new beginning, achieve a new principle. Here for the first time the image world acquires a purely *immanent* validity and truth. It does not aim at something else or refer to something else; it simply "is" and consists in itself. From the sphere of efficacy to which the mythical consciousness clings and the sphere of signification in which the linguistic sign perseveres we are transposed into a sphere where, as it were, only the pure reality, only the intrinsic and inherent essence, of the image is apprehended as such. Thus for the first time the world of the image becomes a self-contained cosmos with its own center of gravity. And only now can the spirit enter into a truly free relation with it. Measured by empirical, realistic criteria, the aesthetic world becomes a world of appearance; but in severing its bond with immediate reality, with the material existence and efficacy which constitute the world of magic and myth, it embodies a new step toward the truth. Thus, although myth, language, and art interpenetrate one another in their concrete historical manifestations, the relation between them reveals a definite systematic gradation, an ideal progression toward a point where the spirit not only is and lives in its own creations, its self-created symbols, but also knows them for what they are. Or, as Hegel set out to show in his *Phänomenologie des Geistes:* the aim of spiritual development is that cultural reality be apprehended and expressed not merely as substance but "equally as subject." In *this* respect the problems growing out of a philosophy of mythology are immediately related to those arising from the philosophy and logic of pure cognition. For what distinguishes science from the other forms of cultural life is not that it requires no mediation of signs and symbols and confronts the unveiled truth of "things in themselves," but that, differently and more profoundly than is possible for the other forms, it knows that the symbols it employs are *symbols* and comprehends them as such. But it does not achieve this at one stroke; on the contrary, here again the typical relation of the spirit to its own creations is repeated at a different level. Here again, freedom toward these creations must be gained and secured by constant critical endeavor. In knowledge, too, the *use* of hypotheses and principles precedes the *knowledge* of their specific function as principles—and until this insight is gained, science can only contemplate and state its own principles in a material, that is, semimythical form.

In these general remarks I have attempted to define provisionally the place occupied by myth in the system of cultural forms. Now let us turn our attention to the specific character of the mythical concept of reality and objectivity.

PART I

Myth as a Form of Thought

Chapter 1

The Mythical Consciousness of the Object

It is one of the first essential insights of critical philosophy that objects are not "given" to consciousness in a rigid, finished state, in their naked "as suchness," but that the relation of representation to object presupposes an independent, spontaneous act of consciousness. The object does not exist prior to and outside of synthetic unity but is constituted only by this synthetic unity; it is no fixed form that imprints itself on consciousness but is the product of a formative operation effected by the basic instrumentality of consciousness, by intuition and pure thought. The *Philosophy of Symbolic Forms* takes up this basic critical idea, this fundamental principle of Kant's "Copernican revolution," and strives to broaden it. It seeks the categories of the consciousness of objects in the theoretical, intellectual sphere, and starts from the assumption that such categories must be at work wherever a cosmos, a characteristic and typical world view, takes form out of the chaos of impressions. All such world views are made possible only by specific acts of objectivization, in which mere impressions are reworked into specific, formed representations. We can follow the *aim* of this objectivization back to strata preceding the theoretical object-consciousness of our experience, of our scientific world view. But when we descend into these strata, the *direction* and *means* of this process of objectivization change. So long as this *direction* is not clearly recognized and defined, no clarity can be obtained with regard to the course of development, its separate stages, its stopping places and turning points. Our investigation has already shown that this direction is by no means "simple" and unique, that the ways in which the diversity of sensory impressions can be synthesized into spiritual unities can reveal the most diverse nuances. And this conclusion is strikingly confirmed when we contrast the mythical process of objectivization with that of theoretical, pure empirical thought.

The logical form of empirical thought stands out most sharply when we consider its highest manifestation, the form and structure of science, and particularly the principles of an "exact" science of nature. But what is here achieved to perfection is already under way in the simplest acts of empirical judgment, in the empirical comparison and coordination of specific contents of perception. The development of science merely carries to full actuality and complete logical specification the principles on which, as Kant said, "the possibility of all perception" rests. In truth, however, what we call the world of our perception is not simple, not given and self-evident from the outset, but "is" only insofar as it has gone through certain basic theoretical acts by which it is apprehended and specified. This universal relationship is perhaps most evident in the intuitive form of our perceptual world, in its *spatial* form. The relations of "together," "separate," "side by side" are not just "given" along with our "simple" sensations, the sensuous "matter" that is ordered in space; they are a highly complex, thoroughly *mediated* product of empirical thought. When we attribute a certain size, position, and distance to things in space, we are not thereby expressing a simple datum of sensation but are situating the sensory data in a relationship and system, which proves ultimately to be nothing other than a relationship of pure *judgment*. Every articulation in space presupposes an articulation in judgment; differences in position, size, and distance can only be grasped and assigned because the separate sensory impressions are differently regarded by the judgment, because a different *significance* is imputed to them. Epistemological and psychological analysis of the problem of space has thrown light on this relationship from all sides and established its fundamental truth. Whether with Helmholtz we speak of "unconscious inferences" or whether we reject this term, which indeed involves certain dangers and ambiguities, the "transcendental" and the physiological-psychological investigations both show that the spatial order of the world of perception, as a whole and in detail, goes back to acts of identification, differentiation, comparison, and coordination which in their basic form are purely intellectual acts. It is only when impressions are articulated through such acts, when they are assigned to different strata of *signification,* that articulation "in" space occurs, as an intuitive reflex, as it were, of this theoretical stratification of signification. And this diverse stratification of impressions, which we observe for example in physiological optics, would not be itself possible unless it were grounded in a general principle. The transition from the world of immediate sensory impression to the mediated world of intuitive, particularly of spatial, "representation," depends on the fact that in the fleeting series of indifferent impressions the constant relations in which they recur must gradually assume an independent character by which they are differentiated from the perpetual flux of sensory contents. These constant relationships constitute the fixed structure and framework of "objectivity." While naive thinking, undisturbed by epistemological questions and doubts, speaks candidly of constant "things" and "attributes," a critical approach follows this notion back to its source and ultimate logical foundations and reduces it to the certainty of such relations, particularly relations of measure and number. It is they which constitute the reality of the objects of experience. And this means that every *apprehension* of a particular empirical thing or specific empirical occurrence contains within it an act of *evaluation*. What distinguishes empirical reality, the constant core of objective being, from the mere world of representation or imagination, is that in it the permanent is more and more clearly differentiated from the fluid, the constant from the variable. The particular sense impression is not simply taken for what it is and immediately gives; instead we ask: will it be confirmed by experience as a *whole*? Only if it stands up under this question and this critical test can we say that it has been received into the realm of reality and determinate objective existence. And in no stage of empirical thought and knowledge is this test, this confirmation, ever at an end; it must always be renewed. Over and over again the constants of our experience prove to be merely relative constants which in turn require the support of other, firmer constants. Thus the limits between the objective and the subjective are not rigidly determined from the first but are formed and determined only in the progressive development of experience and its theoretical principles. It is through a constantly renewed intellectual operation that what we call objective reality changes its shape and is re-created in a new form. This operation has essentially a *critical* character. Elements hitherto accepted as certain, as objective, are continuously rejected when it turns out that they do not fully accord with the unity of experience, or at least that, measured by this unity, they possess only a relative and limited and not an absolute significance. It is at all times the order, the necessity, of phenomena *as a whole* that serves as a criterion for the truth of the *particular* empirical phenomenon and of the "reality" that should be imputed to it. Thus in the theoretical organization of the world of experience each particular is mediately or immediately referred to a universal and measured by it. Fundamentally the "relation of the representation to the object" signifies nothing other than this articulation into a larger systematic relationship, in which a specific place is assigned to it. Thus, in this form of thought, the mere particular is apprehended in accordance with a concept of law. The particular reality or occurrence is and exists; but what secures its existence is that we think it and must think it as an instance of a universal law, or rather of a sum or system of universal laws. Thus the objectivity of this world view is an expression of its fully self-contained character, an expression of the fact that in each particular we must think the form of the whole, that we must regard the particular merely as a special expression, a representative of this total form.

From this task empirical thinking derives the logical tools required for its progressive accomplishment. Although its aim consists in a supreme, universal *synthesis,* in the comprehension of all particulars in the thoroughgoing unity of experience, still the only method by which it can attain to this goal seems to point in the opposite direction. Before the contents can be reordered, before they can enter into the form of the systematic whole, they must undergo a transformation; they must be reduced to—and in a sense dissolved into—ultimate elements which cannot be apprehended by immediate sensory impression but can be postulated only by theoretical thought. Without the postulation of such elements, the law-governed thinking of experience and science would, as it were, lack foundation. For the undifferentiated contents and configurations of perception as such offer this thinking no support or basis. They fit into no universal, fixed order, they nowhere possess the character of truly *unequivocal* determination, but rather, apprehended only in their immediate facticity, represent a pure flux which defies any attempt to draw sharp and accurate boundaries through it. Such boundaries can be drawn only when we go back from the immediate substance and attributes of phenomena to something else which is itself not phenomenal but must rather be thought as the "ground" of phenomena. Thus, for example, there can be no formulation of exact laws of motion as long as we seek the subjects of motion simply in the realm of concrete perceptible objects. It is only when thinking passes beyond this sphere, when it postulates atoms as the true subjects and ideal elements of motion that it can give mathematical formulation to the phenomenon of motion. The *synthesis* toward which empirical thought strives always presupposes a corresponding *analysis* and can only be effected on the basis of such an analysis. Combination presupposes separation, while the separation aims only at making the combination possible and preparing the way for it. In this sense all empirical thinking is intrinsically dialectical—if we take the term dialectical in its original historical meaning, given it by Plato, and make it the unity of combination and differentiation, of συναγωγή and διαίρεσις. The apparent circle of dialectical thinking is merely an expression of the perpetual cycle of empirical thought itself, which must always operate at once analytically and synthetically, progressively and regressively, which must break down the particular contents into their constitutive factors, in order to re-create them genetically.

It is through the reciprocal action, the correlation of these two basic methods, that the world of knowledge gains its characteristic form. What distinguishes it from the world of sense impressions is not the substance from which it is built but the new order in which it is encompassed. This order demands that elements which stand undifferentiated side by side in immediate perception be gradually distinguished, that what is mere coexisting perception be transposed into an orderly system—a system of causes and effects. It is in this category of ground and consequence that thought finds the truly effective instrument of analysis, which in turn makes possible the new mode of synthesis which it now applies to sensory data. Where the sensory world view sees only a peaceable coexistence, a conglomerate of "things," empirical-theoretical thinking finds an interpenetration, a complex of "conditions." And in this gradation of conditions a specific place is assigned to each particular content. Whereas sensory apprehension contents itself with establishing the "what" of the particular contents, this mere "what" is now transformed into a "because"; the mere coexistence or succession of contents in space and time is replaced by an ideal dependency (a being-grounded-in-one-another). Thus a progress is achieved from the simplicity of the first unreflecting view of things to a highly refined and differentiated concept of the object. From the standpoint of the theoretical world view and its ideal of knowledge, "objective" no longer means everything that sensation sets before us in its simple existence and facticity, but only what possesses a guarantee of constancy, of enduring and thoroughgoing determinacy. Since this determinacy—as any phenomenon of illusion shows—is not an immediate property of perceptions, perceptions are gradually removed from the center of objectivity which they seemed originally to occupy, toward the periphery. The objective significance of an element of experience depends no longer on the sensuous force with which it individually strikes consciousness, but on the

clarity with which the form, the law of the whole, is expressed and reflected in it. Yet since this form does not come into being all at once but
is attained by degrees, the empirical concept of truth is subject to differentiations and gradations. Mere sensory appearance is distinguished from
the empirical truth of the object, which cannot be apprehended immediately but can only be achieved by the progress of theory, of scientific,
law-governed thought. Hence this truth itself is not absolute but has only
a relative character, for it stands and falls with the general conditions under which it must be achieved and with the premises, the "hypotheses," on
which these conditions rest. Over and over again the constant is differentiated from the variable, the objective from the subjective, truth from appearance: and it is through this movement that the certainty, the true logical character of empirical thinking is gained. The positive reality of the
empirical object is constituted through a double negation: through its differentiation from the "absolute" on the one hand and from sensory appearance on the other. This object appears "phenomenal" but it is not
"illusory," since it is grounded in necessary laws of knowledge, since it is
a *phaenomenon bene fundatum*. Thus we see that in the sphere of theoretical thought the general concept of objectivity as well as its concrete realiza-
tions rest on a progressive *analysis* of the elements of experience, on a
critical operation of the intellect in which the "accidental" is progressively
differentiated from the "essential," the variable from the constant.

And there is no phase of the empirical consciousness, however primitive,
at which this fundamental character is not clearly discernible. To be sure,
epistemological inquiries often find the beginning of all knowledge in a
state of pure immediacy in which impressions are received and experienced
in their simple sensory properties—without any formation or intellectual
elaboration of any sort. In this state, supposedly, all contents are still
situated on one plane; they are still endowed with a single undifferentiated
character of simple material existence. But it is too readily forgotten that
the purely "naive" stage of the empirical consciousness here presupposed
is itself no fact but a theoretical construction, that it is fundamentally nothing other than a limiting concept created by epistemological reflection.
Even where empirical perception has not yet developed into the empirical
cognition of abstract science, the empirical consciousness contains im-
plicitly those differentiations and distinctions which in scientific cognition
assume explicit logical form. This has already been shown by the example
of the *spatial consciousness,* and what is true of space is no less true of the

other ordering principles by which the "empirical object" is constituted. For every simple perception implies a "taking-for-true" [1]—hence a specific norm and standard of objectivity. On close scrutiny perception is a process of selection and differentiation which consciousness applies to the chaotic mass of "impressions." Out of the mass of impressions which pour in on consciousness in any given moment of time certain traits must be retained as recurrent and "typical" as opposed to others which are merely accidental and transient; certain factors must be stressed and others excluded as nonessential. Upon such a selection, which we apply to the raw material of perception as it presses upon us from all sides, rests the sole possibility of giving it a specific form, hence of obtaining a concrete "object"—the sole possibility of relating perception to any object whatsoever. Thus the objective consciousness of perception and that of scientific experience do not differ fundamentally but only in degree, insofar as distinctions which are already present in perception are in scientific experience raised to the form of knowledge, i.e. stabilized in concept and judgment.[2]

But we are carried one step closer to immediacy when we consider the type of objects and objectivity that confront us in mythical consciousness. Myth too lives in a world of pure forms which it looks upon as thoroughly objective, indeed as objectivity pure and simple. But its relation to this world discloses no sign of that decisive "crisis" with which empirical and conceptual knowledge begin. Its contents, to be sure, are given in an objective form, as "real contents," but this form of reality is still completely homogeneous and undifferentiated. Here the nuances of significance and value which knowledge creates in its concept of the object, which enable it to distinguish different spheres of objects and to draw a line between the world of truth and the world of appearance, are utterly lacking. Myth lives entirely by the presence of its object—by the intensity with which it seizes and takes possession of consciousness in a specific moment. Myth lacks any means of extending the moment beyond itself, of looking ahead of it or behind it, of relating it as a particular to the elements of reality as a whole. Instead of the dialectical movement of thought, in which every given particular is linked with other particulars in a series and thus ultimately subordinated to a general *law* and process, we have here a mere subjection to the impression itself and its momentary "presence." Con-

---

1. German *wahrnehmen* (to perceive) = *wahr* (true) + *nehmen* (to take). Trans.

2. For a more detailed treatment of these epistemological considerations I must refer the reader to my *Substanzbegriff und Funktionsbegriff* (Berlin, 1910), chs. 4, 6. Eng. trans. by William C. and M. C. Swabey, *Substance and Function* (Chicago, 1923).

sciousness is bound by its mere facticity; it possesses neither the impulsion nor the means to correct or criticize what is given here and now, to limit its objectivity by *measuring* it against something not given, something past or future. And if this mediate criterion is absent, all "truth" and reality dissolve into the mere presence of the content, all phenomena are situated on a single plane. Here there are no different *degrees* of reality, no contrasting degrees of objective certainty. The resultant picture of reality lacks the dimension of depth—the differentiation of foreground and background so characteristically effected in the scientific concept with its distinction between "the ground" and that which is founded on it.

This one characteristic of mythical thinking—which for the present is set forth only in the most general terms—implies many other features as its simple and necessary consequences; with it the phenomenology of myth is already indicated in broad outlines. For indeed, a mere glance at the *facts* of mythical consciousness shows that it knows nothing of certain distinctions which seem absolutely necessary to empirical-scientific thinking. Above all, it lacks any fixed dividing line between mere "representation" and "real" perception, between wish and fulfillment, between image and thing. This is most clearly revealed by the crucial significance of dream experience in the genesis and growth of the mythical consciousness. To be sure, the animistic theory which attempts to derive the whole content of myth from this one source, which explains myth primarily as a confusion and mixture of dream experience and waking experience, is unbalanced and inadequate in this form, given it primarily by Tylor.[3] But there can be no doubt that the characteristic structure of certain basic mythical concepts is intelligible only if we consider that for mythical thinking and mythical "experience" there is always a hovering between the world of dream and the world of objective reality. Even in a purely practical sense, in man's action upon reality as well as his mere representations, certain dream experiences are accorded the same force and significance, that is to say the same "truth," as waking experience. The whole life and activity of many primitive peoples, even down to trifling details, is determined and governed by their dreams.[4] And mythical thinking makes no clearer

3. Walter F. Otto, *Die Manen oder Von den Urformen des Totenglaubens* (Berlin, 1923), especially pp. 67 ff., has recently stressed that even the most conspicuous aspects of the primitive concept of the soul, e.g., cannot be fully understood on the basis of dream experience.

4. See the abundant material compiled in Lucien Lévy-Bruhl, *La Mentalité primitive* (Paris, 1922). Eng. trans. by Lilian A. Clare, *Primitive Mentality* (London and New York, 1923). See also Brinton, pp. 65 ff.

distinction between life and death than between sleeping and waking. The two are related not as being and nonbeing, but as two similar, homogeneous parts of the same being. In mythical thinking there is no definite, clearly delimited moment in which life passes into death and death into life. It considers birth as a return and death as a survival. In this sense, all mythical doctrines of immortality have not so much a positive-dogmatic as a negative significance. The undifferentiated, unreflecting consciousness refuses to draw a distinction which is not inherent in the immediate content of experience, but which results only from reflection on the empirical *conditions* of life, that is, from a specific form of *causal analysis*. If all reality is taken only as it is given in the immediate impression, if it is regarded as sufficiently certified by the power it exerts on the perceptive, affective, and active life, then a dead man indeed still "is," even though his outward form may have changed, even though his sensory-material existence may have been replaced by a disembodied shadow existence. Here—where "to be real" and "to be effective" amount to the same thing— the fact that the survivor is still *connected* with him by the emotions of love, fear, etc. can be expressed and explained only by the *survival* of the dead. The analytical discretion which advanced empirical thought exercises in distinguishing between the manifestations of life and death and between their empirical presuppositions is here replaced by an undifferentiated intuition of "existence" as such. In this intuition *physical* existence does not suddenly break off in the moment of death but merely changes its scene. All cults of the dead rest essentially on the belief that the dead also require physical means of preserving their existence, that they require their food, clothing, and possessions. While at the level of *thought,* of metaphysics, the mind must seek proofs for the survival of the soul after death, the contrary relation prevails in the beginnings of human culture. It is not immortality, but mortality that must here be "proved," i.e. that must little by little be ascertained theoretically, through dividing lines which progressive reflection draws in the content of immediate experience.

This characteristic interpenetration, this indifference of all the various levels of objectivization, which are distinguished by empirical thinking and the critical understanding, must be kept constantly in mind if instead of reflecting on the contents of the mythical consciousness from the outside we wish to understand them from within. We are accustomed to view these contents as "symbolic," to seek behind them another, hidden sense to which they mediately refer. Thus, myth becomes mystery: its true

significance and depth lie not in what its configurations reveal but in what
they conceal. The mythical consciousness resembles a code which is intelligible only to those who possess the key to it—i.e. for whom the particular contents of this consciousness are merely conventional signs for something "other," which is not contained in them. From this result the various
types and trends of myth interpretation—the attempts to disclose the
meaning, whether metaphysical or ethical, that is concealed in myths.[5]
Medieval philosophers distinguished three levels of interpretation, a
sensus allegoricus, a *sensus anagogicus* and a *sensus mysticus.* And even the
Romantics, though they strove to replace the allegorical view of myth by
a purely tautegorical interpretation, that is, to understand the basic
phenomena of mythology in themselves and not through their relation
to something else, did not *fundamentally* overcome "allegoresis." Both
Creuzer in his *Symbolik und Mythologie der alten Völker* and Johann von
Görres in his *Mythengeschichte der asiatischen Welt* (1810) looked on
myth as an allegorical, symbolic language concealing a secret meaning,
a purely ideal content which can be glimpsed behind its images. But if
we examine myth itself, what it is and what it *knows* itself to be, we see
that this separation of the ideal from the real, this distinction between a
world of immediate reality and a world of mediate signification, this opposition of "image" and "object," is alien to it. Only observers who no
longer live in it but reflect on it read such distinctions into myth. Where
we see mere "representation," myth, insofar as it has not yet deviated from
its fundamental and original form, sees real identity. The "image" does
not represent the "thing"; it *is* the thing; it does not merely stand for the
object, but has the same actuality, so that it replaces the thing's immediate
presence. Consequently, mythical thinking lacks the category of the ideal,
and in order to apprehend pure signification it must transpose it into a
material substance or being. This is true in all stages of mythical thinking,
but it is nowhere expressed so clearly as in mythical *action.* In all mythical
action a true substantiation is effected at some moment; the subject of the
action is transformed into a god or a demon whom it represents. This
fundamental characteristic of myth can be followed from the most primitive manifestations of the magical world view to the highest expressions of
the religious spirit. It has rightly been stressed that rite precedes *myth.*

---

5. On the history of the interpretation of myths cf. Otto Gruppe, *Geschichte der klassischen
Mythologie und Religionsgeschichte während des Mittelalters im Abendland und während der
Neuzeit* (Leipzig, 1921).

Rites cannot be explained as a mere representation of beliefs; on the contrary, the part of myth which belongs to the world of theoretical representation, which is mere record or accredited narrative, must be understood as a mediate interpretation of the part which resides immediately in the activity of man and in his feelings and will. Seen in this light, rites are not originally "allegorical"; they do not merely copy or represent but are absolutely *real;* they are so woven into the reality of action as to form an indispensable part of it. At the most divergent stages of cultural development we find the belief recurring in innumerable forms that the continuance of human life, indeed the very survival of the world itself, depends on the correct execution of rites. Preuss tells us that the Cora and Uitoto Indians attach more importance to the performance of the sacred rites, the observance of festivals, than to the product of all their agricultural efforts—for it is on the rites that all growth and fertility depend. The cult is the true instrument by which man subjects the world, not so much in a spiritual as in a purely physical sense; the creator's principal benefit to man was to endow him with the various forms of the cult by which he might subject the forces of nature. For despite its regular course nature yields nothing without ceremonies.[6] And this transposition of reality into magical-mythical action as well as the immediate reaction of this practice upon reality occurs in both a subjective and objective sense. It is no mere play that the dancer in a mythical drama is enacting; the dancer *is* the god, he *becomes* the god. This basic sense of identity, of identification, is manifested most particularly in fertility rites celebrating the death and resurrection of the god. What happens in these rites, as in most of the mystery cults, is no mere imitative portrayal of an event but is the event itself; it is a δρώμενον, that is, a real and thoroughly effective action.[7] This

6. Cf. the following by Konrad T. Preuss: "Ursprünge der Religion und Kunst," p. 336; *Die Nayarit-Expedition* (Leipzig, 1912), *I*, lxviii, lxxxix ff.; *Religion und Mythologie der Uitoto*, 2 vols. Göttingen and Leipzig, 1921–23), *I*, 123 ff.; and "Die höchste Gottheit bei den kulturarmen Völkern," *Psychologische Forschung*, *2* (1922), 165.

7. For the ancient mysteries cf. particularly Richard Reitzenstein, *Die hellenistischen Mysterienreligionen* (2d ed. Leipzig, 1920), and the decisive documentation in Hermann K. Usener, "Heilige Handlung," *Kleine Schriften* (4 vols. Leipzig, 1912–14), *4,* 424. Only in one passage in Clement of Alexandria—according to Karel H. E. de Jong, *Das antike Mysterienwesen in religionsgeschichtlicher, ethnologischer, und psychologischer Beleuchtung* (Leyden, 1909), p. 19—are the mythical ceremonies called a drama; usually they are referred to as *dromena,* which as a rule means ceremonies, particularly secret ones—never a theatrical performance. And there is no rite without dancing: when someone betrays the mysteries, he is said not to speak them out but to "dance them out." The same is true of the rites of primitive peoples. "The animal and ghost dances both have a magic purpose," Preuss remarks. "No

form of mime, to which we can trace all dramatic art, is never a mere aesthetic play; it is tragic and serious—with the seriousness characteristic of the sacred action itself. Consequently, the term "analogy magic," commonly used for a certain kind of magic undertaking, does not express the true *meaning* of this magic; for where *we* see mere sign and similarity, magical consciousness and perception see the object itself. Only in this light is belief in magic intelligible: those who believe in it not only believe in the efficacy of magic as a means to something else, but are convinced that in it they possess the very thing itself.

This inability of mythical thinking to apprehend pure ideal signification, is strikingly revealed by its relation to language. Myth and language are inseparable and mutually condition each other. Word and name magic are, like image magic, an integral part of the magical world view. But in all this the basic presupposition is that word and name do not merely have a function of describing or portraying but contain within them the object and its real powers. Word and name do not designate and signify, they are and act. In the mere sensuous matter of language, in the mere sound of the human voice, there resides a peculiar power over things. Primitive peoples "exorcise" threatening events and catastrophe, seek to avert eclipses, storms, etc. by song and loud outcry and noise-making.[8] But the mythical-magical power of language is truly manifested in articulated sound. The formed word is itself restricted and individual: each word governs a specific realm of being, over which it may be said to exert unlimited and sovereign power. And it is most of all the proper name that is bound by mysterious ties to the individuality of an *essence*. Even today we often feel this peculiar awe of the proper name—this feeling that it is not outwardly appended to a man, but is in some way a part of him. "A man's name," reads a familiar passage in Goethe's *Dichtung und Wahrheit*, "is not like a cloak that merely hangs around him, that may be loosened and tightened at will; it is a perfectly fitting garment. It grows over him like his very skin; one cannot scrape and scratch at it without injuring the man himself." But for original mythical thinking the name is even more than such a skin: it expresses what is innermost and essential in the man,

---

mythical narratives are represented, and the purpose is never the mere representation of scenes and ideas. This can only come about when the dances have become profane or reached a higher stage of development." "Ursprung der Religion und Kunst," p. 392.

8. For primitive peoples cf. ibid., p. 384. For documentation of the same phenomenon in ancient literature cf. Erwin Rohde, *Psyche. Seelencult und Unsterblichkeitsglaube der Griechen* (2d ed. Tübingen and Leipzig, 1898), 2, 28, n. 2; 77.

and it positively "is" this innermost essence. Name and personality merge.[9] In rites of initiation a man is given a new name because what he receives in the rite is a new self.[10] The name of a *god* above all constitutes a real part of his essence and efficacy. It designates the sphere of energies within which each deity is and acts. In prayer, hymns, and all forms of religious discourse great care must be taken to address each god by the appropriate name, for he will accept the proffered sacrifice only if he is invoked in the proper way. Among the Romans the ability to invoke the right god in suitable form was developed into an art, which was practiced by the pontifices and set forth in the *indigitamenta* which they administered.[11] And elsewhere in religious history we encounter the view that the true nature of the god, the power and diversity of his action, is contained and, as it were, concentrated in his name. In it rests the secret of divine plenitude: the diversity of God's names, the many names of the divine, indeed, the thousands of names, are a true indication of His omnipotence. The part which this belief in the power of the divine name plays in the books of the Old Testament is well known.[12] In Egypt, which as the classical land of magic and specifically of name magic has most clearly developed this trait in its religious history, the universe is considered to have been created by the divine logos, and the first god himself is held to have been created by the power of his own mighty name: in the beginning was the name, which from out of itself brought forth all being, including divine being. He who knows the true name of a god or demon has unlimited power over the bearer of the name; an Egyptian legend tells how Isis, the great enchantress, tricked Ra, the sun god, into revealing his name to her, and how she thus gained dominion over him and all the other gods.[13]

9. In Roman law slaves had no name, because from a legal point of view they had no personality. See Theodor Mommsen, *Römisches Staatsrecht* (3 vols. Leipzig, 1887–88), *1*, 203, cited in Rudolf Hirzel, *Der Name. Ein Beitrag zu seiner Geschichte im Altertum und besonders bei den Griechen*, Abhandlungen der königlichen Sächsischen Gesellschaft der Wissenschaften, Vol. 26 (Leipzig, 1918).

10. There are numerous examples of this in Brinton, pp. 86 ff.; also in Edwin O. James, *Primitive Ritual and Belief* (London, Methuen, 1917), pp. 16 ff.; Arnold van Gennep, *Les Rites de passage* (Paris, E. Nourry, 1909).

11. See Georg Wissowa, *Religion und Kultus der Römer* (2d ed. Munich, 1912), p. 37. Cf. Eduard Norden, *Agnostos theos. Untersuchung zur Formengeschichte religiöset Rede* (Leipzig and Berlin, 1913), pp. 144 ff.

12. Cf. Friedrich Giesebrecht, *Die alttestamentliche Schätzung des Gottesnamens und ihre religionsgeschichtliche Grundlage* (Königsberg, 1902).

13. Concerning this "omnipotence of the name" and its cosmological significance see my *Sprache und Mythos*. It may be pointed out in passing that the belief in the "substantiality"

And the *image*, like the name, of a person or thing reveals the indifference of mythical thinking toward distinctions in the "stage of objectivization." For mythical thinking all contents crowd together into a single plane
of reality; everything perceived possesses as such a character of reality; the
image like the word is endowed with real forces. It not only represents the
thing for the subjective reflection of a third party, an observer; it is a part
of its reality and efficacy. A man's image like his name is an alter ego: what
happens to the image happens to the man himself.[14] Thus image magic and
object magic are never sharply differentiated. The instrument of magic can
equally well be a man's image or a physical part of him, such as his nails or
his hair. If an enemy's image is stuck with pins or pierced by arrows, he
himself will suffer immediately. And it is not alone this passive efficacy
that images possess. They may exert an active power, equivalent to that of
the object itself. A wax model of an object is the same and acts the same as
the object it represents.[15] A man's shadow plays the same role as his image
or picture. It is a real part of him and subject to injury; every injury to
the shadow affects the man himself. One must not step on a man's shadow
for fear of bringing sickness upon him. Certain primitive peoples are said
to grow terrified at the sight of a rainbow, because they regard it as a net

---

of the word, which dominates all mythical thinking, may be observed in almost unchanged
form in certain pathological phenomena, where it seems to follow from the same mental
condition, an intermingling of stages of objectivization which in critical thinking and analytical concept formation are kept apart. Important and instructive in this respect is a case
reported by Paul Schilder in *Wahn und Erkenntnis, Eine psychopathologische Studie*, Mono-
graphien aus dem Gesamtgebiete der Neurologie und Psychiatrie, Vol. *15* (Berlin, 1918), pp.
66 ff. The patient in question is asked what is most powerful in the world and replies
"words." The heavenly bodies, he says, "give" certain words, and by the knowledge of these
words men dominate things. And not only every word as a whole, but each of its parts,
is effective in the same way. The patient was convinced, e.g., that words such as "chaos"
can be broken apart and that the pieces will also have meaning; his relation "to his words
was the same as that of the chemist to a complex composite substance."

14. A large number of examples for this are cited from the Chinese cultural sphere by
Jan J. M. de Groot, *The Religious System of China* (6 vols. Leyden, E. J. Brill, 1892–1910).
See *4*, 340 ff.: "An image, especially if pictorial or sculptured, and thus approaching close
to the reality, is an *alter ego* of the living reality, an abode of its soul, nay, it is that reality
itself. By myriads are such images made of the dead, expressly to enable mankind to keep
the latter in their immediate presence, as protectors and advisers. . . . Such intense association is, in fact, the very backbone of China's inveterate idolatry and fetish-worship, and,
accordingly, a phenomenon of paramount importance in her Religious System."

15. Characteristic examples of this may be found in E. A. T. W. Budge, "Magical Pictures," in *Egyptian Magic* (2d ed. London, 1901), pp. 104 ff.

thrown out by a mighty magician to catch their shadows.[16] In West Africa a man is sometimes secretly murdered by means of a nail or knife thrust into his shadow.[17] The animistic attempt to account for this importance of the shadow by equating a man's shadow with his soul is probably a later reflection, which we inject into the manifestations of mythical thinking. Actually, we seem to be dealing with a far simpler and more fundamental identification—the identification which joins waking and dreaming, name and thing, etc., and which stands in the way of any strict differentiation between "reality" and "copy." For a distinction of this sort would demand something more than mere intuitive immersion in the content itself; instead of apprehending the particular contents in their mere presence, the understanding would have to trace them back to the conditions of their genesis in consciousness and to the principle of causality governing this genesis: and this in turn would presuppose a kind of logical analysis which is totally absent in mythical thinking.

Mythical thinking is, in general, distinguished from a purely theoretical world view as much by its *concept of causality* as by its *concept of the object*. For the two concepts condition each other: the form of causal thinking determines the form of objective thinking, and vice versa. Mythical thinking is by no means lacking in the universal category of cause and effect, which is in a sense one of its very fundamentals. This is evidenced not only by the mythical cosmogonies and theogonies which seek to answer the question of the origin of the world and the birth of the gods but by any number of mythical legends possessing wholly explicative character, i.e. seeking to provide an "explanation" for the origin of some concrete thing, e.g. the sun, the moon, man, or some species of animal or plant. And the culture myths, which trace a cultural heritage back to a hero or savior, belong to the same class. But mythical causality is distinguished from the scientific principle of causality by the very characteristic to which the opposition between the two concepts of the object ultimately reduces itself. According to Kant the principle of causality is a synthetic principle which enables us to spell out phenomena and so read them as experience. But this causal synthesis, like the synthesis which takes place in the concept of the object, involves a very specific analysis. Here

16. See the abundant ethnological material assembled by James G. Frazer in "Taboo and the Perils of the Soul," *The Golden Bough* (3d ed. London, 1911–15), Vol. *3*, Pt. II, p. 77.
17. Mary H. Kingsley, *West African Studies* (London and New York, 1899), p. 207.

again synthesis and analysis are necessary complements to each other. It is a fundamental flaw in Hume's psychology and his psychological critique of the concept of causality that he does not sufficiently recognize this *analytical* function. According to Hume every representation of causality should ultimately be derived from the representation of mere coexistence. Two contents which have appeared together in consciousness with sufficient frequency are ultimately transposed, through the mediating psychological function of "imagination," from a relationship of mere contiguity, of mere spatial coexistence or temporal succession, into a causal relation. Mere local or temporal contiguity is transformed into causality by a simple mechanism of "association." But in truth, scientific knowledge gains its causal concepts and judgments by an exactly opposite process. Through these concepts and judgments contents which are contiguous for immediate sensory impression are progressively dissected and assigned to different complexes of conditions. In mere perception a specific state A in moment A_1 is followed by another state B in moment A_2. But regardless of how often it is repeated, this succession would not lead to the idea that A is the "cause" of B—the *post hoc* would never become a *propter hoc*—unless a mediating concept intervened. From total state A thought isolates a specific factor a, which it links with a factor β in B. That a and β stand in a necessary relation to each other, a relation of "cause" and "effect," of "condition" and "conditioned," is not passively read from a given perception or number of perceptions: we put it to the test by bringing about the condition by itself and then seeking the effect connected with it. Particularly the physical *experiment* on which causal judgments in physics finally depend is always based on such an analysis of an occurrence into different spheres of conditions, different strata of relations. Through this progressive analysis the spatial-temporal event, which was initially given to us as a mere play of impressions, a "rhapsody of perceptions," takes on the new *meaning* which stamps it as a causal happening. The particular occurrence is no longer considered merely as such: it becomes the vehicle and expression of a universal, comprehensive lawfulness that is represented in it. The twitching of the frog's leg in Galvani's laboratory did not in itself, as an unanalyzed phenomenon, prove the new force of "galvanism" but proved it through the analytical and logical process linked with it. The causal connections created by science do not merely register and repeat sensory, empirical data; on the contrary, they interrupt the mere contiguity of the elements of experience: contents which in empirical existence stand side by side are differentiated according to their "ground" and "essence," while for the conceptual structure of reality others which lie far apart from the immediate sensory view move close together and are related to one another. It was thus that Newton discovered a new causal concept of gravitation, through which such diverse phenomena as the free fall of bodies, the orbit of the planets, and the tides were grasped as a unity and subjected to one and the same universal *rule*.

This isolating abstraction, which singles out a specific factor in a total complex as a "condition," is alien to mythical thinking. Here every simultaneity, every spatial coexistence and contact, provide a real causal "sequence." It has even been called a principle of mythical causality and of the "physics" based on it that one take every contact in time and space as an immediate relation of cause and effect. The principles of *post hoc, ergo propter hoc* and *juxta hoc, ergo propter hoc* are characteristic of mythical thinking. Animals which appear in a certain season are, for example, commonly looked upon as the bringers, the cause of this season: for the mythical view, it is the swallow that *makes* the summer.[18] "Networks of fantastically arbitrary relations," writes Oldenberg in connection with the magical and sacrificial usages of the Vedic religion,

> embrace all the beings whose action is believed to explain the structure of sacrifice and its effect on the world process and on the I. They act on one another by contact, by the number inherent in them, by something attaching to them. . . . They fear one another, penetrate one another, interweave and pair with one another. . . . One passes into the other, becomes the other, is a form of the other, *is* the other. . . . It would seem that once two representations find themselves in a certain proximity, it is impossible to keep them apart.[19]

If this is true, we must come to the astonishing conclusion that Hume, in attempting to analyze the causal judgment of science, rather revealed a source of all mythical explanations of the world. The linguistic term "polysynthetic" has indeed been applied to the mythical imagination, and

18. Cf. Preuss, "Ursprung der Religion und Kunst." For the mythical principle of *juxta hoc, ergo propter hoc* cf. the abundant documentation compiled by Lucien Lévy-Bruhl, *Les Fonctions mentales dans les sociétés inférieures* (Paris, 1910). German trans., *Das Denken der Naturvölker* (Leipzig and Vienna, 1921), pp. 252 ff. Eng. trans. by Lilian A. Clare, *How Natives Think* (New York, 1926).

19. Oldenberg, *Die Lehre der Upanishaden und die Anfänge des Buddhismus* (Göttingen, Vandenhoeck and Ruprecht, 1915), pp. 20 ff.

the term has been explained as meaning that for the mythical imagination there is no separation of a total complex into its elements, but that only a single undivided totality is represented—a totality in which there has been no "dissociation" of separate factors, particularly of the factors of objective perception and subjective feeling.[20] Preuss has illustrated the difference between the mythical-complex view and the analytical conceptual approach by a reference to the cosmological and religious conceptions of the Cora Indians: here no individual star or planet, or the moon or sun, is predominant; the heavenly bodies are worshiped as an undifferentiated whole. The apprehension of the night sky or the daytime sky in its totality, he says, precedes that of the particular heavenly bodies: "the whole was apprehended as a unitary being and the religious conceptions connected with the heavenly bodies often confounded them with the sky as a whole; they could not free themselves from the total view." [21] But in line with our discussion up to this point we now recognize that this often stressed aspect of mythical thinking [22] is not external or accidental but follows necessarily from the structure of such thinking. Here in a sense we have the reverse of the important *epistemological* insight that the basic logical function of the scientific concept of causality does not consist merely in "combining," either by the imagination or by the understanding, elements already given in perception, but must on the contrary first determine these elements as such. As long as this determination is absent we shall lack all those dividing lines which separate the different objects and spheres of objects for our advanced empirical consciousness, shot through as it is with causal inferences.

Whereas empirical thinking is essentially directed toward establishing an unequivocal relation between *specific* "causes" and *specific* "effects," mythical thinking, even where it raises the question of origins as such, has a free selection of causes at its disposal. Anything can *come from* anything, because anything can stand in temporal or spatial contact with anything. Whereas empirical thinking speaks of "change" and seeks to understand it on the basis of a universal rule, mythical thinking knows only a simple metamorphosis (taken in the Ovidian, not in the Goethean sense). When

20. Lévy-Bruhl, *Das Denken der Naturvölker*, p. 30.

21. Preuss, *Die Nayarit-Expedition*, pp. 1 ff. Cf. idem, *Die geistige Kultur der Naturvölker* (Leipzig and Berlin, 1914), pp. 9 ff.

22. Cf. Richard Thurnwald, "Das Problem des Totemismus," *Anthropos, 13* (1918), 1094–1113. Thurnwald speaks not of a "complex" thinking but of a "thinking in full-page pictures" *Denken in Vollbildern*.

scientific thinking considers the fact of change, it is not essentially concerned with the transformation of a single given *thing* into another; on the contrary, it regards this transformation as possible and admissible only insofar as a universal law is expressed in it, insofar as it is based on certain functional relations and determinations which can be regarded as valid independently of the mere here and now and of the constellation of things in the here and now. Mythical "metamorphosis," on the other hand, is always the record of an individual event—a change from one individual and concrete material form to another. The cosmos is fished out of the depths of the sea or molded from a tortoise; the earth is shaped from the body of a great beast or from a lotus blossom floating on the water; the sun is made from a stone, men from rocks or trees. All these heterogeneous mythical explanations, chaotic and lawless as they may seem in their mere content, reveal one and the same *approach* to the world. Whereas the scientific causal judgment dissects an event into constant elements and seeks to understand it through the complex mingling, interpenetration, and constant conjunction of these elements, mythical thinking clings to the total representation as such and contents itself with picturing the simple course of what happens. In this event certain typical traits may be repeated, but still there can be no question of a rule, of specific limiting formal conditions.

However, even the contrast between law and arbitrariness, necessity and contingency must be critically analyzed and more closely defined before it is applicable to the relation between mythical and scientific thinking. Leucippus and Democritus seem to express the very principle of a scientific explanation of the world and its definitive break with myth when they set forth the proposition that nothing in the world happens at random, that everything happens out of reason and by necessity (οὐδὲν χρῆμα μάτην γίνεται, ἀλλὰ πάντα ἐκ λόγου τε καὶ ὑπ' ἀνάγκης). And yet at first glance this principle of causality seems to apply no less, but indeed to an even greater degree, to the structure of the mythical world. Inability to conceive of an event that is in any sense "accidental" has, in any case, been called characteristic of mythical thinking. Often where *we* from the standpoint of science speak of "accident," mythical consciousness insists on a cause and in every single case postulates such a cause. For primitive peoples a catastrophe that descends on the land, an injury which a man suffers, sickness, and death are never "accidental"; they always go back to magical interventions as their true causes. Death in particular never occurs "of itself" but is always brought about by magic influence.[23] In this light, mythical thinking seems to be so far from an arbitrary lawlessness that on the contrary we are tempted rather to speak of a kind of hypertrophy of the causal "instinct" and of a need for causal explanation. Indeed, the proposition that nothing in the world happens by accident and everything by conscious purpose has sometimes been called fundamental to the mythical world view.[24]

Here again it is not the concept of causality as such but the specific form of causal explanation which underlies the difference and contrast between the two spiritual worlds. It is as though the conceptual consciousness and the mythical consciousness applied the lever of explanation at entirely different points. Science is content if it succeeds in apprehending the individual event in space and time as a special instance of a general law but asks no further "why" regarding the individualization as such, regarding the here and now. The mythical consciousness, on the other hand, applies its "why" precisely to the particular and unique. It "explains" the individual event by postulating individual acts of the will. Even though our causal concepts are directed toward the apprehension and specification of the particular, although in fulfilling this purpose they differentiate themselves and complement and determine one another, nevertheless they always leave a certain sphere of indeterminacy surrounding the particular. For precisely *as* concepts they cannot exhaust concrete-intuitive existence and events; they cannot exhaust all the countless "modifications" of the general rule, which may occur at any particular time. Here every particular is indeed subject to the universal but cannot be fully deduced from it alone. Even the "special laws of nature" represent something new and specific as opposed to the general principle, the principle of causality as such. They are subject to this principle; they fall *under* it, but in their concrete formulation they are not postulated *by* it and they cannot be determined by it alone.

Here theoretical thinking and natural science encounter the problem of the "accidental"—for in this connection "accidental" does not mean what deviates from the form of universal necessity but what rests on a modification of this form that is not wholly deducible. If theoretical thought wishes in some way to apprehend and specify this element which, from the

23. For examples from African religions see Carl Meinhof, "Schriftlose Religionen," in *Die Religionen der Afrikanen* (Oslo, 1926), pp. 15 ff.

24. Cf. Brinton, pp. 47 ff.; Lévy-Bruhl, *La Mentalité primitive*.

standpoint of the general law of causality, is "accidental," it must—as the *Kritik der Urtheilskraft* has shown in detail—move into another category. The purely causal principle is now replaced by the principle of purpose: what we call purposiveness is really the "lawfulness of the accidental." [25]

Myth, however, takes the opposite path. It begins with the intuition of purposive action—for all the forces of nature are for myth nothing other than expressions of a demonic or divine will. This principle constitutes the source of light, which for myth progressively illuminates the whole of reality and outside of which there is no possibility of understanding the world. For scientific thought, to "understand" an event means nothing else than to reduce it to certain universal conditions, to subordinate it to that universal complex of conditions which we call "nature." A phenomenon such as the death of a man is understood if we succeed in assigning a place to it within this complex—if we can recognize it as necessary on the basis of the physiological conditions of life. But even if myth could conceive this necessity of the universal "process of nature," the mythical consciousness would regard it as mere accident because it leaves unexplained precisely what holds the interest and attention of myth, namely the here and now of the particular case, the death of precisely *this* man, at *this* particular time. This individual aspect of the event seems to become understandable only if we can reduce it to something no less individual, to a personal act of the will, which as a free act requires and is susceptible of no further explanation. Pure cognition tends to think of all freedom of action as determined by an unequivocal causal order; myth, on the contrary, dissolves all determination of events into a freedom of action: both have "explained" an occurrence when they have interpreted it from their own specific point of view.

Linked with this form of causality is another trait which has always been stressed as characteristic of the mythical world view, namely the peculiar relation it assumes between the *whole* of a concrete object and its particular *parts*. For our empirical apprehension the whole *consists* of its parts; for the logic of natural science, for the logic of the analytical-scientific concept of causality, it *results* from them; for the mythical view neither of these propositions applies; here there prevails a true indifference, both in thought and practice, between the whole and its parts. The whole does not "have" parts and does not break down into them; the part *is* immediately the

25. Cf. the analysis of the *Kritik der Urtheilskraft* in my *Kants Leben und Lehre* (3d ed. Berlin, 1922), pp. 310 ff.

whole and functions as such. This relationship, this principle of the *pars pro toto* has also been designated as a basic principle of primitive logic. However, the part does not merely represent the whole, but "really" specifies it; the relationship is not symbolic and intellectual, but real and material. The part, in mythical terms, is the same thing as the whole, because it is a real vehicle of efficacy—because everything which it incurs or does is incurred or done by the whole at the same time. The consciousness of the part as such, as a "mere" part, does not belong to the immediate, naive intuition of reality but is achieved only by that analytical and synthetic function of mediating thought which goes back from objects as concrete material units to their constitutive conditions. If one follows the history of scientific thinking, the concept of causality and the category of the whole and the parts are seen to develop hand in hand; both belong to one and the same direction of analysis. The question of the origin of being as set forth in the beginnings of Greek speculation is distinguished from the same question of origins as embodied in the mythical cosmogonies by its concern with the "elements" of being. The ἀρχή in its new *philosophical* sense, in the sense of "principle," now signifies both origin and element. Not only does the world originate in the primal water as in myth; water is also its substance, its material constituent. And even though this constituent is still sought in a single concrete original substance, the concept of the element soon begins to shift as the physical view of the world is replaced by mathematical intuition and the basic form of *mathematical analysis*. It is no longer earth, air, water, and fire that constitute the "elements" of things—and it is no longer the semimythical forces of "love" and "hate" which fuse and sunder these elements; the new mathematical-physical cosmos is constituted by the simplest spatial figures and movements and the necessary laws according to which they are ordered. In the genesis of the ancient atomic theory one can clearly see how it is the new concept of "the ground," of causality that demanded and called forth a new concept of "element" and a new relation between the whole and its parts. The idea of the atom is only a single factor in the development of the general view manifested in Democritus' concept of natural law, of etiology.[26] And the ulterior development of the concept of the atom in the course of scientific history fully confirms this relationship. Atoms were regarded as the ultimate, irreducible parts of matter only as long as the

26. Cf. my account of the history of Greek philosophy in *Lehrbuch der Philosophie*, ed. Max Dessoir (Berlin, 1925), Vol. *1*.

analysis of *change* seemed to find an ultimate foundation in them. But once the causal analysis of change into its particular factors advanced beyond these foundations, the picture of the atom changed. It broke down into other, simpler elements which were then postulated as the true vehicles of change, the basis on which the determining causal relations could be formulated. Thus we see that the divisions and subdivisions of reality which scientific cognition undertakes are merely an expression and as it were a conceptual cloak for the necessary relations by which science seeks to comprehend and unambiguously determine the world of change. Here the whole is not so much the sum of its parts as a construct of their mutual relation; it signifies the unity of the dynamic connection in which each one participates and which it helps to accomplish.

Here myth shows us the opposite side of this relationship, permitting us to prove our point inversely. Because myth lacks the form of causal analysis, it cannot know the sharp dividing line which only this form of thought creates between the whole and its parts. Even where empirical intuition seems, of itself so to speak, to give us inwardly differentiated things, myth replaces this sensuous separation and contiguity by a characteristic form of interpenetration. The whole and its parts are interwoven, their destinies are linked, as it were—and so they remain even after they have been detached from one another in pure fact. Even after such separation the fate of the part hangs over the whole as well. Anyone who acquires the most insignificant bodily part of a man—or even his name, his shadow, his reflection in a mirror, which for myth are also real "parts" of him—has thereby gained power over the man, has taken possession of him, has achieved magical power over him. From a purely formal point of view the whole phenomenology of magic goes back to this one basic premise, which clearly distinguishes the complex intuition of myth from the abstract, or more precisely abstracting and analytical, concept.

The workings of this form of thought can be followed in respect to *time* as well as *space:* it makes over the intuition of succession and simultaneity in its own mold. In both cases mythical thinking has a tendency to thwart that analytical dissection of reality into independent partial factors and partial conditions, with which the scientific approach to nature begins and which remains typical of it. According to the view underlying "sympathetic magic" there is a general link, a true causal nexus, between all things whose spatial proximity or whose membership in the same material whole designates them, however externally, as "belonging together." To leave remnants of food about, or the bones of animals one has eaten, involves grave dangers, for anything that happens to these remains through hostile magic influences will at the same time happen to the food in the body and to the man who has eaten it. The cuttings of a man's hair and nails and his excrement must be buried or burned to prevent them from falling into the hands of a hostile magician. Among certain Indian tribes if an enemy's spittle can be obtained, it is enclosed in a potato and hung in the chimney: as the spittle dries in the smoke, the enemy's strength dwindles with it.[27] As we see, the "sympathetic" relationship assumed to exist between the different parts of the body is totally indifferent to their physical and spatial separation. This relationship annuls any breakdown of a total organism into its parts, any clear specification of what the parts are for themselves and what they mean for the whole. Whereas science in its exposition and explanation of biological phenomena splits the total process of the organism into characteristic activities and functions, myth accomplishes no such breakdown into elementary processes, hence no true "articulation" of the organism itself. Any part of the body, however "inorganic," e.g. the nail or the little toe, is equal to any other in its *magical* significance for the whole; instead of organic development, which always presupposes organic differentiation, simple equivalence prevails. Here again we have a simple coexistence of material *pieces* without any superordination and subordination of *functions* differentiated according to their particular conditions. And just as the physical parts of the organism are not sharply distinguished according to their importance, so the temporal specifications of the process, the particular moments in time, are not differentiated according to their causal significance. If a warrior is wounded by an arrow, he can, according to magical conceptions, heal or diminish his pain by hanging the arrow in a cool place or smearing it with an ointment.

Strange as this kind of "causality" may seem to us, it becomes comprehensible when we consider that here arrow and wound, "cause" and "effect," are still simple, unanalyzed material units. From the standpoint of science one thing is never simply the cause of another; its effect on this thing is produced only under very specific determining circumstances and above all in a rigidly delimited *moment of time*. The causal relation is not so much a relation between things, as a relation between *changes* which occur in certain objects at specific times. Through this attention to the

27. Cf. Frazer, *Golden Bough*, Vol. *3*, Pt. II, pp. 126 ff., 258 ff., 287 ff., etc.

temporal course of a process and its dissection into different, clearly delimited "phases," causal relationships become more and more complex and mediate as science progresses. The arrow can no longer be considered as the cause of the wound; what happens is rather that in a certain moment (t_1) in which it penetrates the body the arrow provokes a certain change in it and that this change is followed (in the ensuing moments t_2, t_3, etc.) by other specific changes and series of changes in the bodily organism, all of which must be considered necessary partial conditions of the wound. Because myth and magic nowhere undertake this analysis into partial conditions, each possessing only a specific *relative* value within the causal relationship as a whole, they fundamentally recognize no specific barriers between either the moments of time or the parts of a spatial whole. Sympathetic magic passes over spatial as well as temporal differences: the dissolution of spatial contiguity, the physical separation of a part from the whole of the body does not annul the causal relationship between them, and similarly, "before" and "after," "earlier" and "later" merge with one another. In more precise terms, magic has no need to *create* a connection between spatially and temporally separate elements (such a connection is only a mediate, reflexive expression of their relationship); on the contrary magic forestalls such a separation into elements from the very outset; and even where *empirical* intuition seems to present such a separation, it is at once annulled by magical intuition. The tension between elements separated in space and time is dissolved in the simple identity of the magical "cause." [28]

A further consequence of this barrier which confronts mythical thinking is evident in the material-substantial view of action that is everywhere characteristic of it. The logical-causal analysis of action is essentially directed toward breaking down the given into simple isolated *processes* whose regularity we can observe; but even where the mythical view turns its attention to the process, even where it inquires into the genesis and origin, it links this "genesis" with a concrete, given substance. It knows and apprehends the process of action only as a simple change from one concrete, individual substance to another. In scientific analysis the road runs from the "thing" to the "condition," from "substantial" to "functional"

---

28. In my study *Die Begriffsform im mythischen Denken*, Studien der Bibliothek Warburg, Vol. *1* (Leipzig and Berlin, 1922) I have attempted to show how this form of mythical causality operates not only in magic but also in the highest levels of mythical thinking, particularly in the system of astrology.

intuition; in the magical view the intuition of change remains confined within the intuition of simple substance. The more cognition advances, the more it limits itself to inquiring into the pure how of change, i.e. into its necessary form; myth, on the contrary, inquires solely into its what, whence, and whither, and it insists on seeing both the whence and the whither in the form of determinate things. Here causality is no relational form of mediating thought, an independent entity which situates itself, as it were, between the particular elements in order to combine and divide them; here the factors into which the change is dissected still possess a true character of *original objects* (*Ur-Sachen; Ursachen = causes*), of concrete, independent things. While conceptual thought splits a continuous series of events into causes and effects and is thus oriented essentially toward the mode, the constancy, the rule of the *change,* the mythical need of explanation is satisfied if the *beginning* and *end* of the process are clearly differentiated. A great number of creation myths relate how the world issued from a simple, original thing, from the cosmic egg or an ash tree. In Nordic mythology it is formed from the body of the giant Ymir: from Ymir's flesh the earth is made, from his blood the roaring sea, from the bones the mountains, from his hair the trees, from his skull the dome of heaven. And this is a typical conception, as is shown by the analogy with a Vedic hymn of creation which describes how the living creatures, the beasts of the air and wilderness, the sun, the moon, and the air issued from the parts of the Purusha, the man who was offered up as a sacrifice by the gods. And here the characteristic hypostatization essential to all mythical thinking stands out even more sharply; for it is not only concrete, perceptible objects whose genesis is explained in this way but highly complex, mediated formal relations. The songs and melodies, the meters and sacrificial formulas also issued from different parts of the Purusha; and the social orders disclose the same concrete, material origin. "The Brahmin was his mouth, his arms were made the Rājanya (warrior), his two thighs the Vaiśya (trader and agriculturist), from his feet the Sūdra (servile class) was born." [29] While scientific thought seeks to dissolve all reality into relations and understand it through them, mythical thinking answers the question of origins by reducing even intricate complexes of relations—such as

29. Rigveda, x, 90. Eng. trans. by Edward J. Thomas, *Vedic Hymns* (London, John Murray, 1923), p. 122. Cf. *Lieder des Ṛgveda,* German trans. by Alfred von Hillebrandt (Göttingen and Leipzig, 1913), pp. 130 ff. For a German trans. of the song of Edda, describing the creation of the world from the body of the giant Ymir, see Wolfgang Golther, *Handbuch der germanischen Mythologie* (Leipzig, 1895), p. 517.

musical rhythms or the organization of the castes—to a pre-existing material substance. And because of this fundamental form of thought, all mere properties or attributes must for myth ultimately become *bodies*. The distinction between the Brahman, the Warrior, and the Sudra is understandable only on the supposition that they contain different substances, the Brahman, the Kshatra, the Sudra, each of which lends its specific property to those who partake of it. According to Vedic theology, the "husband-killing body" dwells in an evil, faithless woman, the "body *(tanu)* of son-lessness dwells in a barren woman." [30] In such concretions the immanent conflict, the dialectic in which the mythical imagination moves, becomes particularly evident. The mythical fantasy drives toward animation, toward a complete "spiritualization" of the cosmos; but the mythical *form of thought,* which attaches all qualities and activities, all states and relations to a solid foundation, leads to the opposite extreme: a kind of materialization of spiritual contents.

It is true that mythical thinking seeks to create a kind of *continuity* between cause and effect by intercalating a series of middle links between the initial and the ultimate states. But even these middle links preserve a merely material character. From the standpoint of analytical, scientific causality a process is regarded as constant if a unitary law, an analytical function, is demonstrated under which the whole of the process can be logically subsumed and by which its progress from moment to moment can be determined. With each moment in time a specific state of the process, expressible in specific mathematical quantities, is coordinated; but taken together, all these *different* quantities constitute a *single* series of change, because the change which they undergo is subject to a universal rule and is thought as issuing necessarily from that rule. In this rule both the unity and the differentiation, the "continuity" and the "discreteness," of the separate factors of the process is represented. Mythical thinking, however, knows such a unity neither of combination nor of separation. Even where it seems to divide an action into a number of stages, it considers the action in an entirely substantial form. It explains any attribute of the action by a specific material quality which passes from one thing in which it is inherent to other things. Even what in empirical and scientific thought appears to be a mere dependent attribute or momentary property here obtains a character of complete substantiality and hence of transferability. It is reported that the Hupa Indians look on pain as a sub-

30. Cf. Hermann Oldenberg, *Religion des Veda* (Berlin, W. Hertz, 1894), 2d ed. pp. 478 ff.

stance.[31] And even purely "spiritual," purely "moral" attributes are in this sense regarded as transferable substances, as is shown by a number of ritual rules regulating this transference. Thus a taint, a miasma that a community has brought on itself, can be transferred to an individual, a slave for example, and destroyed by the sacrifice of the slave. The Greek Thargelia and certain Ionian festivals included a similar ritual of atonement,[32] going back to the most ancient mythical origins.[33] Originally these rites of purification and atonement were based not on a symbolic substitution but on a real, physical transference.[34] A Batak suffering under a curse can "make it fly away" by transferring it to a swallow.[35] And the transfer may be to a mere object as well as an animate subject, as is shown, for example, by a Shinto usage. Here a man desiring to be relieved of guilt receives from the priest a sheet of white paper cut in the form of a human garment, called *katashiro,* "representative of the human form." On it he writes the year and month of his birth and his family name; then he rubs it over his body and breathes on it, whereupon his sins are transferred to the *katashiro.* At the end of the purification ceremony these "scapegoats" are thrown into a river or sea, in order that the four gods of purification may guide them into the underworld, where they will disappear without trace.[36] And all other spiritual attributes and faculties are, for mythical thinking, bound up with some specific material substratum. In connection with the Egyptian coronation ceremonies we have exact instructions governing transference of the god's attributes to the Pharaoh through the regalia, the scepter, the scourge, the sword. These are looked upon not as mere symbols

---

31. Pliny E. Goddard, *Life and Culture of the Hupa,* University of California Publications, American Archaeology and Ethnology, Vol. *1* (Berkeley, 1903–4).

32. Cf. Rohde, *Psyche,* 2, 78.

33. On the widespread conception of the scapegoat cf. Frazer, "The Scapegoat," *Golden Bough,* Vol. 9, Pt. IV.

34. Cf. Lewis R. Farnell, *The Evolution of Religion* (London and New York, 1905), pp. 88 ff., 117 ff.

35. Johannes G. Warneck, *Die Religion der Batak* (Leipzig, T. Weicher, 1909), p. 13. We find similar conceptions in Indian and Germanic folk superstition. "Every peasant woman in India," says E. Washburn Hopkins, *Origin and Evolution of Religion* (New Haven, Yale Univ. Press, 1923), p. 163, "who is afflicted leaves a rag infected with her trouble on the road, hoping someone else will pick it up, for she has laid her sickness on it and when another takes it she herself becomes free of the sickness." For the Germanic sphere cf. Karl Weinhold, *Die mystische Neunzahl bei den Deutschen, Abhandlungen der philosophische-historischen Classe der königlichen Akademie der Wissenschaften zu Berlin* (1897), p. 51.

36. Karl Florenz, "Die Religionen der Japaner: 1. der Shintoismus," in *Die orientalischen Religionen,* Die Kultur der Gegenwart, Vol. *1*, Pt. III (Leipzig and Berlin, 1906), pp. 194–219.

but as true talismans—vehicles and guardians of divine forces.[37] In general, the mythical concept of force differs from the scientific concept in that it never looks on force as a dynamic *relation*, the expression for a sum of causal relations, but always as a material substance.[38] This substance is distributed throughout the world, but it seems concentrated, as it were, in certain powerful personalities, in the magician and the priest, the chieftain and the warrior. And from this substantial whole, from this store of force, parts can detach themselves and enter into another individual by mere contact.

The magical force characteristic of the priest or chieftain, the *mana* that is concentrated in them, is not bound to them as individual subjects but can be communicated to others in many ways. Thus mythical force is not, like physical force, a mere comprehensive term, a mere "resultant" of causal factors and conditions which can be viewed as "effective" only in their relation to one another; it is, on the contrary, an independent substantial reality which as such moves from place to place, from subject to subject. Among the Ewes, for example, the vessels and secrets belonging to the magician can be acquired by purchase, but an individual can acquire the magic force itself only by physical transference, which is accomplished

37. Cf. Alexandre Moret, *Du Caractère religieux de la royauté pharaonique* (Paris, 1902). The same is true in connection with other rites, e.g. of marriage. Van Gennep, p. 191, writes: "Ils doivent être pris non pas dans un sens symbolique, mais au sens strictement matériel: la corde, qui attache, l'anneau, le bracelet, la couronne, qui ceignent etc. ont une action réelle coexercitive."

38. This view of mythical thinking seems to be directly contradicted by Fritz Graebner's thesis, put forward in *Das Weltbild der Primitiven* (Munich, E. Reinhardt, 1924), that for mythical thinking "the attributes of a particular object, its effects and relations to other objects enter consciousness with greater force . . . than its substance" (p. 23). "In primitive thinking the attributes play a far greater, the substances a far lesser role than with us" (p. 132). But if we consider the concrete examples by which Graebner seeks to support this thesis, we find that the contradiction lies far less in fact than in formulation. For these examples show unmistakably that mythical thinking does not know any sharp distinction between substances on the one hand, and attributes, relations, and forces on the other, but condenses what from our standpoint is mere attribute or a mere dependent relation into independent things. The critical, scientific view of substance—according to which, as Kant put it, the "permanence" of the real in time is the schema of the substance and the characteristic by which it is empirically recognized—is indeed alien to mythical thinking, which permits of an unlimited "transformation" of substances into one another. But this fact should not lead us to conclude with Graebner "that of the two most important categories of human thought, those of causality and of substance, the former is far more pronounced than the latter in mythical thinking" (p. 24). For as we have shown above, the distance between what can be called "causality" in the mythical sense and its scientific concept is just as great as the distance between the two concepts of substance.

mainly by mixing the blood and spittle of the seller and purchaser.[39] Likewise a sickness which assails a man is never, in mythical terms, a *process* operating in his body under empirically known and universal conditions but is a demon which has taken possession of him. And the emphasis is less animistic than substantial, for although the sickness can be interpreted as an animated demonic being, it can equally well be a kind of foreign *body* which enters into a man.[40] The profound cleavage between this mythical form of medicine and the empirical-scientific form which found its first basis in Greek thought becomes apparent when, for example, we compare the Hippocratic corpus with the lore of the priests of Asclepias at Epidaurus. Throughout mythical thinking we encounter a hypostatization of properties and processes, or forces and activities, often leading to their immediate materialization.[41] Certain writers have spoken of a mythical principle of "emanism" to explain this characteristic detachability and transferability of attributes and properties.[42] But perhaps we can best appreciate the meaning and origin of this way of thinking if we consider that even in scientific knowledge the sharp distinction between thing on the one hand and attribute, state, and relation on the other results only

39. Jakob Spieth, *Die Religion der Eweer in Süd-Togo* (Göttingen and Leipzig, 1911), p. 12. This transference of the mana, the magical force—which according to mythical conceptions is no transference, since the force is preserved in full substantial *identity*—is excellently illustrated by a Maori tradition. It is reported that the Maoris reached their present home in a canoe, known as Kurahoup or Kurahoupo. "According to the version communicated by the Maori Te Kahui Kararehe the canoe was wrecked on the coast of Hawaiki, soon after setting out for the new home, through magic inspired by envy of the boat's special *manakura*. But the enemies' intention of destroying the boat's *mana* was thwarted, for the chieftain of the Kurahoupo canoe, Te Moungaroa, who is called the 'embodiment of the *mana* of the Kurahoupo canoe,' reached New Zealand, though in a differrent canoe. . . . On his arrival Te Moungaroa (in accordance with this theory of embodiment) introduced himself to the other Maori tribes with the words: 'I am the Kurahoupo canoe.'" "The Kurahoupo Canoe," *Journal of the Polynesian Society,* 2 (1893), 186 ff. Quotation from Friedrich R. Lehmann, *Mana. Der Begriff des "ausserordentlich Wirkungsvollen" bei Südseevölkern* (Leipzig, 1922), p. 13.

40. Cf. Thilenius, *Globus,* 87 (1905), 105 ff.; Vierkandt, *Globus,* 92 (1907), 45; also Alfred W. Howitt, *The Native Tribes of South-East Australia* (London and New York, 1904), pp. 380 ff.

41. Thus, e.g., the manitou of the Algonquin tribes of North America is characterized as a kind of mysterious force-susbtance which can manifest itself and penetrate everywhere. "A man in a steam bath often makes incisions on his arms and legs in order that the manitou which is awakened in the stone by the heat and dispersed in the steam of the water poured on the stone may enter into his body." Preuss, *Geistige Kultur,* p. 54.

42. Cf. Richard Karutz, "Der Emanismus," *Zeitschrift für Ethnologie, 45* (1913), 545–611. Cf. Friedrich Lehmann, pp. 14, 25, 111.

gradually from unremitting intellectual struggles. Here too the boundaries between the "substantial" and the "functional" are ever and again blurred, so that a semimythical hypostasis of purely functional and relational concepts arises. The physical concept of force, for example, freed itself but slowly from this involvement. In the history of physics we frequently encounter attempts to understand and classify the different forms of action by attaching them to specific *substances* and their transference from one point in space to another, from one "thing" to another. The physics of the eighteenth and early nineteenth century still spoke of a "thermal substance," an electrical or magnetic "matter." But while the true tendency of scientific, analytical-critical thinking is toward liberation from this substantial approach, it is characteristic of myth that despite all the "spirituality" of its *objects* and *contents,* its "logic"—the *form* of its contents— clings to bodies. So far we have attempted to characterize this logic in its most universal lines. Now we shall seek to determine how the specific object concept and causal concept of mythical thinking are manifested in the *individual* configuration and how they decisively determine all the *special* categories of myth.

Chapter 2

Particular Categories of Mythical Thinking

WHEN we compare the empirical-scientific and the mythical world views, it becomes evident that the contrast between them does not reside in their use of entirely different categories in contemplating and interpreting reality. It is not the quality of these categories but their *modality* which distinguishes myth from empirical-scientific knowledge. The modes of synthesis which they employ to give the form of unity to the sensuous manifold, to imprint a shape on disparate contents, disclose a thorough-going analogy and correspondence. They are the same universal forms of intuition and thought which constitute the unity of consciousness as such and which accordingly constitute the unity of both the mythical conscious-ness and the consciousness of pure knowledge. In this respect it may be said that each of these forms, before taking on its specific logical form and character, must pass through a preliminary mythical stage. The astronomi-cal picture of the cosmos and of the articulation of bodies in the cosmos originated in the astrological view of space and of processes in space. Before the general doctrine of motion developed into a pure mechanics—a mathematical representation of the phenomena of motion—it had sought to answer the question of the source of motion, which took it back to the mythical problem of creation, the problem of the "prime mover." And no less than the concepts of space and time, that of number, before becoming a purely mathematical concept, was a mythical concept which, though alien to the primitive mythical consciousness, underlies all its higher con-figurations. Long before number became a pure unit of measurement it was revered as "sacred number," and an aura of this reverence still attended the beginnings of scientific mathematics. Thus, taken abstractly, both the mythical and the scientific explanations of the world are dominated by the same kinds of relation: unity and multiplicity, coexistence, contiguity and succession. Yet each of these concepts, as soon as we place it in the mythical sphere, takes on a very special character, one might say a specific "tonality." This tonality assumed by the particular concepts within the mythical consciousness seems at first glance totally individual, something which can only be felt but in no way known and understood. And yet beneath this individual phenomenon there lies a universal. On closer scrutiny the special character of each particular category reveals a specific *type* of thought. The basic structure of mythical thinking—which manifests itself in the direction of mythical object consciousness and in the character of its concepts of reality, substance, and causality—goes farther: it also encompasses and determines the particular configurations of this thinking and, as it were, sets its imprint upon them.

The objective relation and the specification of the object within pure cognition go back to the basic form of the synthetic judgment: "We say that we know the *object* as soon as we have achieved synthetic unity in the manifold of intuition." But synthetic unity is essentially systematic unity: its production stands still at no point but progressively seizes upon the whole of experience, to refashion it into a single logical context, a totality of causes and effects. In the structure, in the hierarchy of these causes and effects, a special position is assigned to each particular phenomenon, to each being and event, by which it is distinguished from all others and at the same time *related* to all others. This is most clearly manifested in the mathematical view of the world. The particularity of a thing or action is designated when specific and characteristic numerical and quantitative values are assigned to it; but all those values are linked to one another in definite equations, in functional relationships, so that they form a series articulated according to law, a fixed network of exact quantitative determinations. In this sense modern physics, for example, "apprehends" the totality of actions by expressing each particular action in its four space-time coordinates x_1, x_2, x_3, x_4 and reducing the changes of these coordinates to ultimate invariant laws. This example shows once again that for scientific thinking synthesis and analysis are not different or opposite operations but it is through one and the same process that the particulars are sharply differentiated, and comprehended in the systematic unity of the whole. The reason for this is to be sought in the nature of the synthetic judgment itself. For what distinguishes synthetic judgment from analytical judgment is that it considers the unity it effects not as a conceptual *identity* but as a unity of *different* entities. Each element postulated in it is thus characterized: it is not solely "in itself," nor does it remain logically in itself, but rather it is correlative to some other element. To give a schematic expression of this relationship let us call the elements of the relation *a* and *b* and the relation by which they are held together *R*. Every such relationship shows a threefold *articulation*. The two elements (*a* and *b*) are clearly differentiated through the relation into which they enter. Moreover, the *form* of the relation itself (*R*) signifies something new and specific as opposed to the contents that are ordered in it. It belongs, so to speak, to a different plane of signification from the particular contents; it is not itself a particular content, a specific thing, but a universal, purely ideal *relation*. Such ideal relations form the foundation of what scientific cognition calls the "truth" of phenomena, for what is meant by this truth is nothing other than the totality of the phenomena themselves, insofar as they are not taken in their concrete existence but are transposed into the form of a logical *relationship,* a relationship which is based to an equal degree and with equal necessity on acts both of logical synthesis and of logical analysis.

Myth, too, strives for a "unity of the world" and in this striving moves in very specific channels prescribed by its spiritual "nature." Even in lowest levels of mythical thinking, which seem wholly subject to immediate sensory impression and elementary sensory drives, even in magic, which disperses the world into a confused multiplicity of demonic forces, we find traits pointing to a kind of articulation, a future "organization" of these forces. And as myth rises to higher configurations, as it transforms the demons into gods, each with his own individuality and history, the nature and efficacy of these forces become more and more clearly differentiated. Just as scientific cognition strives for a hierarchy of laws, a systematic superordination and subordination of causes and effects, so myth strives for a hierarchy of forces and gods. The world becomes more intelligible in proportion as its parts are assigned to the various gods, as special spheres of material reality and human activity are placed under the guardianship of particular deities. But though the mythical world is thus woven into a whole, this intuitive whole discloses a very different character from that conceptual whole in which cognition strives to comprehend reality. Here there are no ideal, relational forms which constitute the objective world as a world thoroughly determined by law; here, on the contrary, all reality is smelted down into concrete unifying images. And this contrast, visible in the *result,* rests ultimately on an opposition in *principle*. Every *particular* synthesis effected by mythical thinking embodies this character which only becomes fully evident in the whole. Whereas scientific cognition can combine elements only by differentiating them in the same basic critical act, myth seems to roll up everything it touches into unity without distinction. The relations it postulates are such that the elements which enter into them not only enter into a reciprocal ideal relationship, but become positively identical with one another, become one and the same *thing*. Things which come into contact with one another in a mythical sense—whether this contact is taken as a spatial or temporal contiguity or as a similarity, however remote, or as membership in the same class or species—have fundamentally ceased to be a multiplicity: they have acquired a substantial unity. And this is evident even at the lowest stages of myth. Concerning this basic mythical trend Preuss has written, for example: "It is as though a particular object cannot be regarded as distinct once it has aroused magical interest but always bears within it an appurtenance to other objects with which it is identified, so that its outward appearance constitutes only a kind of veil, a mask." [1] Along this line mythical thinking shows itself to be concrete in the literal sense: whatever things it may seize upon undergo a characteristic concretion; they grow together. Whereas scientific cognition seeks a synthesis of distinctly differentiated elements, mythical intuition ultimately brings about a *coincidence* of whatever elements it combines. In place of a synthetic unity, a unity of *different* entities, we have a material indifference. And this becomes understandable when we consider that for the mythical view there is fundamentally but one dimension of relation, one single "plane of being." In cognition the pure relational concept comes, as it were, *between* the elements which it links. For it is not of the same world as these elements—it has no material *existence* comparable to theirs, but only an ideal *signification*. The history of philosophy and the history of science show that the first awareness of this special position of pure relational concepts brought about a new epoch in scientific thought. The first strictly logical characterization of these concepts stressed this opposition as the crucial factor: the pure "forms" of intuition and thought were designated as a "not-being," a μὴ ὄν, to distinguish them from the mode of existence pertaining to things, to sensuous phenomena. But for myth there is no such not-being in which the being, the "truth" of the phenomenon is grounded: it knows only immediate existence and immediate efficacy. Hence the relations which it

1. *Geistige Kultur*, p. 13.

postulates are not logical relations in which those things which enter into them are at once differentiated and linked; they are a kind of glue which can somehow fasten the most dissimilar things together.

This characteristic law of the *concrescence or coincidence of the members of a relation in mythical thinking* can be followed through all its categories. To begin with the category of *quantity,* we have already seen how mythical thinking makes no sharp dividing line between the whole and its parts, how the part not only *stands for* the whole but positively *is* the whole. For scientific thought, which takes quantity as a synthetic relational form, every magnitude is a one in many, i.e. unity and multiplicity are equally necessary, strictly correlative factors in it. The synthesis of elements into a whole presupposes their sharp differentiation *as* elements. Thus number is defined by the Pythagoreans as that which brings all things into harmony within the soul, which thus lends them body and "divides the different relationships of things, whether they be nonlimited or limiting, into their separate groups." [2] And precisely on this division rest the necessity and possibility of all harmony, for "the things which were alike and related needed no harmony, but the things which were unlike and unrelated and unequally arranged are necessarily fastened together by such a harmony, through which they are destined to endure in the universe." [3] Instead of such a harmony, which is the "unity of many mixed elements and an agreement between disagreeing elements," mythical thinking knows only the principle of the equivalence of the part with the whole. The whole is the part, in the sense that it enters into it with its whole mythical-substantial essence, that it is somehow sensuously and materially "in" it. The whole man is contained in his hair, his nail-cuttings, his clothes, his footprints. Every trace a man leaves passes as a real part of him, which can react on him as a whole and endanger him as a whole.[4] And the same mythical law of "participation" which holds for empirical things prevails for purely ideal relations (in *our* sense). Similarly, the genus, in its relation to the species or individuals it comprises, is not a universal which logically determines the particular but is immediately present, living and acting in this particular. Here we have no mere logical subordination but an actual sub-

2. Philolaus of Tarentum. Fragment 11 in Hermann Diels, *Die Fragmente der Vorso-kratiker, griechisch und deutsch* (6th ed. 3 vols. Berlin, Weidmann, 1951–52). Eng. trans. by Kathleen Freeman, *Ancilla to the Pre-Socratic Philosophers* (Cambridge, Harvard Univ. Press, 1948), p. 75.

3. Freeman, p. 74.

4. For examples see above, pp. 50 ff.

jection of the individual to its generic concept. The structure of the totemic world view, for example, can scarcely be understood except through this essential trait of mythical thinking. For in the totemic organization of men and the world as a whole there is no mere coordination between on the one hand the classes of men and things and on the other, specific classes of animals and plants; on the contrary, here the individual is truly regarded as dependent on his totemic ancestor, in fact as identical with him. According to Karl von den Steinen's well-known report the Trumais of Northern Brazil say, for example, that they are aquatic animals, while the Bororos call themselves red parrots.[5] Mythical thinking does not know that relation which we call a relation of logical subsumption, the relation of an individual to its species or genus, but always forms a material relation of action and thus—since in mythical thinking only "like" can act on "like"—a relation of material equivalence.

The same tendency becomes still more evident when we consider it from the standpoint of quality rather than quantity—i.e. when, instead of the relation between the whole and its parts, we consider that between the thing and its attributes. Here again we observe the same characteristic coincidence of the members of the relation: for mythical thinking the attribute is not one defining the aspect of the thing; rather, it expresses and contains within it the whole of the thing, seen from a different angle. For scientific cognition, the reciprocal determination created in it rests, as before, on an opposition which in this determination is reconciled but not effaced. The subject of the attributes, the substance in which they inhere, is not itself immediately comparable with any attribute, cannot be apprehended and demonstrated as a concrete thing, but confronts each particular attribute as well as the sum of attributes as something "other," something independent. Here "accidents" are not actual material "parts" of the substance; the substance on the contrary forms the ideal center and mediation through which they are related to one another and through which they are united. But in myth the unity it creates is here again immediately diffused into mere equivalence. For myth, which sees reality on a single plane, one and the same substance does not "have" different attributes; on the contrary each specification as such *is* substance, i.e. it can be apprehended only in immediate concretion, in direct hypostatization. We have already

5. Karl von den Steinen, *Unter den Naturvölkern Zentral-Brasiliens* (2d ed. Berlin, 1897), p. 307. Other characteristic examples of this mythical "law of participation" may be found in Lévy-Bruhl, *Das Denken der Naturvölker*, ch. 2.

seen how all mere properties and attributes, all activities and all relations, undergo this hypostatization (see above, pp. 52 ff.). But far more sharply than at the primitive levels of mythical thinking, the characteristic principle here at work is manifested where myth is on its way to allying itself and permeating itself with the basic principle of scientific thought, where in conjunction with this principle it creates a kind of hybrid, a semimythical "science" of nature. Just as the mythical concept of *causality* can perhaps be most clearly illustrated by the structure of astrology,[6] so the specific tendency of the mythical concept of the attribute is most evident in the structure of alchemy. And this gives us a systematic explanation of the relation between alchemy and astrology, which can be followed throughout their history:[7] the two are merely different expressions of the same form of thought, a mythical identity-thinking in the form of substance. Here every similarity in the sensuous manifestation of different things or in their mode of action is ultimately explained by the supposition that one and the same material cause is in some way "contained" in them. Alchemy, for example, looks on bodies as complexes of simple qualities from which they arise through mere aggregation. Each attribute represents a specific elementary thing, and from the sum of these elementary things the composite world, the world of empirical bodies, is built. He who knows the mixture of these elementary things consequently knows the secret of their changes and is lord over them, for he not only understands these changes but can by his own action bring them about. The alchemist can produce the "philosopher's stone" from common quicksilver by first extracting a water, i.e. that mobile, fluid element which detracts from the true perfection of the quicksilver. His next task is to "fixate" the body thus obtained, i.e. to free it from its volatility by removing an airy element which it still contains. In the course of its history, alchemy developed this addition and subtraction of attributes into a highly ingenious and intricate system. In these extreme refinements and sublimations we still clearly discern the mythical root of the whole process. All alchemic operations, regardless of their individual type, have at their base the fundamental idea of the transferability and material detachability of attributes and states—the same idea which is disclosed at a more naive and primitive stage in such notions as

6. Cf. my *Die Begriffsform im mythischen Denken*, pp. 29 ff.
7. For documentation of this fact see Hermann F. M. Kopp, *Die Alchimie in älterer und neuerer Zeit* (Heidelberg, 1886); Edmund O. von Lippmann, *Entstehung und Ausbreitung der Alchimie* (Berlin, 1919).

that of the "scapegoat" (above, pp. 55 ff.). Every particular property that matter possesses, every form it can assume, every efficacy it can exert is hypostatized into a special substance, an independent being.[8] Modern science, and particularly modern chemistry in the form given it by Lavoisier, succeeded in overcoming this semimythical alchemic concept of the attribute only by fundamentally reforming the whole question. For modern science the "attribute" is not simple but highly complex; not original and elementary but derived; not absolute but thoroughly relative. What, according to a sensationalist view, one calls an attribute of things and seeks to apprehend and understand immediately as such is interpreted by critical analysis as a determinate mode of efficacy, a specific reaction, which, however, arises only under very definite *conditions*. Thus the inflammability of a body no longer implies the presence of a specific substance, *phlogiston,* in it, but signifies its reaction to oxygen; while the solubility of a body signifies its reaction to water or an acid, etc. The particular quality appears no longer as a substance but as something thoroughly contingent which, under causal analysis, dissolves into a mesh of relations. And from this it follows obversely that until this form of logical analysis is developed, "thing" and "attribute" cannot be sharply differentiated; the categorical spheres of the two concepts must inevitably move together and ultimately merge.

The typical contrast between myth and cognition can be shown in the category of *similarity* no less than in the categories of the *whole and the part* and the *attribute*. The articulation of the chaos of sensory impressions, in which definite groups based on similarities are picked out and specific series are formed, is, again, common to both logical and mythical thinking; without it myth could no more arrive at stable configurations than logical thought at stable concepts. But the similarities of things are, once again, apprehended in different directions. In mythical thinking any similarity of sensuous manifestation suffices to group the entities in which it appears into a single mythical "genus." Any characteristic, however external, is as good as another; there can be no sharp distinction between "inward" and "outward," "essential" and "nonessential," precisely because for myth every perceptible similarity is an immediate expression of an identity of *essence*. This similarity is never a mere concept of relation and reflection but is a real force—absolutely actual because absolutely effective. All so-

8. For details cf. the accounts of Lippmann (especially pp. 318 ff.) and Marcellin P. E. Berthelot, *Les Origines de l'alchimie* (Paris, 1885).

called analogy magic reveals this basic mythical view, which, indeed, is more obscured than clarified by the false name of analogy magic. For where we see a mere analogy, i.e. a mere *relation,* myth sees immediate existence and presence. For myth there is no mere sign which suggests something distant and absent; for myth the thing is present with a part of itself, i.e. in the mythical view; the thing is present as a whole, as soon as anything similar to it is given. In the tobacco smoke rising from a pipe the mythical consciousness sees neither a mere symbol nor a mere instrument for making rain—it sees the tangible image of a cloud and in this image the thing itself, the desired rain. It is a general principle of magic that one can gain possession of things by a mere mimetic representation of them, without performing any action which we would call purposive,[9] because for the mythical consciousness there is no such thing as *mere* mimesis, *mere* signification. Scientific thinking again shows its dual character in its postulation of similarities and its creation of similar series: it proceeds at once synthetically and analytically. In similar contents it emphasizes the factor of dissimilarity as well as the factor of similarity; indeed it gives special emphasis to the factor of dissimilarity, since in setting up its genera and species it is less concerned with bringing out the common element in them than with the principle on which differentiation and gradation within one and the same genus are based. The interpenetration of these two tendencies is demonstrable for example in the structure of any *mathematical* class concept. When mathematical thinking subsumes the circle and the ellipse, the hyperbola and parabola under *one* concept, this subsumption is not grounded in any immediate similarity of forms, which from the standpoint of the senses are as dissimilar as possible. But in characterizing all these forms as "conic sections," mathematical thinking apprehends a unity of *law,* a unity of structural principle in the midst of dissimilarity. The expression of this law, the general formula for curves of the second order, fully represents their common principle as well as their inner differences, for it shows how, through the simple variation of certain magnitudes, one geometric form passes into another. This principle, which determines and regulates the change, is here no less necessary and in the strict sense "constitutive" of the concept than the positing of the common factor. Thus the view of traditional logicians—which ordinarily

---

9. Abundant examples can be found in Frazer, "The Magic Art and the Evolution of Kings," *Golden Bough,* Vols. *1–2,* Pt. I. Cf. also Preuss, *Geistige Kultur,* p. 29. See above, pp. 48 ff.

attributes the formation of logical classes and genera to abstraction, and by abstraction means nothing other than the selection of those characteristics in which a multiplicity of contents agree—is just as one-sided as the view which sees the function of causal thinking solely in the combination, or association, of representations. In neither case are given and stably delimited contents merely combined; it is rather this logical act of delimitation itself that is *accomplished*. And here again myth shows that this delimitation—this differentiation of the individual, the species, and the genus in the sense of logical subordination, of abstraction and determination—is alien to it. Just as it sees the whole in every part, so in every specimen of a genus it immediately sees the genus with all its mythical characteristics, i.e. forces. Thus, whereas the logical class divides and unites at the same time—since it endeavors to derive the particular from the general by means of an all-inclusive principle—myth binds particulars together in the unity of an image, a mythical figure. Once the parts, the specimens, the species have thus become enmeshed, all differentiation ceases; there is only a total indifference in which they continuously merge with one another.

And yet it might seem as though our efforts thus far to distinguish between the mythical and the logical form of thought contributed little or nothing to an understanding of myth as a whole, to an insight into the original spiritual stratum in which it arose. For is it not a *petitio principii*, a false rationalization of myth, to attempt to understand it through its *form of thought?* Admitted even that such a form exists—is it anything more than an outward shell which conceals the core of myth? Does myth not signify a unity of intuition, an *intuitive* unity preceding and underlying all the explanations contributed by *discursive* thought? And even this form of intuition does not yet designate the ultimate stratum from which it rises and from which new life continuously pours into it. For nowhere in myth do we find a passive contemplation of things; here all contemplation starts from an attitude, an act of the feeling and will. Insofar as myth condenses into lasting configuration, insofar as it sets before us the stable outlines of an objective world of forms, the significance of this world becomes intelligible to us only if behind it we can feel the dynamic of the life feeling from which it originally grew. Only where this feeling is aroused from within, only where it manifests itself in love and hate, fear and hope, joy and grief, is that mythical fantasy engendered which creates a world of specific representations. But from this it seems to follow that any characterization of the mythical forms of thought applies only to something mediated and derived—that it must remain inadequate unless it succeeds in going back from the mere mythical form of *thought* to the mythical form of *intuition* and its characteristic form of *life*. For these forms are nowhere distinct from one another; from the most primitive productions to the highest and purest configurations of myth they remain interwoven; and this is what makes the mythical world so characteristically self-contained and gives it its specific imprint. This world, too, shapes and articulates itself according to the basic forms of "pure intuition": it, too, breaks down into unity and multiplicity, into a "coexistence" of objects and a succession of events. But the mythical intuition of space, time, and number that thus arises is differentiated by highly characteristic boundaries from what space, time, and number signify in theoretical thought and the theoretical structure of the objective world. These boundaries can only become clear and visible if we succeed in reducing the mediated divisions which we encounter in mythical thinking as in the thinking of pure cognition to a kind of primordial division from which they issue. For myth, too, presupposes a spiritual crisis of this sort—it, too, takes form only when a division occurs in consciousness as a whole and introduces into men's intuition of the world as a whole a specific differentiation which divides this whole into diverse strata of meaning. It is this first division which contains all others in germ and through which they remain determined and dominated—and it is in this division if anywhere that we shall find the specific character not so much of mythical thinking as of mythical intuition and the mythical life feeling.

PART II

Myth as a Form of Intuition. Structure and Articulation of the World of Time and Space in the Mythical Consciousness

Chapter 1

The Basic Opposition

THE *theoretical* structure of men's world view begins at the point where consciousness first makes a clear distinction between illusion and truth, between what is merely perceived or represented and what truly "is," between the subjective and the objective. The criterion for truth and objectivity here employed is the factor of permanence, of logical constancy and logical necessity. Each particular content of consciousness is referred to this postulate of thoroughgoing lawfulness and measured by it. Thus, spheres of being are differentiated: the relatively transient is distinguished from the relatively permanent, the accidental and unique from the universally valid. Certain elements of experience prove to be necessary and fundamental, the framework supporting the whole edifice. To others only a dependent and mediate reality is assigned; they "are" only insofar as the particular conditions of their occurrence are realized, and by these conditions they are restricted to a specific sphere or sector of being. Thus, theoretical thought progresses by continuously postulating specific differences of logical value, one might say logical "rank," in the data of sensory experience. And the universal criterion it here employs is the principle of sufficient reason, which it retains as its supreme postulate, its primary requirement. In it is expressed the essential direction, the characteristic modality of knowledge. To "know" is to advance from the immediacy of sensation and perception to the purely cogitated and mediated "cause," to dissect the simple matter of sensory impressions into strata of "grounds" and "consequences."

As we have seen, such a differentiation and stratification is totally alien to the mythical consciousness. This consciousness lives in the immediate impression, which it accepts without measuring it by something else. For the mythical consciousness the impression is not merely relative but absolute; the impression is not through something else and does not depend on something else as its condition; on the contrary it manifests and confirms itself by the simple intensity of its presence, by the irresistible force with which it impresses itself upon consciousness. Whereas scientific thought takes an attitude of inquiry and doubt toward the "object" with its claim to objectivity and necessity, myth knows no such opposition. It "has" the object only insofar as it is overpowered by it; it does not possess the object by progressively building it but is simply possessed by it. It has no will to understand the object by encompassing it logically and articulating it with a complex of causes and effects; it is simply overpowered by the object. But this very intensity, this immediate power with which the mythical object is present for consciousness, removes it from the mere series of uniform being and uniform recurrence. Instead of being bound by the schema of a rule, a necessary law, each object that engages and fills the mythical consciousness pertains, as it were, only to itself; it is incomparable and unique. It lives in an individual atmosphere and can only be apprehended in its uniqueness, its immediate here and now. Yet on the other hand the contents of the mythical consciousness do not disperse into mere disconnected particulars; they, too, are governed by a universal principle—which, however, is of an entirely different kind and origin from the universal principle of the logical concept. For precisely through their special character all the contents of the mythical consciousness are rejoined into a whole. They form a self-enclosed realm and possess a common tonality, by which they are distinguished from the contents of common, everyday, empirical existence. This trait of isolation, this character of the egregious, is essential to every content of the mythical consciousness as such; it can be traced from the lowest to the highest levels, from the magical world view which still understands magic in a purely practical, hence semitechnical, sense up to the highest manifestations of religion, in which all miracles are ultimately dissolved in the one miracle of the religious spirit. It is this characteristic *transcendence* which links the contents of the mythical and the religious consciousness. In their mere immediate existence they all contain a revelation and at the same time retain a kind of mystery; it is this interpenetration, this revelation which both reveals and conceals, that gives the mythical-religious content its basic trait, its character of the "sacred." [1]

---

1. On the concept of the sacred as a fundamental religious category cf. Rudolf Otto, *Das Heilige. Über das Irrationale in der Idee des Göttlichen und sein Verhältnis zum Rationalen* (Göttingen, 1917).

The significance of this fundamental character and its bearing on the structure of the mythical world are perhaps most evident where it is still found in a totally unmingled state, where it is not yet permeated with other shadings of signification and value or, above all, with ethical implications. For original mythical feeling the meaning and power of the sacred are limited to no particular sphere of reality or value. This meaning is rather imprinted upon the immediate concrete totality of existence and events. There is no sharp boundary dividing the world spatially, as it were, into a "here" and a "beyond," a purely "empirical" and a "transcendent" sphere. The differentiation effected in the consciousness of the sacred is, on the contrary, purely qualitative. Any content of existence, however commonplace, can gain the distinguishing character of the sacred, provided only that it fall under the specific mythical-religious *perspective,* provided only that instead of remaining within the accustomed sphere of actions and events it captures mythical interest and enthusiasm from one angle or another. The characteristic of the sacred is consequently not limited from the very outset to specific objects or groups of objects; on the contrary, any content, however indifferent, can suddenly participate in it. It designates a specific ideal relation rather than a specific objective property. Myth, too, begins by introducing certain differentiations into indistinct, "indifferent reality," by dividing it into different spheres of meaning. It, too, gives form and meaning by interrupting the indifferent uniformity of the contents of consciousness—by introducing certain distinctions of "value" into this indifference. All reality and all events are projected into the fundamental opposition of the sacred and the profane, and in this projection they assume a new meaning, one which they do not simply have from the very beginning but which they acquire in this form of contemplation, one might say in this mythical "illumination."

These general considerations throw considerable light on certain basic phenomena of mythical thinking, certain distinctions and stratifications which have been disclosed in the last decades, particularly by the empirical study of mythology. Ever since Codrington in his well-known work on the Melanesians pointed to mana as a central concept of primitive mythical thinking, the problems grouped around this concept have attracted increasing interest among ethnologists, psychologists, and sociologists. First it became evident that from the standpoint of pure content the representation expressed in the mana of the Melanesians and Polynesians, has its exact correlate in other mythical concepts distributed over the whole earth in diverse variants. The *manitou* of the Algonquin tribes of North America, the *orenda* of the Iroquois, the *wakanda* of the Sioux disclose such complete and striking parallels with the mana that a truly elementary mythical idea seemed to have been found.[2] The mere phenomenology of mythical thinking seemed to suggest that mana represented not a mere *content* of the mythical consciousness but one of its typical *forms*, perhaps indeed its most fundamental form. Some scholars went so far as to treat the notion of mana as a category of mythical-religious thinking, or even as the basic religious category.[3] Mana was linked with the closely related, negative concept of "taboo"; and with these two antithetical concepts an original stratum of the mythical-religious consciousness seemed to have been laid bare. The mana-taboo formula was looked upon as a "minimum definition of religion," as one of its primary constitutive conditions.[4] But with the extension of the mana concept the difficulty of defining it sharply became increasingly evident. The attempts to do so by situating it among the various hypotheses concerning the origin of mythical thinking proved more and more unsatisfactory. Codrington interpreted mana essentially as a "spiritual power," which he further qualified as "supernatural." But this attempt to reduce mana ultimately to the soul and so interpret it through the presuppositions of animism did not stand up under criticism. The more closely scholars defined the signification of the *word* "mana" and the content of its concept, the more evident it became that both belonged to another stratum, to a pre-animistic direction of mythical thinking. The use of the *word* mana seemed in truth to have its place in a sphere where there can be no question of a highly developed concept of the soul

2. The copious literature on the concept of mana (up to 1920) has been carefully compiled and critically discussed in Friedrich Lehmann, *Mana*. See above, p. 56. On the manitou of the Algonquins cf. William Jones, "The Algonkin Manitou," *Journal of American Folklore, 18* (1905), 183–190; on the orenda of the Iroquois see J. N. B. Hewitt, "Orenda and a Definition of Religion," *American Anthropologist*, n.s., 4 (1902), 33–46; on the wakanda see W. J. McGee, "The Siouan Indians," *Fifteenth Annual Report of the [U.S.] Bureau of [American] Ethnology*, 1893–94 (Washington, 1897), pp. 157–204. See also Karl Beth, *Religion und Magie bei den Naturvölkern. Ein religionsgeschichtlicher Beitrag zur Frage nach den Anfängen der Religion* (Leipzig, 1914), pp. 211 ff.

3. The concept of mana is, e.g., treated as a fundamental category of mythical thinking by Henri Hubert and Marcel Mauss, "Esquisse d'une théorie générale de la magie," *Année sociologique*, 7 (1902–03), 1–146.

4. Cf. in particular Robert R. Marett, "The Taboo-mana Formula as a Minimum Definition of Religion," *Archiv für Religionswissenschaft, 12* (1909), 186–194; idem, *Threshold of Religion* (2d ed. 1914), pp. 99 ff.

or the personality, or at least where there is no clear dividing line between physical and psychic, spiritual-personal and impersonal reality.[5]

And this usage preserves a characteristic indifference toward other contrasts of either advanced logical or mythical thinking. Most particularly it draws no sharp distinction between the concepts of substance and force. Thus, neither the "substantial" theory which interprets mana simply as a magic substance, nor the "dynamistic" theory which places the emphasis on the concept of power, on potency and efficacy, seems to arrive at the true significance of the concept of mana. This significance lies rather in its characteristic "fluidity," in its merging of properties which to our way of thinking are clearly distinguished. In this stratum, even where we seem to be dealing with spiritual reality and spiritual forces, these are still permeated with substantial images. The spirits at this stage, it has been said, are "of an extremely indefinite kind, without distinction between natural and supernatural, real and ideal, between persons and other existences and entities." [6] Thus what seems to remain as the relatively solid core of the idea of mana is simply the impression of the extraordinary, the unusual, the uncommon. The essential is not *what* bears this specification, but precisely this specification itself, this character of the uncommon. The idea of mana, like the negatively corresponding idea of taboo,, represents a sphere distinct from and opposed to the sphere of daily life, of customary processes. Here other criteria prevail, other possibilities, forces, and modes of efficacy than those manifested in the common course of things. But at the same time this realm is filled with constant threats, with unknown dangers which surround men on all sides. Thus the content of the notions of mana and taboo can never be fully apprehended purely through inquiry into their objects. They do not serve to designate specific classes of objects, but represent the characteristic accent which the magical-mythical con-

5. Thus, e.g., mana can be attributed to any physical thing whatsoever, even if it is not regarded as the seat of a spirit or demon, provided that the thing is distinguished by any special characteristic (e.g. its size) from the sphere of the customary and common. On the other hand, *all* psychic reality is by no means held to be endowed with mana. The souls of the dead usually have no mana, but only the souls of those who were gifted with mana in their lifetime—who were distinguished by special powers which make them sought after or feared after their death. Cf. Robert H. Codrington, *The Melanesians* (Oxford, 1891), p. 253.

6. Alfred E. Crawley, *The Idea of the Soul* (London, A. and C. Black, 1909); quoted from Edvard Lehmann, *Die Anfänge der Religion und die Religion der primitiven Völker*, Die Kultur der Gegenwart, Vol. *1*, Pt. III (2d ed. Leipzig, 1913), p. 15.

sciousness places on objects. This accent divides the whole of reality and action into a mythically significant and mythically irrelevant sphere, into what arouses mythical interest and what leaves it relatively indifferent. Thus there is neither more nor less justification for regarding the taboo-mana formula as the "foundation" of myth and religion than for regarding the interjection as the foundation of language. Both concepts represent, as it were, primary interjections of the mythical consciousness. They still have no independent function of signification and representation but resemble cries of mythical emotion.[7] They designate that amazement, that θαυμάζειν, with which myth as well as scientific cognition and "philosophy" begins. When mere bestial terror becomes an astonishment moving in a twofold direction, composed of opposite emotions—fear and hope, awe and admiration—when sensory agitation thus seeks for the first time an issue and an *expression,* man stands on the threshold of a new spirituality. It is this characteristic spirituality which is in a sense reflected in the idea of the sacred. For the sacred always appears *at once* as the distant and the near, as the familiar and protective but at the same time absolutely inaccessible, as the *mysterium tremendum* and the *mysterium fascinosum*.[8] The consequence of this twofold character is that in differentiating itself from empirical, profane substance, the sacred does not simply *repel* it but progressively *permeates* it; in its opposition it still retains the ability to give form to its opposite. The general concept of taboo and the concrete abundance of taboo regulations mark the first steps on the road to this form-giving, this configuration. In a purely negative sense they represent the first limitation which the will and the immediate sensory drive impose on themselves; but this negative barrier contains the germ and the first precondition for a positive limitation, a positive configuration. However, the direction in which this primary configuration moves remains sharply differentiated from other fundamental directions of the cultural consciousness. There are characteristic differences of mythical "valence," just as there

7. Thus it is reported, particularly of the Algonquin manitou, that the term is used wherever the imagination is aroused by something new and unusual. If, e.g., a fisherman catches a new variety of fish, the term "manitou" is immediately applied to it. Cf. Marett, *Threshold of Religion* (3d ed.), p. 21. Cf. also Nathan Söderblom, *Das Werden des Gottesglaubens. Untersuchungen über die Anfänge der Religion* (Leipzig, 1916), pp. 95 ff. The words "wakan" and "wakanda" among the Sioux also seem to go back etymologically to interjections of astonishment. See Brinton, p. 61.

8. This twofold character of the sacred has been particularly stressed by Rudolf Otto, *Das Heilige.*

are similar original differences of logical or ethical dignity. The original mythical concept of holiness coincides so little with that of ethical purity that a remarkable opposition, a characteristic tension, can arise between the two. That which is hallowed in a mythical and religious sense has thereby become forbidden, an object of awe, hence unclean. This double meaning, this peculiar ambivalence is still expressed in the Latin *sacer* and the Greek ἅγιος, ἅζεσθαί, for these terms designate both the holy and the accursed or forbidden, but in both cases something consecrated and set apart.[9]

We shall see that this basic trend of the mythical consciousness, this original division between the sacred and profane, the consecrated and the unconsecrated, is by no means limited to particular, eminently primitive creations but is confirmed even in the supreme configurations of myth. It is as though everything that myth grasps were drawn into this division, which seems to impregnate the entire world, insofar as it represents a mythically formed whole. All derived and mediated forms of the mythical world view, regardless of their complexity and spiritual elevation, remain in some part conditioned by this primary division. The entire wealth and dynamism of the mythical forms result from the development of this accentuation of existence expressed in the concept of the sacred, from its progressive extension to new spheres and contents of consciousness. When we study this development, we find an unmistakable analogy between the growth of the mythical objective world and the growth of the empirical objective world. In both the isolation of the immediate datum is overcome; in both we must seek to understand how particulars are woven into a whole. And in both cases the concrete expressions of this wholeness, its intuitive schemata, prove to be the fundamental forms of space, time, and finally of number in which the factors which appear separate in space and time, the factor of "coexistence" and the factor of "succession," permeate each other. Any relationship into which the contents of mythical as of empirical consciousness gradually enter is attainable only in and through these forms of space, time, and number. But the *mode* of this grouping again shows the fundamental difference between logical and mythical synthesis. In empirical knowledge the intuitive structure of empirical reality is mediately determined by the general goal that it sets itself—by its theoretical con-

9. Cf. Nathan Söderblom, "Holiness," in Hastings' *Encyclopaedia of Religion and Ethics,* 6, 376 ff. For the Greek ἅγιος cf. Eduard Williger, *Hagios, Untersuchungen zur Terminologie des Heiligen in den hellenisch-hellenistischen Religionen* (Giessen, 1922).

cept of truth and reality. The concepts of space, time, and number are formed in accordance with the general logical idea toward which pure cognition aims more and more resolutely and consciously. Space, time, and number stand out as the logical media through which a mere aggregate of perceptions is gradually formed into a system of experience. The representations of order in coexistence, of order in succession, and of a stable numerical, quantitative order of all empirical contents form the foundation for an ultimate synthesis of all these contents into a lawful or causal world order. In this respect space, time, and number are, for theoretical knowledge, nothing other than the vehicles of the principle of causality. They are the basic constants to which all variables are referred, the universal systems of coordinates in which all particulars must in some way be located and assigned the fixed position which guarantees their fixed and unambiguous value. Thus as theoretical knowledge progresses, the purely intuitive qualities of space, time, and number recede more and more into the background. They themselves appear less as concrete contents of consciousness than as its universal *ordinative forms*. Leibniz, the logician and philosopher of the "principle of sufficient reason," was the first to state his relationship with full clarity, defining space as the ideal condition of "order in coexistence" and time as the ideal condition of "order in succession," and interpreting them, on the basis of this purely ideal character, not as contents of reality but as "eternal truths." And similarly for Kant the true explanation, the "transcendental deduction" of space, time, and number consists in showing them to be pure principles of mathematical cognition, hence mediately of all empirical knowledge. As the conditions of experience they are at the same time conditions of the objects of experience. The space of pure geometry, the number of pure arithmetic, the time of pure mechanics are, in a sense, original forms of the theoretical consciousness; they constitute logical schemata, which mediate between the sensory particular and the universal law of thought, of the pure understanding.

Mythical thinking reveals the same process of schematization; as it progresses it, too, discloses an increasing endeavor to articulate all substance in a common spatial order and all happenings in a common order of time and destiny. This striving found its highest mythical fulfillment in the structure of the astrological world view; but its true root goes deeper, extending down into the original, fundamental stratum of the mythical consciousness. We have seen that in the progress of *linguistic*

concept formation the working out of clear spatial distinctions was pre-
requisite to the designation of universal logical relations. We have seen
how the simplest spatial terms, the designations of the here and there,
the near and distant, contain a fruitful germ which with the progress
of language unfolds into a surprising wealth of intellectual terms. By the
intermediary of spatial terms the two ends of language formation seemed
in a sense truly linked for the first time; a purely spiritual factor seemed
to have been disclosed in sensuous expression, and a sensuous factor in
spiritual expression.[10] Space—and time as well—proves to be a similar
medium of spiritualization in the mythical sphere. The first clear articulations of the mythical world are linked with spatial and temporal distinctions. But the mythical consciousness is not, like the theoretical consciousness, concerned with gaining fundamental constants by which to
explain variation and change. This differentiation is replaced by another,
which is determined by the characteristic perspective of myth. The mythical consciousness arrives at an articulation of space and time not by stabiliz-
ing the fluctuation of sensuous phenomena but by introducing its specific
opposition—the opposition of the sacred and profane—into spatial and
temporal reality. This fundamental and original accent of the mythical
consciousness also dominates all the particular divisions and combina-
tions within space as a whole and time as a whole. At primitive levels of
mythical consciousness "power" and "sacredness" still appear as kinds
of things: sensuous, physical somethings which adhere to specific persons or things as their vehicle. But in the progressive development of the
mythical consciousness this character of sacredness is gradually transferred
from particular persons or things to other determinations which are
purely ideal in *our* sense. Now, this character appears above all in holy
places, in holy days and seasons, and finally in sacred numbers. The
contrast between sacred and profane is viewed no longer as a particular
but as a truly *universal* opposition. Because all existence is articulated in
the form of space and all change in the rhythm and periodicity of time,
every attribute which adheres to a specific spatial-temporal *place* is immediately transferred to the *content* that is given in it; while conversely,
the special character of the content gives a distinguishing character to
the place in which it is situated. Through this mutual determination all
reality and all events are gradually spun into a network of the subtlest
mythical relations. Just as space, time, and number can be shown to be basic

10. Cf. *1*, 198 ff.

instruments and stages in the process of *objectivization*, so they also represent the three essential phases in the process of mythical apperception. Here a perspective is opened upon a specific morphology of myth which complements our inquiry into the general form of mythical thinking and fills it with concrete content.

Chapter 2

Foundations of a Theory of Mythical Forms. Space, Time, and Number

1. The Articulation of Space in the Mythical Consciousness

WE MAY arrive at a provisional and general characterization of the mythical intuition of space by starting from the observation that it occupies a kind of middle position between the space of sense perception and the space of pure cognition, that is, geometry. It is self-evident that the space of perception, the space of vision and touch, does not coincide with the space of pure mathematics, that there is indeed a thoroughgoing divergence between the two. The determinations of mathematical space do not follow simply from those of sensory space (the former cannot even be derived from the latter in an unbroken logical sequence); on the contrary, we require a peculiar reversal of perspective, a *negation* of what seems immediately given in sensory perception, before we can arrive at the "logical space" of pure mathematics. Particularly, a comparison between "physiological" space and the "metric" space upon which Euclidean geometry bases its constructions shows this antithetical relationship in every detail. What is established in the one seems negated and reversed in the other. Euclidean space is characterized by the three basic attributes of continuity, infinity, and uniformity. But all these attributes run counter to the character of sensory perception. Perception does not know the concept of infinity; from the very outset it is confined within certain spatial limits imposed by our faculty of perception. And in connection with perceptual space we can no more speak of homogeneity than of infinity. The ultimate basis of the homogeneity of geometric space is that all its elements, the "points" which are joined in it, are mere determinations of position, possessing no independent content of their own outside of this relation, this position which they occupy in relation to each other. Their reality is exhausted in their reciprocal relation: it is a purely functional and not a substantial reality. Because fundamentally these points are devoid of all content, because they have become mere expressions of ideal relations, they can raise no question of a diversity in content. Their homogeneity signifies nothing other than this similarity of structure, grounded in their common logical function, their common ideal purpose and meaning. Hence homogeneous space is never given space, but space produced by construction; and indeed the geometrical concept of homogeneity can be expressed by the postulate that from every point in space it must be possible to draw similar figures in all directions and magnitudes.[1] Nowhere in the space of immediate perception can this postulate be fulfilled. Here there is no strict homogeneity of position and direction; each place has its own mode and its own value. Visual space and tactile space are both anisotropic and unhomogeneous in contrast to the metric space of Euclidean geometry: "the main directions of organization—before-behind, above-below, right-left—are dissimilar in both physiological spaces."[2]

If we start from this standard of comparison, there would seem to be doubt that *mythical* space is closely related to the space of perception and strictly opposed to the logical space of geometry. Both mythical space and perceptive space are thoroughly concrete products of consciousness. Here the distinction between *position* and *content,* underlying the construction of "pure" geometric space, has not yet been made and cannot be made. Position is not something that can be detached from content or contrasted with it as an element of independent significance; it "is" only insofar as it is filled with a definite, individual sensuous or intuitive content. Hence in sensory as in mythical space, no "here" and "there" is a mere here and there, a mere term in a universal relation which can recur identically with the most diverse contents; every point, every element possesses, rather, a kind of tonality of its own. Each element has a special distinguishing character which cannot be described in general concepts but which is immediately experienced as such. And this characteristic difference adheres to the diverse directions in space as it does to the diverse positions. We have seen that *physiological* space differs from *metric* space

1. Cf. Hermann Grassmann, "Die Ausdehnungslehre von 1844," *Gesammelte mathematische und physikalische Werke* (3 vols. Leipzig, 1894–1911), *1,* 65.

2. Ernst Mach, *Erkenntnis und Irrtum* (Leipzig, J. A. Barth, 1905), p. 334.

in that here right and left, before and behind, above and below are not interchangeable, since motion in any of these directions involves specific organic sensations—and similarly, each of these directions carries specific mythical feeling values. In contrast to the homogeneity which prevails in the conceptual space of geometry every position and direction in mythical space is endowed as it were with a particular *accent*—and this accent always goes back to the fundamental mythical accent, the division between the sacred and the profane. The limits which the mythical consciousness posits and through which it arrives at its spatial and intellectual articulations are not, as in geometry, based on the discovery of a realm of fixed figures amid the flux of sensory impressions; they are fixed on man's self-limitation in his immediate relation to reality, as a willing and acting subject—on the fact that in confronting this reality he sets up specific barriers to which his feeling and his will attach themselves. The primary spatial difference, which in the more complex mythical configurations is merely repeated over and over and increasingly sublimated, is this difference between two *provinces* of being: a common, generally accessible province and another, sacred, precinct which seems to be raised out of its surroundings, hedged around and guarded against them.

But although the mythical intuition of space is distinguished from the abstract space of pure cognition by this foundation of individual feeling on which it rests and from which it seems inseparable, even here a universal tendency and a universal function are manifested. On the whole, the mythical world view effects a construction of space which, though far from being identical in content, is nevertheless analogous in form to the construction of geometrical space and the building up of empirical, objective "nature." It, too, operates as a schema through whose mediation the most diverse elements, elements which at first sight seem utterly incommensurate, can be brought into relation with one another. We have seen that the progress of objective knowledge rests essentially on the reduction of all the merely sensuous distinctions provided by immediate sensation to pure distinctions of space and magnitude, which fully represent them; in the mythical world view there is a similar representation, a "copying" in space of what is intrinsically unspatial. Here every qualitative difference seems to have an aspect in which it is also spatial, while every spatial difference is and remains a qualitative difference. Between the two realms there occurs a kind of exchange, a perpetual transition from one to the other. The investigation of language has already indicated the form of this transition: it has shown us that a vast number of the most diverse relations, particularly qualitative and modal relations, come within the scope of language only indirectly, by way of spatial determinations. The simple spatial terms thus became a kind of original intellectual expression. The objective world became intelligible to language to the degree in which language was able, as it were, to translate it back into terms of space. (See *1*, 200 ff.)

A similar translation, a similar transference of perceived and felt qualities into spatial images and intuitions, also occurs constantly in mythical thinking. Here, too, we find that peculiar schematism of space through which space assimilates the most dissimilar elements and so makes them mutually comparable and in some way similar.

The further back we go in our study of specifically mythical configurations, and the closer we come to the truly primordial mythical forms and articulations, the more distinct this relation seems to become. In totemism we see a primordial articulation of this sort, a first primitive division and particularization of all existence into rigidly determined classes and groups. Not only are human individuals and groups sharply differentiated from one another by their membership in a particular totem; the whole world is permeated by this form of classification. Every thing, every occurrence is understood by being endowed with some characteristic totemic "badge." And, as in all mythical thinking, this badge is not a *mere* sign but the expression of relationships which are felt and understood to be quite real. But the immense complexity which results from this, the weaving of all individual, social, spiritual, and physical-cosmic reality into the most diverse relations of totemic kinship, becomes relatively transparent as soon as mythical thinking begins to give it a spatial expression. Now this whole elaborate division of classes seems to break down according to the main spatial directions and dividing lines and so to gain intuitive clarity. In the mythical-sociological world view of the Zuñis, for example, which Cushing has described in detail, the sevenfold form of the totemic organization, which runs through the whole world, is particularly reflected in the conception of space. Space as a whole is divided into seven zones, north and south, east and west, the upper and the lower world, and finally the center of the world; and every reality occupies its unequivocal position, its definitely prescribed place, within this general classification. The elements of nature, the physical substances as well as the separate phases of the world process, are differentiated accordingly. To the north belongs the air, to the south fire, to the east earth, to the west water; the north is the home of winter, the south of summer, the east of autumn, the west of spring; etc. And the various human classes, occupations, and institutions enter into the same basic schema: war and warriors belong to the north, the hunt and the hunter to the west, medicine and agriculture to the south, magic and religion to the east. Strange and eccentric as these classifications may appear at first glance, it is certain that they did not arise by chance but are an expression of a very definite and typical outlook. The Jorubas, like the Zuñis, have a totemic organization which also finds its characteristic expression in the conception of space. Here again a specific color, a specific day of the five-day week, and a specific element is assigned to each region in space; here, too, the sequence of prayers, the order in which the cult implements are employed, and the seasonal sacrifices performed—in short the whole sacral system—goes back to certain fundamental spatial differences, particularly the fundamental distinction between right and left. Similarly, the structure of their city and its division into sections is, one might say, merely a spatial projection of their general totemic view.[3]

In Chinese thought we again encounter, in a different form but developed with the greatest subtlety and precision, the notion that all qualitative distinctions and oppositions possess some sort of spatial "correspondence." Once again all things and occurrences are in some way distributed among the diverse cardinal points. Each has a particular color, element, season, and sign of the zodiac, a particular organ of the human body, a particular basic emotion, etc., which belongs to it specifically; and through this common relation to a determinate position in space the most heterogeneous elements enter, as it were, into contact with one another. All species and varieties of things have their "home" somewhere in space, and their absolute reciprocal strangeness is thereby annulled:

3. For details see Leo Frobenius, *Und Afrika sprach* (Berlin *ca.* 1912), pp. 198 ff., 280 ff. Eng. trans. by Rudolf Blind, *The Voice of Africa* (London, 1913). From the quadriform "system" underlying the religion of the Jorubas Frobenius attempts to derive a kind of primordial relationship between them and the Etruscans, among whom he assumes this system to have first developed. However, the above considerations show the problematic character of such an inference. The fact that similar systems are found all over the world shows that what we have here is not an isolated offshoot of mythical thinking but one of its typical and fundamental intuitions—not a mere content of mythical thinking but one of its determining factors.

local mediation leads to a spiritual mediation between them, to a composition of all differences in a great whole, a fundamental mythical plan of the world.[4]

Thus the universality of spatial intuition becomes once again a vehicle for the "universalism" of a world view. But here, too, myth differs from cognition in the *form* of the whole toward which it strives. The totality of the scientific cosmos is a totality of laws, i.e. of relations and functions. Space and time, though at first taken as substances, as things existing in themselves, are, as scientific thinking develops, recognized more and more as ideal schemata, as systems of relations. Their objective being signifies merely that it is they which first make empirical intuition possible, that they are the principles in which it is grounded. And ultimately the whole reality of space and time, all the modes in which they are manifested, are brought into relation with this function of grounding. Thus the intuition of pure geometric space is also governed by the law formulated in the "principle of sufficient reason." It serves as an instrument and organ for an explanation of the world; and what happens in this explanation is simply that a merely sensuous content is poured into a spatial mold in which, one might say, it is re-formed and through which it is apprehended in accordance with the universal laws of geometry. Thus, space is an ideal factor which takes its place in the general work of knowledge—and this systematic position also determines its character. In the space of pure cognition the relation of the spatial whole to the spatial part is seen not materially but, fundamentally, in purely functional terms: the whole of space is not pieced together out of its elements but is built up from them as constitutive conditions. The line is "generated" from the point, the surface from the line, the body from the surface: thought makes one grow from another in accordance with a specific law. The complex spatial forms are understood in their genetic definition, which expresses the manner and the rule of their production. Accordingly, an understanding of the spatial whole requires a return to the producing elements, to points and the motions of points.

In contrast to the *functional* space of pure mathematics the space of myth proves to be *structural*. Here the whole does not "become" by growing genetically from its elements accordingly to a determinate rule; we find rather a purely static relationship of inherence. Regardless of how far

---

4. For more detailed treatment cf. my *Begriffsform im mythischen Denken*, with fuller documentation drawn from ethnological literature; see especially pp. 16 ff., 54 ff.

we divide, we find in each part the form, the structure, of the whole. This form is not, as in the mathematical analysis of space, broken down into homogeneous and therefore formless elements; on the contrary, it endures as such, unaffected by any division. The whole spatial world, and with it the cosmos, appears to be built according to a definite model, which may manifest itself to us on an enlarged or a reduced scale but which, large or small, remains the same. All the relations of mythical space rest ultimately on this original *identity;* they go back not to a similarity of efficacy, not to a dynamic law, but to an original identity of essence. This fundamental view has found its classical expression in astrology. For astrology every occurrence in the world, every genesis and new formation is fundamentally illusion; what is expressed in the world process, what lies behind it, is a predetermined fate, a uniform determination of being, which asserts itself identically throughout the moments of time. Thus, the whole of a man's life is contained and decided in its beginning, in the constellation of the hour of his birth; and in general, growth presents itself not as a genesis but as a simple permanence and an explanation of this permanence. The form of existence and life is not produced from the most diverse elements, from an interweaving of the most diverse causal conditions; from the very outset it is given as a finished form which need only be explained, which for us onlookers seems to unfold in time. And this law of the whole is repeated in each of its parts. The predetermination of being applies to the individual as it applies to the universe. The formulas of astrology often make this relationship clear by transforming the *efficacy* of the planets, which forms the basic principle of the astrological view, into a kind of *substantial inherence.* In each of us there *is* a definite planet: ἐστί δ'ἐν ἡμῖν Μήνη Ζεὺς, Ἄρης Παφίη Κρόνος Ἥλιος Ἑρμῆς.[5] Herein we see how the astrological conception of efficacy is ultimately grounded in that mythical view of space which astrology developed to its supreme, one might say, "systematic" consequence. In accordance with the fundamental principle which dominates all mythical thinking, astrology can interpret coexistence in space only as an absolutely *concrete* coexistence, as a specific position of *bodies* in space. Here there is no detached, no merely abstract, form of space; instead, all intuition of form is melted down into the intuition of content, into the aspects of the planetary world. But these are not unique and merely individual; in them the structural law of the whole, the form of the universe, emerges in

5. Cf. Franz Boll, *Die Lebensalter* (Leipzig, 1913), pp. 37 ff.

intuitive clarity and concretion. And regardless of how far we advance toward the particular, regardless of how much we split this form, its true essence remains untouched; it remains an indivisible unity. Space possesses a determinate structure of its own, which recurs in all its separate configurations, and no particular thing or process can depart or, as it were, fall away from the determinacy, the fatality, of the whole. We may examine the order of the natural elements or the order of the seasons, the mixtures in bodies or the typical temperaments of men, but always we find in them one and the same original schema, one and the same "articulation" through which the seal of the whole is imprinted on every particular.[6]

Of course this grandiose, self-contained intuition of the spatial-physical cosmos that we find in astrology is not the beginning of mythical thinking but is one of its late achievements. Even the mythical world view starts from the most restricted sphere of sensuous-spatial existence, which is extended only very gradually. We have seen in our investigation of language that the terms of spatial orientation, the words for "before" and "behind," "above" and "below" are usually taken from man's intuition of his own body: man's body and its parts are the system of reference to which all other spatial distinctions are indirectly transferred (see *1, 207* ff.). Myth travels the same road: wherever it finds an organically articulated whole which it strives to understand by its methods of thought, it tends to see this whole in the image and organization of the human body. The objective world becomes intelligible to the mythical consciousness and divides into determinate spheres of existence only when it is thus analogically "copied" in terms of the human body. Often it is the form of this copying which is actually thought to contain the answer to the mythical question of origins and which hence dominates all mythical cosmography and cosmology. Because the world is formed from the parts of a human or superhuman being, it retains the character of a mythical organic unity, however much it may seem to disperse into particulars. As mentioned above, one of the hymns of the Rigveda describes how the world issued from the body of man, the Purusha. The world *is* the Purusha, for it arose when the gods offered him up as a sacrifice and brought forth the various creatures from the parts of his body, which was dismembered in accordance with the laws of sacrifice. Thus the parts of the world are nothing other than the organs of the human body.

6. Concerning this form of astrology cf. *Begriffsform im mythischen Denken*, pp. 25 ff.

The Brahmin was his mouth, his arms were made the Rājanya (warrior), his two thighs the Vaiśya (trader and agriculturist), from his feet the Sūdra (servile class) was born.

The moon was born from his spirit (*manas*), from his eye was born the sun, from his mouth Indra and Agni, from his breath Vāyu (wind) was born.

From his navel arose the middle sky, from his head the heaven originated, from his feet the earth, the quarters from his ear. Thus did they fashion the worlds.[7]

Thus here, too, in the early age of mythical thinking, the unity of microcosm and macrocosm is so interpreted that it is not so much man who is formed from parts of the world, as the world from parts of man. We find this same attitude, though in reverse, in the Christian-Germanic view that Adam's body was formed of eight parts, so that his flesh resembles the earth, his bones the rocks, his blood the sea, his hair the plants, his thoughts the clouds.[8] In both cases myth starts from a spatial-physical *correspondence* between the world and man and from this correspondence infers a unity of *origin*. This transference is not limited to the relationship between world and man, which despite its vast importance remains *particular*, but is universally applied to the most diverse spheres of existence. As we have seen, mythical thinking in general knows no purely ideal similarities but looks upon any kind of similarity as an indication of an original kinship, an essential identity;[9] and this is particularly true in regard to similarities or analogies of spatial structure. The mere possibility of coordinating certain spatial totalities part for part suffices to make them coalesce. From this point on they are only different expressions of one and the same essence, which can assume entirely different dimensions. By virtue of this peculiar principle mythical thinking seems to negate and suspend spatial distance. The distant merges with what is close at hand, since the one can in some way be copied in the other. So deeply rooted is this trait that with all its progress pure knowledge, the "exact" view of space, has never fully overcome it. As late as the eighteenth century Swedenborg, in his *Arcana coelestia,* attempted to construct a

7. Rigveda, x, 90. Eng. trans. by Thomas, p. 122. Cf. Paul Deussen, "Allgemeine Einleitung und Philosophie des Veda," *Allgemeine Geschichte der Philosophie mit besonderer Berücksichtigung der Religionen* (7 vols. Leipzig, 1894–1920), Vol. *1*, Pt. I, pp. 150 ff.

8. See Golther, *Handbuch der germanischen Mythologie*, p. 518.

9. See above, pp. 67 ff.

system of the intelligible world according to this category of universal cor-respondence.[10] Here all spatial barriers ultimately drop—for as man can be copied in the world, so the small can be copied in the large, the distant in the near, and the two are essentially the same. Thus, just as there is a magical anatomy in which particular parts of the human body are equated with particular parts of the world, there is also a mythical geography and cosmography in which the structure of the earth is de-scribed and defined in accordance with the same basic intuition. Often the two, magical anatomy and mythical geography, merge into one. The seven-part map of the world in the Hippocratic book on the number seven represents the earth as a human body: its head is the Peloponnesus, the Isthmus is its spinal cord, while Ionia appears as the diaphragm, i.e. the true center, the "navel of the world." And all the intellectual and moral qualities of the peoples inhabiting these regions are regarded as in some way dependent on this form of "localization." [11] Here on the threshold of classical Greek philosophy we find a view which can only be under-stood through its widespread mythical parallels. One need only compare this schema of the earth and of space as a whole with the universal spatial schematism of the Zuñis in order to perceive the fundamental relation between the two.[12] For mythical thinking the relation between what a thing "is" and the place in which it is situated is never purely external and accidental; the place is itself a part of the thing's being, and the place confers very specific inner ties upon the thing. In totemic organiza-tions, for example, the members of a given clan stand in this relation of original kinship not only to one another but also, for the most part, to certain zones in space. To each clan, above all, belongs an often precisely defined spatial direction and sector.[13] When a member of a clan dies,

10. That even in modern thought this manner of thinking has not lost its attraction and importance is shown by Wilhelm Müller-Walbaum's remarkable and instructive work, *Die Welt als Schuld und Gleichnis. Gedanken zu einem System universeller Entsprechungen* (Vienna and Leipzig, 1920).

11. Cf. Wilhelm H. Roscher, *Die Hippokratische Schrift von der Siebenzahl in ihrer vierfachen Überlieferung,* Abhandlungen der philosophisch-historischen Klasse der könig-lichen Sächsischen Gesellschaft der Wissenschaften, Vol. *28* (Leipzig, 1911), pp. 5 ff., 107 ff.

12. For a detailed treatment of the spatial schematism of the Zuñis see Frank H. Cushing, "Outlines of Zuñi Creation Myths," (*Thirteenth Annual Report of the* [*U.S.*] *Bureau of American Ethnology,* 1891–92 (Washington, 1896), pp. 367 ff.

13. See the characteristic examples given by Alfred W. Howitt for the Australian aborigi-nes in "Further Notes on the Australian Class System," *Journal of the Anthropological In-stitute, 18* (1889), 62 ff., reprinted as append. 2 of my *Begriffsform im mythischen Denken,* pp. 54 ff.

care is taken to bury him in the spatial position and direction peculiar and essential to his clan.[14] In all this we see the two fundamental features of the mythical feeling of space—the thorough qualification and particularization from which it starts and the systematization toward which it nevertheless strives. The systematization has found its clearest expression in the form of "mythical geography" which grew out of astrology. As early as the old Babylonian period the terrestrial world was divided, according to its relation with the heavens, into four different realms: Akkad, i.e. south Babylonia, was governed and guarded by Jupiter; Amurru, the west country, was governed by Mars; Subartu and Elam in the north and east were ruled over by the Pleiades and Perseus.[15] Later, the system of the seven planets seems to have led to a sevenfold organization of the whole world, such as we encounter in Babylonia, India, and Persia. Here we seem far removed from those primitive divisions which project and copy all human reality in the human body; here the narrow sensuous view seems to be overcome by a truly cosmic and universal perspective; but the principle of coordination has remained the same. Mythical thinking seizes upon a very specific and concrete spatial structure in order to carry through its whole "orientation" of the world. In "What Does It Mean to Orient Ourselves in Thought?"—an article which despite its brevity is highly characteristic of his manner of thinking—Kant attempted to define the origin of the concept of "orientation" and follow its development: "However high we may place our concepts and much as we may abstract them from the sensuous world, still images adhere to them. . . . For how should we give meaning and signification to our concepts if some intuition . . . did not underly them?" Kant then goes on to show how all orientation begins with a sensuously *felt* distinction—namely the feeling of the distinction between the right and the left hand—and how it then rises to the sphere of pure mathematical *intuition* and ultimately to the orientation of thought as such, of pure reason. If we examine the peculiarity of mythical space and compare it with the space of sensory intuition and the *logical* space of mathematics, we can follow these stages of orientation down to a still deeper spiritual level; and we can clearly discern the point of transition at which an opposition intrinsically rooted in mythical feeling begins to shape itself, to take on an objective form, through which the general process of objec-

14. Howitt, p. 62.
15. Cf. Jastrow, *Aspects of Religious Belief*, pp. 217 ff., 234 ff.

tivization, the intuitive-objective apprehension and interpretation of the world of sense impressions, assumes a new direction.

2. Space and Light. The Problem of Orientation

We have seen that the intuition of space is a basic factor in mythical thinking, since this thinking is dominated by a tendency to transform all the distinctions which it postulates and apprehends into spatial distinctions and to actualize them in this form. Thus far we have essentially regarded spatial distinctions as directly given, i.e. we have assumed the divisions and separations of spatial direction, of right and left, above and below, etc. to be effected in the primary sense impression without the need of a special intellectual effort, a specific "energy" of consciousness. But precisely this assumption now requires a correction, for on closer scrutiny, it contradicts what we have recognized as a fundamental characteristic of the process of symbolic formation. We have seen that the essential and characteristic achievement of all symbolic form—whether of language, myth, or pure cognition—does not lie simply in receiving given material impressions (which in themselves possess a fixed and definite character, a given quality and structure) and then grafting onto them, as though from outside, another form originating in the independent energy of consciousness. The characteristic achievement of the spirit begins much earlier than this. On sharper analysis even the apparently "given" proves to have passed through certain acts of linguistic, mythical, or logical-theoretical apperception. Only what is *made* in these acts "is"; even in its seemingly simple and immediate nature, what is thus made proves to be conditioned and determined by some primary meaning-giving function. And it is this primary, not the secondary, formation which contains the true secret of all symbolic form, which must forever arouse new philosophical amazement.

Here again the basic philosophical problem does not consist of understanding by means of what spiritual mechanism mythical thinking succeeds in relating purely qualitative distinctions to spatial distinctions, into which it transposes them, as it were. It consists rather in ascertaining the fundamental motive by which mythical thinking is guided in its original *setting up* of these same spatial distinctions. How, in mythical space as a whole, do particular "regions" and directions come to be singled out—how does it come about that one region and direction is opposed to the others, "stressed" over against them, and endowed with a particular distinguishing mark? That this is no idle question becomes evident once we consider that in this differentiation mythical thinking proceeds according to entirely different criteria from those employed by theoretical-scientific thinking in mastering the same task. The latter establishes a determinate spatial order by relating the sensuous diversity of impressions to a system of purely logical, purely ideal, forms. The empirical straight line, the empirical circle, and the empirical sphere are determined and understood in reference to the ideal world of purely geometrical figures, in reference to the straight line "as such," the circle "as such," and the sphere "as such." An aggregate of geometrical relations and laws is set up which supplies the norm for all apprehension and interpretation of empirical things in space. The theoretical view of *physical* space shows itself to be governed by the same intellectual motive. Here, to be sure, sensory intuition as well as immediate sensation seem to play a part; here particular zones and directions in space seem to become distinguishable only when we link them with some material distinctions of our bodily organization, our physical body. But although the physical view of space cannot dispense with this support, it strives more and more to free itself from it. All progress in "exact," strictly scientific physics is directed toward eradicating the "anthropomorphic" ingredients of the physical world view. Thus, in particular, the sensuous antithesis of "above" and "below" loses its significance in the cosmic space of physics. "Above" and "below" are no longer absolute opposites. They have validity only in relation to the empirical phenomenon of gravity and the empirical regularity of this phenomenon. Physical space is in general characterized as a *space relevant to forces:* but in its purely mathematical formulation the concept of force goes back to the concept of law, hence of the function. In the structural space of myth, however, we see an entirely different line of thought. Here the universal is not distinguished from the particular and accidental, the constant from the variable, through the basic concept of law; here we find the *one* mythical value accent expressed in the opposition between the sacred and profane. Here there are no purely geometrical or purely geographical, no purely ideal or merely empirical distinctions; all thought and all sensory intuition and perception rest on an original foundation of feeling. However subtle and particularized its structure may become, mythical space as a whole remains embedded, or one might say, immersed in this feeling. In this

space, specific boundaries and distinctions are thus not arrived at by
progressive logical thinking through intellectual analysis and synthesis;
they go back to distinctions already made on the basis of such feeling.
The zones and directions in space stand out from one another because
a different accent of meaning is connected with them, and they are mythically evaluated in different and opposite senses.

In this appraisal a spontaneous act of the mythical consciousness is
performed; but objectively considered, it is also tied to a specific and fundamental physical fact. The development of the mythical feeling of space
always starts from the opposition of *day* and *night, light* and *darkness.*
The dominant power which this antithesis exerts on the mythical consciousness can be followed down to the most highly developed religions.
Some of these religions, particularly that of the Iranians, may even be
designated as complete systematizations of this *one* opposition. But even
where the antithesis does not take on this logical form, this almost dialectical sharpness, it may be recognized as one of the latent factors in the
religious structure of the cosmos. Among the religions of primitive peoples that, for example, of the Cora Indians—described in detail by Preuss
—is¯ totally dominated and permeated by this opposition of light and
darkness. Around it unfolds the mythical feeling and the whole mythical
world view peculiar to the Coras.[16] And in the creation legends of nearly
all peoples and religions the process of creation merges with the dawning of the light. In the Babylonian creation legend the world arises from
the struggle waged by Marduk, god of the morning sun and the spring
sun, against chaos and darkness, represented by the monster Tiamat. The
victory of the light is the origin of the world and the world order. The
Egyptian story of the creation has also been interpreted as an imitation of
the daily sunrise. The first act of creation begins with the formation of
an egg which rises out of the primal water; from the egg issues Ra, the
god of light, whose genesis is described in the most diverse versions, all
of which however go back to the one original phenomenon—the bursting
forth of light out of darkness.[17] And it is the living intuition of this original phenomenon which gives the Biblical story of the creation its full
concrete "meaning"—as Herder first pointed out and as he set forth with

16. Cf. Preuss, *Die Nayarit-Expedition, 1,* xxiii ff.

17. Cf. Heinrich K. Brugsch, *Religion und Mythologie der alten Ägypter* (Leipzig, 1888),
p. 102; Franz Lukas, *Die Grundbegriffe in den Kosmogonien der alten Völker* (Leipzig,
1893), pp. 48 ff.

sensitive eloquence. Perhaps Herder's gift of not seeing spiritual phenomena as mere facts but of transposing himself into the creative process from which they spring is nowhere so brilliantly revealed as in this interpretation of the first chapter of Genesis. For him the narrative of the creation is nothing other than the story of the birth of the light—as experienced by the mythical spirit in the rising of every new day, the coming of every new dawn. This dawning is for mythical vision no mere process; it is a true and original creation—not a periodically recurring natural process following a determinate rule but something absolutely individual and unique. Heraclitus' saying, "The sun is new each day," is spoken in a truly mythical spirit. Here we have, as it were, the first characteristic beginning of mythical thinking; and in all its further progress the antithesis of light and darkness, day and night, proves to be a living and enduring motif. In his fine and moving book Troels-Lund followed the growth of this motif from the first primitive beginnings to that universal elaboration which it underwent in astrology. "We start from the assumption," he writes,

> that sense of place and receptivity to impressions of light are the two most fundamental and deep-seated manifestations of the human intelligence. It is by these two roads that the individual and the race achieve their most essential spiritual development. It is from this perspective that the great questions have been answered with which existence itself confronts each one of us: Who are you? What are you? What should you do? . . . For each inhabitant of the earth, this sphere which is itself not luminous, the interchange of light and darkness, day and night, is the earliest impulse and the ultimate end of his faculty of thought. Not only our earth but ourselves, our own spiritual I, from our first blinking at the light to our highest religious and moral feelings, are born and nurtured of the sun. . . . The progressive view of the difference between day and night, light and darkness, is the innermost nerve of all human cultural development.[18]

Every separation of the zones of space and hence every kind of articulation within mythical space as a whole is connected with this contrast. The characteristic mythical accent of the sacred and profane is distributed in different ways among the separate directions and zones and lends each

18. Troels F. Troels-Lund, *Himmelsbild und Weltanschauung im Wandel der Zeiten* (3d ed. Leipzig, 1908), p. 5.

of them a definite mythical-religious imprint. East, west, north, and south are not essentially similar zones which serve for orientation within the world of empirical perception; each of them has a specific reality and significance of its own, an inherent mythical life. The directions are taken not as abstract and ideal relations but rather as independent *entities,* each endowed with a life of its own—as can be seen, for example, from the fact that they often experience the highest concrete formation and embodiment of which myth is capable, i.e. they are raised to the level of gods. Even at relatively low levels of mythical thinking we encounter these gods of direction: gods of the east and north, of the west and south, of the lower and upper world.[19] And perhaps there is no cosmology, however primitive, in which the contrast of the four main directions does not in some way emerge as the cardinal point of its understanding and explanation of the world.[20] Thus Goethe's saying, "God's is the orient, God's is the occident; north and south rest in the peace of His hands,"— applies in the strictest sense to mythical thinking. But before it could arrive at this unity, this universal feeling of space and of God in which all particular distinctions seem dissolved, mythical thinking had to pass through these same distinctions and set them off against one another. Each particular spatial determination thus obtains a definite divine or demonic, friendly or hostile, holy or unholy "character." The east as the origin of light is also the source of life—the west as the place of the setting sun is filled with all the terrors of death. Wherever we find the idea of a realm of the dead, spatially separate and distinguished from the realm of the living, it is situated in the west of the world. And this opposition of day and night, light and darkness, birth and death, is also reflected in countless ways in the mythical interpretation of concrete events of life. They all take on a different cast, according to the relation in which they stand to the phenomenon of the rising or setting sun. "The worship of light," writes Usener in his *Götternamen,*

> is woven into the whole of human existence. Its basic features are common to all the members of the Indo-European family of peoples; indeed they extend much farther; even today, often unconsciously, we are dominated by it. Out of the half-death of sleep the light of day awakens us to life: "to see the light," "to behold the light of the sun,"

19. Such gods of direction are found for example among the Coras. Cf. Preuss, *Die Nayarit-Expedition, 1,* lxxiv ff.

20. Cf. Brinton, pp. 118 ff.

"to be in the light" mean to live; "to see the light" means to be born, "to depart from the light" means to die. . . . As early as the Homeric epics the light represents salvation. . . . Euripides calls the light of the day "pure." The cloudless blue sky with its unobstructed light is the divine prototype of purity and became the basis for the conceptions of the land of the gods and the sojourn of the blessed. . . . And this intuition was directly transposed into the supreme moral concepts of truth and justice. . . . From this fundamental view it followed that sacred actions for which the gods of heaven could be invoked as helpers or witnesses could be performed only under the open daytime sky. . . . The oath, whose sanctity is based on the invocation of the all-seeing, all-knowing, punishing gods as witnesses, could originally be taken only under the open sky. The Germanic assembly in which the community of free men who dwelt in houses were united for counsel and judgment took place "in the sacred ring," under the open sky. . . . All these are simple, involuntary notions; they arise under the irresistible power of sense impressions to which we have not yet grown impervious and which form a closed circle of their own. In them springs up an original and inexhaustible well of religiosity and morality.[21]

In all these transitions we are again immediately aware of that dynamic which belongs to the essence of every true spiritual form of expression. In every such form the rigid limit between "inside" and "outside," the "subjective" and the "objective," does not subsist as such but begins, as it were, to grow fluid. The inward and outward do not stand side by side, each as a separate province; each, rather, is reflected in the other, and only in this reciprocal reflection does each disclose its own meaning. Thus in the spatial form which mythical thinking devises the whole mythical *life form* is imprinted and can, in a certain sense, be read from it. This relationship found its classical expression in the Roman sacral order. In a basic work Nissen has elucidated this reciprocal transposition from all sides and shown how the mythical-religious feeling of the sacred found its first objectivization by turning outward, by representing itself in the intuition of spatial relations. Hallowing begins when a specific zone is detached from space as a whole, when it is distinguished from other zones and one might say religiously hedged around. This concept of a religious hallowing manifested concur-

21. Usener, *Götternamen*, pp. 178 ff.

rently as a spatial delimitation has found its linguistic deposit in the word *templum*. For *templum* (Greek τέμενος) goes back to the root τεμ, "to cut," and thus signifies that which is cut out, delimited. It first designates the sacred precinct belonging to the god and consecrated to the god and then, by extension, every marked-off piece of land, every bounded field or orchard, whether it belongs to a god, king, or hero. But by a primal and basic religious intuition the heavens as a whole appear as just such an enclosed, consecrated zone; as a temple inhabited by one divine being and governed by one divine will.

Then a sacral ordering of this unity sets in. The whole of heaven breaks down into four parts, determined by the zones of the cosmos: a hither part in the south, a nether part in the north, a left part in the east, and a right part in the west. From this first purely local partitioning developed the entire system of Roman theology. In searching the sky for omens of man's undertakings on earth the augur began by dividing it into definite sectors. The east-west line, established by the course of the sun, was bisected by a vertical from north to south. With this intersection of the two lines the *decumanus* and the *cardo,* as they were called in the language of the priests, religious thinking created its first basic schema of coordinates. Nissen has shown in detail how this schema was transferred from religious life to every sector of juridical, social, and political life, and how in this transference it became more and more precisely and subtly differentiated. It formed the basis for the development of the concept of property and the symbolism by which property was designated and safeguarded as such. For the fundamental act of "limitation," through which fixed property was first established in the juridical-religious sense, is everywhere related to the sacral order of space. In the books of the Roman *agrimensores* limitation was attributed to Jupiter and related directly to the act of creation—as though the strict limitation prevailing in the universe had thus been transferred to the earth and to all earthly relations. Limitation is also based on the world zones, on the division of the cosmos designated by the lines from east to west and north to south, the decumanus and the cardo. It begins with the simplest natural division into a diurnal and nocturnal aspect, followed by a second division into morning and evening, the waxing and waning day. Roman political law is closely bound up with this form of limitation; upon it is based the distinction between *ager publicus* and *ager divisus et adsignatus,* between public and private property. For only land enclosed in fixed boundaries, in immutable mathematical lines, passes as private property. Like the god before them, the state, the community, and the individual now acquired a definite space through the intermediary of the idea of the templum, and in this space they made themselves at home.

> It is not a matter of indifference how the augur limits the sky; for although the will of Jupiter extends over the whole of it, just as the *pater-familias* governs the whole household, other gods dwell nevertheless in the various regions, and the lines are drawn according as one interprets the will of this one or that one. Once the lines are drawn the space thus hedged about is immediately occupied by a spirit. . . . Not only the city but also the *compitum* and house, not only the land as a whole but every field and vineyard, not only the house as a whole but every room within it, has its own god. The godhead is recognized by its workings and surroundings. Consequently every spirit which is confined within a given space gains an individuality, and a specific name by which man can invoke him.[22]

This system—which also dominated the structure of the Italic cities, the grouping and order within the Roman camp, and the ground plan and inner arrangement of the Roman house—makes it clear how progressive spatial limitation, like every new boundary established in space by mythical thinking and mythical-religious feeling, became an ethical and cultural boundary. This relationship can be followed down to the very beginnings of theoretical science. The beginnings of Roman scientific mathematics, as Moritz Cantor has shown in a monograph, went back to the books of the Roman agrimensores and their system of spatial orientation.[23]

Throughout the classical mathematical demonstrations of the Greeks we also discern an echo of primordial mythical notions; we feel the breath of that awe which surrounded the spatial "limit" from the very beginning. The form of logical-mathematical definition developed through the idea of spatial limitation. In the Pythagoreans and Plato limit and the unlimited, πέρας and ἄπειρον, are set off against each other as the determinant and the indeterminate, form and formlessness, good and evil. Thus the purely intellectual orientation of the cosmos grew from this spatial orientation of the mythical beginnings. Language has in many instances preserved the

22. Heinrich Nissen, *Das Templum. Antiquarische Untersuchungen* (Berlin, Weidmann, 1869), p. 8; idem, *Orientation. Studien zur Geschichte der Religion* (Berlin, 1906), Pt. I.

23. Moritz Cantor, *Die römischen Agrimensoren und ihre Stellung in der Geschichte der Feldmesskunst* (Liepzig, 1875). Cf. Cantor's *Vorlesungen über die Geschichte der Mathematik* (2d ed. Leipzig, 1894–1908), *1*, 496 ff.

traces of this connection; for example, the Latin term for pure theoretical thought and vision, *contemplari,* goes back to the idea of the templum, the marked-off space in which the augur carried on his observation of the heavens.[24] And from the ancient world this same theoretical and religious orientation entered into Christianity and the system of medieval Christian theology. The ground plan and structure of the medieval Church show the characteristic features of the old mythical symbolism of the cardinal points. Sun and light are no longer the godhead itself, but they still serve as the most immediate emblems of the divine, of the divine will to salvation and power of salvation. The historical effectiveness and historical triumph of Christianity were indeed closely bound up with its ability to assimilate and refashion the basic conceptions of the pagan cults of the sun and the light. The cult of *sol invictus* was now replaced by faith in Christ as the "sun of righteousness." [25] Accordingly, the early Christians retained the eastward orientation of their church and altar, while the south became the symbol of the Holy Ghost and the north conversely of estrangement from God, faith, and the light. Before baptism the novice was turned toward the west to renounce the devil and his works, and then toward the east, toward paradise, that he might profess faith in Christ. The four ends of the Cross were also identified with the four celestial and cosmic directions. And upon this simple plan was constructed the increasingly subtle and profound symbolism in which the whole of man's inner faith turned outward as it were, objectifying itself in elementary spatial relations.[26]

If we look back over all these examples, we cannot fail to recognize that although they belong to the most diverse cultures and stages in the development of mythical-religious thinking, they reveal the same basic characteristics of the mythical consciousness of space. This consciousness is comparable to a fine ether which pervades the most diverse manifestations of the mythical spirit and binds them to one another. Cushing writes that thanks to the sevenfold organization of their space the whole world view of the Zuñis and their whole life and activity are completely systematized, so that, for example, when they occupy a new campsite the position of the different groups and clans is determined in advance. To this the structure

24. Cf. Franz Boll's fine lecture, *Vita contemplativa* (Heidelberg, 1920).

25. Cf. Usener, *Götternamen,* p. 184; Franz Cumont, "La Théologie solaire du paganisme romain," *Mémoires presentés par divers savants à l'Académie des inscriptions et belles-lettres de l'Institut de France, 12,* Pt. II (1913), 449.

26. Cf. Joseph Sauer, *Symbolik des Kirchengebäudes und seiner Ausstattung in der Auffassung des Mittelalters* (Freiburg, Herder, 1902).

and order of the Roman camp presents a perfect analogy, for the plan of the camp was drawn up according to that of the city, while the city in turn was constructed according to the general plan of the world and the different spatial zones of the cosmos. Polybius tells us that when the Roman army entered the site selected for their camp, it was as though citizens, returning to their native city, each sought out his own house.[27] In both cases the local ordering of the different groups was not looked upon as something merely outward and accidental but was required and predetermined by definite sacral notions.

Everywhere such sacral conceptions are bound up with the general view of space and distinct spatial boundaries. A primordial mythical-religious feeling is linked with the fact of the spatial "threshold." Men's veneration of the threshold and awe of its sanctity are expressed almost everywhere in similar usages. Even among the Romans Terminus was a special god, and at the festival of the Terminalia the boundary stone itself was crowned with a garland and sprinkled with the blood of a sacrificial beast.[28] From the veneration of the temple threshold, which spatially separates the house of the god from the profane world, the fundamental juridical-religious concept of property seems to have developed along similar lines in totally different cultural spheres. Just as it originally protected the house of the god, the sanctity of the threshold (in the form of land markings) safe-guarded house and fields against hostile trespass and attack.[29] Often the terms coined by language for the expression of religious awe and veneration go back to a basic sensuous-spatial idea, the idea of shrinking back from a particular spatial zone.[30] And this spatial symbolism is transferred to the intuition and expression of circumstances of life bearing only the most indirect relation, if any, to space. Wherever mythical thinking and mythical feeling endow a content with particular value, wherever they distinguish it from others and lend it a special significance, this qualitative distinction tends to be represented in the image of spatial separation. Every mythically significant content, every circumstance of life that is raised out of the sphere of the indifferent and commonplace, forms its own ring of existence, a walled-in zone separated from its surroundings by fixed limits, and only

27. Polybius, ch. 41, line 9. Cf. Nissen, *Das Templum*, pp. 49 ff.

28. Ovid, *Fasti*, Bk. II, lines 641 ff. Cf. Wissowa, *Religion und Kultus der Römer*, pp. 136 ff.

29. Cf. the copious material assembled by H. C. Trumbull, *The Threshold Covenant; or, the Beginning of Religious Rites* (Edinburgh, 1896).

30. Thus, e.g., the Greek σέβεσθαι is derived etymologically from a root represented in Sanskrit at *tyaj* (to leave, to thrust back). Cf. Williger, *Hagios*, p. 10.

in this separation does it achieve an individual religious form. All movements into and out of this ring are governed by very definite sacral regulations. Transition from one mythical-religious sphere to another involves *rites of passage* which must be carefully observed. These rites govern moves from one city to another, from one country to another, and changes from one phase of life to another—childhood to puberty, celibacy to marriage, childlessness to motherhood, etc.[31] Here again we find confirmed that universal norm which is discernible in the development of all forms of cultural expression. The purely inward must be objectified, must transform itself into something outward; but on the other hand, all intuition of the outward remains enmeshed in inward determinations. Even where contemplation seems to move entirely in the outward sphere, the pulsebeat of an inner life can be felt in it. The barriers which man sets himself in his basic feeling of the sacred are the starting point from which begins his setting of boundaries in space and from which, by a progressive process of organization and articulation, the process spreads over the whole of the physical cosmos.

3. The Mythical Concept of Time

Yet significant as the form of space may be for the structure of the mythical objective world, it nevertheless seems that if we stop here, we cannot enter into the real being, the actual "heart" of this world. The mere term by which language designates such a world gives an intimation of this, for in its basic signification *"mythos"* embodies not a spatial but a purely temporal view; it designates a distinctly temporal "aspect," in which the world as a whole is seen. True myth does not begin when the intuition of the universe and its parts and forces is merely formed into definite images, into the figures of demons and gods; it begins only when a genesis, a becoming, a life in time, is attributed to these figures. Only where man ceases to content himself with a static contemplation of the divine, where the divine explicates its existence and nature in time, where the human consciousness takes the step forward from the figure of the gods to the history, the narrative, of the gods—only then have we to do with "myths" in the restricted, specific meaning of the word. And if we break down the concept "history of the gods" into its component factors, the emphasis is not on the second, but on the first factor, the intuition of the temporal. Its primacy

31. A summary of such rites may be found in Van Gennep, *Rites de passage*.

rests on the fact that it proves to be one of the conditions for the full develop-ment of the concept of the divine. Only by his history is the god constituted; only by his history is he singled out from all the innumerable impersonal powers of nature and set over against them as an independent being. Only when the world of the mythical begins as it were to flow, only when it becomes a world not of mere being but of action, can we distinguish individual, independent figures in it. Here it is the specific character of change, of acting and being acted upon, which creates a basis for delimita-tion and definition. True, a first step is presupposed, namely the universal differentiation underlying all mythical-religious consciousness, the differ-entiation between the worlds of the sacred and the profane. But within this universal differentiation, which finds its expression in purely spatial divisions and limitations, the mythical world achieves its true and specific articulation only when its dimension of depth, so to speak, opens up with the form of time. The true character of mythical being is first revealed when it appears as the being of origins. All the sanctity of mythical being goes back ultimately to the sanctity of the origin. It does not adhere im-mediately to the content of the given but to its coming into being, not to its qualities and properties but to its genesis in the past. By being thrust back into temporal distance, by being situated in the depths of the past, a particular content is not only established as sacred, as mythically and reli-giously significant, but also justified as such. Time is the first original form of this spiritual justification. Specifically human existence—usages, customs, social norms, and ties—are thus hallowed by being derived from institutions prevailing in the primordial mythical past; and existence itself, the "nature" of things, becomes truly understandable to mythical feeling and thinking only when seen in this perspective. A conspicuous trait of nature, a striking characteristic of a thing or species, is held to be "explained" as soon as it is linked with a unique event in the past, which discloses its mythical genera-tion. The mythical tales of all times and peoples are rich in concrete ex-amples of this kind of explanation.[32] Here a stage has been reached at which man's thinking no longer contents itself with the mere givenness of

---

32. For examples of this form of explicative mythical tale, relating especially to the origin of particular species of plants and animals and their peculiarities, see Graebner, *Das Weltbild der Primitiven*, p. 21: "Red spots in the plumage of the black cockatoo and of a certain hawk originated in a great fire, the spout hole of the whale in a spear thrust which he once—while still a man—received in the back of his head. The sandpiper came by his strange gait—alternately running and standing still—when he attempted to follow the guardian of the waters unobserved and was compelled to stand still each time the guardian turned around."

things, customs, and ordinances, with their simple existence and simple presence; it is not satisfied until it succeeds in somehow transposing this presence into the form of the past. The past itself has no "why": it *is* the why of things. What distinguishes mythical time from historical time is that for mythical time there is an absolute past, which neither requires nor is susceptible of any further explanation. History dissolves being into the never-ending sequence of becoming, in which no point is singled out but every point indicates the way to one farther back, so that regression into the past becomes a *regressus in infinitum*. Myth, to be sure, also draws a line between being and having-become, between present and past; but once this past is attained, myth remains in it as in something permanent and unquestionable. For myth time does not take the form of a mere relation, in which the factors of present, past, and future are persistently shifting and interchanging; here, on the contrary, a rigid barrier divides the empirical present from the mythical origin and gives to each its own inalienable "character." Thus it is understandable that the mythical consciousness—despite the fundamental and truly constitutive importance which the universal intuition of time possesses for it—has sometimes been called a timeless consciousness. For compared with objective time, whether cosmic or historical, mythical time is indeed timeless. In its early phases the mythical consciousness retains the same indifference toward relative stages of time as characterizes certain phases of the linguistic consciousness.[33] In it, to quote Schelling, there still prevails "an absolutely prehistoric time," a

> time which is indivisible by nature and absolutely identical, which therefore, whatever duration may be imputed to it, can only be regarded as a moment, i.e. as time in which the end is like the beginning and the beginning like the end, a kind of eternity, because it is itself not a sequence of time but only One Time, which is not in itself an objective time, i.e. a sequence of times, but only becomes time (that is, the past) relative to the time which follows it.[34]

If we now seek to trace the process of how this mythical "primordial time" gradually turns into "real" time, into a consciousness of sequence, we find confirmed that fundamental relation to which our inquiry into language has already called our attention. Here again the expression of temporal relations develops only through that of spatial relations. Between

33. Cf. *1*, 220 ff.
34. Schelling, *Philosophie der Mythologie*, p. 182.

the two there is at first no sharp differentiation. All orientation in time presupposes orientation in space, and only as the latter develops and creates definite means of expression are temporal specifications distinguishable to feeling and consciousness. One and the same concrete intuition, the interchange of light and darkness, day and night, underlies both the primary intuition of space and the primary articulation of time. And the same schema of orientation, the same purely felt distinctions between the quarters of the heavens and the directions, governs the division both of space and time into clear-cut sections. We have seen that the simplest spatial relations, such as left and right and forward and backward, are differentiated by a line drawn from east to west, following the course of the sun, and bisected by a perpendicular running from north to south—and all intuition of temporal intervals goes back to these intersecting lines. Among the peoples who developed this system to the greatest clarity and perfection this relation is often echoed in the most common linguistic term for time. The Latin *tempus*, to which corresponds the Greek τέμενος and *τέμπος (preserved in the plural, τέμπεα), grew out of the idea and designation of the templum.

> The basic words τέμενος *(tempus), templum* signified nothing other than bisection, intersection: according to the terminology of later carpenters two crossing rafters or beams still constituted a templum; thence the signification of the space thus divided was a natural development; in *tempus* the quarter of the heavens (e.g. the east) passed into the time of day (e.g. morning) and thence into time in general.[35]

The division of space into directions and zones runs parallel to the division of time into phases; both represent merely different factors in that gradual illumination of the spirit which starts from the intuition of the fundamental physical phenomenon of light.

And by virtue of this relationship a particular mythical-religious "character," a special accent of "holiness," is given to time as a whole and to every phase of time in particular. As we have seen, mythical feeling looks on position and direction in space not as the expression of a mere relation but as a particular being, a god or demon, and the same is true of time and its subdivisions. Even highly developed religions have preserved this basic intuition and this belief. In the Persian religion the cult of time and the segments of time, of the centuries, the years, the four seasons, the twelve

35. Usener, *Götternamen*, p. 192.

months, and particular days and hours, developed from the general worship of light. Particularly in the development of Mithraism this cult
achieved great importance.[36] In general, the mythical intuition of time,
like that of space, is altogether qualitative and concrete, and not quantitative
and abstract. For myth there is no time "as such," no perpetual duration
and no regular recurrence or succession; there are only configurations of
particular content which in turn reveal a certain temporal *gestalt,* a coming
and going, a rhythmical being and becoming.[37] Thus, time as a whole is
divided by certain boundaries akin to musical bars. But at first its "beats"
are not measured or counted but immediately felt. Above all, man's religious
activities show a rhythmic articulation of this sort. Specific sacral acts are
meticulously assigned to definite times and seasons, outside of which they
would lose all sacral power. All religious activity is organized according
to very definite time intervals, e.g. periods of seven or nine days, weeks, or
months. The "holy days," the times of festival, interrupt the uniform flow
of life and introduce distinct lines of demarcation. The phases of the moon
play a particular role in determining "critical dates." According to Caesar,
Ariovistus postponed hostilities until the new moon; the Lacedaemonians
waited until the full moon before taking the field. The intuition underlying all this is that temporal, like spatial, intervals and dividing lines are
not mere conventional distinctions of thought but possess an inherent
quality and particularly, an essence and efficacy of their own. They do not
form a simple and uniform, purely extensive series; to each of them, rather,
there belongs an intensive content which makes them similar or dissimilar,
corresponding or contrasting, friendly or hostile to one another.[38]

The fact is that long before the human consciousness forms its first concepts concerning the basic objective differentiations of number, time, and
space, it seems to acquire the subtlest sensitivity to the peculiar periodicity
and rhythm of human life. Even at the lowest stages of culture, even among
primitive peoples who have barely arrived at the first beginnings of enu-
meration and who consequently cannot possibly have any exact quantitative
conception of temporal relations, we often find this subjective feeling for

36. Cf. Franz Cumont, ed., *Textes et monuments figurés relatifs aux mystères de Mithra*
(2 vols. Brussels, 1899, 1896), *1,* 18 ff., 78 ff., 294 ff.; idem, *Astrology and Religion among
the Greeks and Romans* (London and New York, 1912), p. 110.

37. For this concept of "temporal gestalt" cf. the corresponding remarks on language in
1, 177 ff.

38. Cf. Henri Hubert and Marcel Mauss, "Étude sommaire de la représentation du temps
dans la religion et la magie," in *Mélange d'histoire des religions* (Paris, 1909), pp. 189 ff.

the living dynamic of the temporal process developed in astonishing subtlety and precision. These peoples have what one might call a special mythical-religious "sense of phases" which applies to all the occurrences of life, particularly to the most important transitions from one age or status to another. Even at the lowest levels these transitions, the most important changes in the life of the species as of the individual, are in some way distinguished by the cult, are somehow lifted out of the uniform course of events. Any number of carefully observed rites safeguard their beginning and end. Through these rites the monotonous course of existence, the mere "flow" of time, undergoes a kind of religious division; through them each phase of life acquires a particular religious stamp which gives it a specific meaning. Birth and death, pregnancy and motherhood, puberty and marriage—all are marked by specific rites of passage and initiation.[39] The religious particularization of the different phases of life brought about by these rites is often so sharp as to break the continuity of life. It is a widespread notion, recurring in various forms, that in passing from one sphere of life to another man acquires a new I—that the child, for example, dies with the coming of puberty; he dies to be reborn as a youth and as a man. In general, two significant stages of life are separated by a "critical phase" of greater or lesser duration, which is manifested in a number of positive prescriptions and negative prohibitions and taboos.[40]

Thus we see that for mythical consciousness and feeling a kind of biological time, a rhythmic ebb and flow of life, precedes the intuition of a properly cosmic time. Actually, cosmic time itself is first apprehended by myth in this peculiar biological form, for to the mythical consciousness the regularity of the natural process, the periodicity of the planets and the seasons, appears entirely as a life process. At first the mythical consciousness apprehends the change of day into night, the flowering and fading of plants, and the cyclical order of the seasons only by projecting these phenomena into human existence, where it perceives them as in a mirror. This reciprocal relation gives rise to a mythical feeling of time which creates a bridge between the subjective form of life and the objective intuition of nature. Even at the magical stage the two forms are closely inter-

39. Concerning these "rites of initiation" see the abundant material offered on the Australian aborigines in Baldwin Spencer and Francis J. Gillen, *The Native Tribes of Central Australia* (London, 1938), p. 212; idem, *The Northern Tribes of Central Australia* (New York, 1904), pp. 382 ff. Cf. Van Gennep; and Brinton, pp. 191 ff. For the South Sea peoples cf. Walter W. Skeat, *Malay Magic* (London, 1900), pp. 320 ff.

40. Cf. Marett, *Threshold of Religion* (3d ed.), pp. 194 ff.

woven, and this explains how objective processes can be determined by magic. The path of the sun and the course of the seasons are not regulated by an immutable law; they are subject to demonic influences and accessible to magical powers. The most diverse forms of analogy magic serve to influence, reinforce, or coerce the powers that are here at work. The popular customs which even today are associated with the principal turning points in the rise and fall of the year, particularly with the winter and summer solstices, still disclose this original intuition, obscured only by the lightest of veils. The imitative games and rites connected with the various festivals—the Maypole dances, the crowning with wreaths, the fires lighted in the nights of May Day and Christmas, Easter, and the summer solstice—are based on the notion that the life-giving power of the sun and the vegetative forces of nature must be aided, and guarded against hostile powers, by human activity. The general distribution of these customs (Wilhelm Mannhardt has compiled copious material for the Greek and Roman as well as the Slavic and Germanic worlds, while Hillebrandt has given a detailed description of the solstice festivals of ancient India [41]) shows that we have to do with conceptions going back to a fundamental form of the mythical consciousness. The primary mythical "sense of phases" can apprehend time only in the image of life, and consequently it must transpose and dissolve everything which moves in time, everything which comes and goes in set rhythm, into the form of life.

Thus myth knows nothing of that kind of objectivity which is expressed in the mathematical-physical concept or of Newton's absolute time which "flows in and for itself, without regard to any outward object." It knows historical time no more than it does mathematical-physical time. For even the historical consciousness of time contains very definite objective factors. It is based on a fixed chronology, a strict distinction of the earlier and later, and the observation of a determinate, unequivocal order in the sequence of the moments of time. Myth is aware of no such division of the stages of time, no such ordering of time into a rigid system where any particular event has one and only one position. As we know, it lies in the essence of mythical thinking that wherever it posits a relation, it causes the members of this relation to flow together and

41. Wilhelm Mannhardt, *Wald- und Feltkulte* (2 vols. Berlin, Gebrüder Borntraeger, 1875–77). For the Indian solstice rites see Alfred Hillebrandt, "Die Sonnwendfeste in Alt-Indien," *Romanische Forschungen,* 5 (1890), 299–340. A compilation of these rites for the Aryan world as a whole is given by Leopold von Schröder, *Arische Religion* (2 vols. Leipzig, 1914–16), Vol. 2.

merge; and this rule of concrescence, this growing together of the members of a relation,[42] prevails also in the mythical consciousness of time. The stages of time—past, present, future—do not remain distinct; over and over again the mythical consciousness succumbs to the tendency and temptation to level the differences and ultimately transform them into pure identity. Magic in particular extends its general principle of *pars pro toto* from space to time. And just as in magic each spatial part not only stands for the whole but is the whole, so the magical relation passes over all temporal differences and dividing lines. The magical "now" is by no means a *mere* now, a simple, differentiated present, but is, to quote Leibniz, "chargé du passé et gros de l'avenir"—laden with the past and pregnant with the future. In this sense, divination, in which this peculiar qualitative interpenetration of all temporal factors is most clearly disclosed, forms an integral part of the mythical consciousness.

However, this consciousness rises to a new level once it ceases to content itself, like magic, with producing a particular effect; it orients itself toward being and becoming as a whole and is more and more imbued with the intuition of this whole. Now it gradually frees itself from immediate confinement in sense impression and momentary sensory emotion. Instead of living in the present as an isolated point—or in a series of such points, a simple sequence of separate phases of action—it turns more and more to the contemplation of the eternal cycle of events. This cycle is still immediately felt more than thought; but even in this feeling the certainty of a universal world order dawns upon the mythical consciousness. No longer, as in the mythical animation of nature, is a particular thing, a particular physical substance, filled with specific psychic contents, with personal, individual forces; now, an everywhere recurring measure is felt in the world process as a whole. The more this feeling gains in strength, the more it awakens mythical thought, which it confronts with a new problem. For now, contemplation is directed not toward the mere content of change but toward its pure form. Here again the time motif operates as a middle link: although time is apprehended by myth only concretely, only through a definite physical process, particularly through the changes of the planets, it nevertheless contains within it another factor which belongs to a different, purely ideal "dimension." It is a different matter whether the forces of nature are particularized and made an object of mythical interpretation and religious worship, or

42. On the mythical concrescence of the members of a relation cf. above, pp. 62 ff.

whether they are looked upon only as the vehicles, as it were, of a universal temporal order. In the first case we are still wholly within the sphere of the substantial view: sun, moon, and stars are animated divine beings, but they are nevertheless individual things, endowed with very definite individual powers. In this respect these divine beings are distinguished only in degree but not in kind from the subordinate nature demons. But in the second case, when the mythical-religious feeling is no longer oriented solely toward the immediate existence of the various objects in nature and the immediate action of the particular natural forces, when both of these gain a characteristic expressive meaning in addition to their direct substantial signification—when they become a medium through which the idea of a lawful order governing and permeating the universe is apprehended—a new conception and meaning of the divine emerge. Now, consciousness is no longer oriented toward any particular natural phenomenon, however overpowering; every natural phenomenon serves rather as a sign for something else, something more comprehensive, which is revealed in it. Where sun and moon are not considered solely according to their physical being and physical effects, where they are not worshiped for the sake of their radiance or as producers of light and warmth, moisture and rain, but are taken instead as the constant measures of time from which the course and the rule of all change are read—here we stand at the threshold of a fundamentally different and more profound view of the world. From the rhythm and periodicity which can be felt in all immediate life and existence the mind of man now rises to the idea of the temporal order as a universal order of destiny, governing all reality and all change. Only thus seen as destiny does mythical time become a truly cosmic potency—a power binding not only man but also the demons and gods, because only in it, and through its inviolable measures and norms, are the life and action of men and even of the gods made possible.

At low levels the idea of this bond may clothe itself in naive sensuous images and expressions. The Maoris of New Zealand have a mythical tale relating how Maui, their tribal ancestor and culture hero, once trapped the sun, which had previously moved through the heavens without any fixed rule, and compelled it to take a regular course.[43] But as consciousness progressed and the strictly religious view of the world became more sharply distinguished from the magical view, this basic relationship

43. Theodor Waitz, *Anthropologie der Naturvölker* (6 vols. Leipzig, 1859–72), *6,* 259; William W. Gill, *Myths and Songs of the South Pacific* (London, 1876), p. 70.

achieved a purer, more spiritual expression. This turn from the sensuous and particular, from the deification of particular natural powers, to the universal, can be followed with special clarity in Babylonia and Assyria, the home and source of all "astral" religion. The beginnings of the Babylonian-Assyrian religion point back to the sphere of a primitive animism. Here again the basic stratum consists in a belief in demons, in friendly and hostile powers which intervene arbitrarily and capriciously in events. Sky demons and storm demons, demons of meadow and field, and of mountain and spring stand side by side with hybrids still preserving traces of animal worship and older totemistic views. But as Babylonian thought concentrated increasingly on the contemplation of the stars, its general form changed. The primitive demon mythology was not done away with, but it was relegated to a low level of popular faith. The religion of the wise men, of the priests, became the religion of the "sacred epochs" and "sacred numbers." The true basic phenomenon of the divine is represented in the definiteness of the astronomical process, in the temporal rule that governs the course of the sun, moon, and planets. The individual heavenly body is not conceived and worshiped as a godhead in its immediate corporeity; it is rather apprehended as a partial revelation of the universal divine power which acts according to constant norms in the whole as in the particular, in the greatest as in the smallest sphere of events. From the heavens, which are its clearest manifestation, this divine order may be followed in constant gradations down to the order of earthly, specifically human (political and social) reality as one and the same fundamental form which realizes itself in the most diverse spheres of existence.[44] Thus the movements of the planets as the visible image of time expressed the new unity of meaning in which mythical-religious thinking was beginning to encompass the whole of reality and change. The creation myth of the Babylonians represents the rise of the world order from the formless primal source in the image of the struggle waged by the sun god Marduk against the monster Tiamat. After his victory Marduk established the planets as the seats of the great gods and determined their course; he introduced the signs of the zodiac, the year, and the twelve months; he set up firm barriers lest any of the days deviate or lose its way. Thus, all movement and with it all life began when the

44. Cf. Morris Jastrow, *Die Religion Babyloniens und Assyriens* (2 vols. in one, Giessen, 1905); Bezold, *Himmelsschau und Astrallehre;* and Winkler, *Himmelsbild und Weltenbild der Babylonier* (2d ed. Leipzig, 1903).

luminous figure of time penetrated absolutely formless being, differentiating it and breaking it up into separate phases. And since, for mythical thought and feeling, outward and inward events are closely intertwined, this regularity of the cosmos implied an inviolable rule and norm appointed over the actions of men. "Marduk's word is constant, his command is not changed, what issues from his mouth no God can transform." Thus he became the supreme guardian of justice, "who looks into that which is innermost, who does not let the malefactor escape, who bends the recalcitrant and causes justice to prosper." [45]

The same relation between the universal temporal order, which governs all events, and the external order of justice, which likewise presides over all happenings—the same link between the astronomical and ethical cosmos—is found in nearly all the great religions. In the Egyptian pantheon it is the moon god Thoth who, as the measurer, the divider of time, is also lord over just measurement. The sacred ell used in drawing up the plan of temples and in land measurement is consecrated to him. He is the scribe of the gods and the judge of the heavens, who has bestowed language and writing on mankind and who, through the arts of counting and reckoning, has given gods and men to know what is their due. Here, too, the name for the exact, unchanging measure (maāt) becomes the name for the eternal and immutable order prevailing in nature as in ethical life. This concept of measure in its twofold signification has indeed been designated as the foundation of the whole Egyptian religious system; [46] and the religion of China was equally rooted in that basic feature of thinking and feeling which De Groot has called "universism": the conviction that all norms of human activity are grounded in the original law of the world and the heavens and can be directly derived from it. Only he who knows the course of the heavens and of time and who orders his activity accordingly—only he who has learned how to center his doings around fixed dates, months, and days—can properly accomplish his human career. "What the heavens determine, that is the nature of man; to follow human nature is man's Tao. The cultivation of this

45. On the Babylonian legend of the creation cf. Peter Jensen, *Die Kosmologie der Babylonier* (Stuttgart, 1890), pp. 279 ff. For a German translation of the above quotation see Hermann Gunkel, *Schöpfung und Chaos in Urzeit und Endzeit* (Göttingen, Vandenhoeck and Ruprecht, 1895), pp. 401 ff.

46. Cf. Peter Le Page Renouf, *Lectures on the Origin and Growth of Religion as Illustrated by the Religion of Ancient Egypt* (London, 1880). German trans., *Vorlesungen über Ursprung und Entwicklung der Religion* (1881), p. 233. Cf. also Alexandre Moret, *Mystères Égyptiens* (Paris, A. Colin, 1913), pp. 132 ff.

Tao is called instruction." Here again the ethical bonds governing men's acts merge with the temporal, in fact with the calendarial regulation of these acts, and the various segments of time—the "great year," the year, the seasons, and the months—are accordingly worshiped as divine. Men's duty and virtue consist simply in knowing and observing the "path" which the macrocosm imposes upon the microcosm.[47]

The same characteristic development can be followed in the religious intuitions of the Indo-Germanic peoples; here again the particularization of the divine, prevailing in the polytheistic religion of nature, is replaced by the idea of a universal order of nature, which appears at the same time as a spiritual and ethical order. And again, it is the intuition of time which acts as an intermediary between these two basic meanings and ultimately brings about their conjunction. In the Vedas this process of religious development is represented by the concept of the Rita, in the Avesta by the substantially and etymologically corresponding concept of the Asha. Both are expressions of the regular "course," the prescribed order of events, apprehended equally from the standpoint of reality and duty—a cosmic order which is at the same time an order of justice. "According to the Rita the rivers flow," runs a song of the Rigveda, "according to the Rita, the dawn rises: the Rita follows the path of order; knowing, it does not miss the directions of heavens." [48] And the same order governs the progress of the year. Around the heavens runs the twelve-spoked wheel of the Rita which never grows old: the year. In a well-known song of the Atharvaveda it is time itself, Kâla, who runs like a horse with many reins:

> his chariot wheels are all the worlds of creatures. This Time hath rolling wheels and seven naves: immortality is the chariot's axle. This Time brings hitherward all worlds about us: as primal Deity is he entreated. . . . He carries from us all these worlds of creatures. They call him Kâla in the loftiest heaven. He only made the worlds of life, he only gathered the worlds of living things together. Their son did he become who was their Father: no other higher power than he existeth.[49]

47. Cf. Jan J. M. de Groot, *Universismus. Die Grundlage der Religion und Ethik, des Staatwesens und der Wissenschaften Chinas* (Berlin, G. Reimer, 1918), amplified from *Religion in China. Universism* (New York and London, 1912). See also James Legge, *The Sacred Books of China: the Texts of Taoism*, The Sacred Books of the East, ed. F. Max Müller, Vols. 39, 40 (Oxford, 1891).

48. Rigveda, I, 124, 3.

49. Atharvaveda, XIX, 53. Eng. trans. by Ralph T. H. Griffith, *The Hymns of the Atharva-Veda* (2 vols. Benares, Lazarus, 1895–96), 2, 309–10.

In this intuition of time we can discern the struggle between two fundamental religious motifs: destiny and creation. There is a peculiar dialectical opposition between destiny, which though manifested in time is essentially a supratemporal power, and creation, which must always be thought
of as a single act in time. In the later Vedic literature we find the conception of Prajapati as the creator of the worlds, of the gods and men, but
his relation to time is twofold and contradictory. On the one hand Prajapati,
from whom all things have issued, is identified with the year, or more generally with time; he *is* the year, for he has created it in his own image.[50]
But in other passages, as in the song of the Atharvaveda, mentioned above,
the relation is reversed. It is not Prajapati who creates time but time which
creates Prajapati. Time is the first of the gods, who has brought forth all
beings and who will survive them all. Here, as we see, the divine
power of time is beginning to become, as it were, supradivine, because suprapersonal. It is as in Goethe's *Prometheus:* wherever al-
mighty time and eternal fate enter the stage, they dethrone the polytheistic gods, even the supreme creator-god. Insofar as the polytheistic
gods endure, they are worshiped not for themselves but as guardians and
administrators of the universal order of destiny, to which they are subordinated. The gods are no longer the absolute legislators of the physical
and ethical world; they and their actions are now subject to a higher law.
Over the Homeric Zeus stands the impersonal power of Moira; and in
Germanic mythology the power of destiny, of becoming (Wurd) appears
at once as the woof of the Norns, the weavers of fate, and as primal law
(*urlagu,* OHG *urlag,* Old Saxon, *orlag*). Here it is also the power of
measurement; in the Nordic myth of creation, for example, the world
ash tree Yggdrasil is represented as the tree with the right measure, the
tree which gives the measure.[51] In the Avesta, where the pure creation
motif is most sharply delineated, Ahura Mazda, the supreme ruler, is
worshiped as the originator and lord of all things, but at the same time
conceived as the executor of a suprapersonal order of the Asha, which is
both a natural and an ethical order. Although the Asha is created by
Ahura Mazda, it is an independent primal power, which helps the god of
light in his victorious battle against the powers of darkness and falsehood.

50. A survey of the passages in which this identification is made may be found in Deussen,
"Allgemeine Einleitung und Philosophie des Veda," p. 208.

51. Cf. Mogk in Hermann Paul, *Grundriss der germanischen Philologie* (2d ed. 4 vols.
Strassburg, 1900–9), *1,* 281 ff.; Golther, *Handbuch der germanischen Mythologie,* pp. 104 ff.,
529.

As helpers in his war against Ahriman, the god of the good has created the six archangels, the Amesha Spenta, headed by the "best honesty," Asha Vahishta, and "good opinion" (Vohu Manah).

With the creation and designation of these spiritual powers—in Plutarch's Greek translation rendered as εὔνοια and ἀλήθεια—we have attained to a sphere of religious ideas which is more than a mere mythical image-world, which is indeed shot through with truly dialectical and speculative motifs. And once again these motifs are most clearly developed in the determination of the concept of time. It is here that the tension between the idea of eternity and the idea of creation becomes strongest—so that it gradually seems to transform the whole religious system from within and give it a new character. The Avesta distinguishes two basic forms of time: limitless time, or eternity, and the "prevailing time of the long period," which Ahura Mazda has appointed as the time for the history of the world, as the epoch of his battle against the spirit of darkness. This epoch of the "long time, subject to its own law" is in turn divided into four main sections. With the creation begins the first era of three millennia: (1) a "time before time" in which the world, though already luminous, is not yet perceptible but exists only spiritually; (2) a "primordial age" in which the world is refashioned in perceptible form on the basis of its already existing configurations; and (3) an "era of battle," in which Ahriman and his companions invade the pure creation of Ormazd and in which the history of mankind on earth begins; until finally, in (4) the "era of the end," the power of the evil spirit is broken and the "prevailing time of the long period" is again dissolved into endless time and the time of the world into eternity. In the system of Zruvanism (the literary records of which are relatively late), which seems merely to have revived certain original motifs of the Iranian faith that had been submerged by the Zoroastrian reform, Endless Time (Zruvan Akarano) is expressly put forward as the ultimate and supreme principle, as the primal source from which arose all things, including the two warring powers of good and evil. Endless Time splits in two, thus creating the powers of Good and Evil, his twin sons who belong to each other but must forever combat each other. This system, in which "time" and "destiny" are expressly equated—the Greek reports render Zruvan by τύχη—shows the peculiar twofold character of a conception which sometimes rises to the most difficult and subtle abstractions and yet fully preserves the color of the specifically mythical feeling of time. Here cosmic historical time is never what it is for theoretical and particularly mathematical cognition: a purely ideal, ordering form, a system of reference and coordinates; it is the basic power of history itself, endowed with divine and demonic, creative and destructive forces.[52] To be sure, its order is apprehended as universal and inviolable, but on the other hand, this order seems to be decreed—the law of time to which all change is subservient appears as a law ordained by a half-personal, half-impersonal power. Myth cannot pass beyond this last barrier because of the contingency of its form and means of expression, but within this form an extensive differentiation of the concept and feeling of time is possible, insofar as mythical-religious intuition can lend varying emphasis to the particular factors of time—insofar as it can endow them with varying values and so confer a varying gestalt upon time as a whole.

4. The Formation of Time in the Mythical and Religious Consciousness

It is characteristic of the road followed by theoretical cognition, by mathematics and mathematical physics, that in them the idea of the homogeneity of time is more and more sharply defined. Only through this idea can the aim of mathematical-physical inquiry, the progressive quantification of time, be achieved. All individual specifications of time are referred to the concept of pure number, and ultimately time seems to dissolve in it entirely. In the modern development of mathematical-physical thinking, in the development of the general theory of relativity, this is expressed in the fact that here time has actually cast off all its specific particularity. Every point in the universe is determined by its space-time coordinates x_1, x_2, x_3, x_4; and these signify mere numerical values, which are no longer distinguished from one another by any special characteristics and which are accordingly interchangeable. For the mythical-religious world view, time never becomes a uniform quantum of this sort; however universal its concept may ultimately become, it is and remains given as a peculiar *quale*. And it is precisely in this qualification that the characteristic differences between the various epochs and cultures as well as the various directions of religious development consist. What we have found to be true of mythical space applies also to mythical time;—its form depends on the

52. On the concept of time in the Iranian religion and the system of "Zruvanism" see particularly Heinrich F. Junker's lecture, *Über iranische Quellen der hellenistischen Aion-Vorstellung* (Leipzig, 1923), pp. 125 ff. Cf. James Darmesteter, *Ormazd et Ahriman* (Paris, 1877), pp. 316 ff., 78 ff., 294 ff.

characteristic mythical-religious accentuation, the distribution of the accents of the sacred and profane. From a religious point of view time is never a simple, uniform process of change but obtains its meaning only through the differentiation of its phases. The gestalt assumed by time as a whole depends on how the religious consciousness distributes the light and shadow, on whether it dwells on and immerses itself in one phase of time or in another upon which it sets a mark of special value. Present, past, and future, it is true, are the basic factors in any picture of time, but the mode and the lighting of this picture vary according to the energy with which consciousness turns now to the one, now to the other factor. For the mythical-religious approach is not concerned with a purely logical synthesis, which fuses the "now" with the "earlier" and the "later" in the "transcendental unity of appreciation"; here everything depends, rather, on which direction of temporal consciousness gains predominance over all others. In the concrete mythical-religious consciousness of time there always lives a specific dynamic of feeling—a varying intensity with which the I devotes itself to the present, past, or future and so places them in a definite relation of affinity to or dependence on one another.

It would be tempting to follow these diversities and changes in the feeling of time through the whole of religious history and to show how this changing aspect of time—men's changing conception of the nature, duration, and process of time—constitutes one of the profoundest distinctions between the various religions. Here we shall not follow this diversity in detail but only attempt to characterize it by a few typical examples. The emergence of the idea of pure monotheism represents an important turning point in the religious attitude toward time. For in monotheism the fundamental revelation of the divine does not occur in the form of time which nature discloses in the transformation and periodic recurrence of its forms. This form of change can provide no image for God's imperishable being. Particularly in the religious consciousness of the Prophets, there is, consequently, a sharp turn away from nature and from the temporal orders of the natural process. While the Psalms praise God as the creator of nature, as Him to whom day and night belong, who assigns a fixed course to the sun and the planets, who has made the moon to divide the year by, the Prophetic view, although these great images appear in it, takes an entirely different road. Since the divine will has created no symbol of itself in nature, nature becomes a matter of indifference for the purely ethical-religious pathos of the Prophets. Belief in God is seen as superstition if, whether in hope or fear, it clings to nature. "Learn not the way of the heathen," says Jeremiah, "and be not dismayed at the signs of heaven; for the heathen are dismayed at them" (Jeremiah 10:2). And for the Prophetic consciousness the whole of cosmic, astronomical time disappears along with nature; in its place arises a new intuition of time which has reference solely to the history of mankind. Moreover, this history is not seen as past history but as a religious history of the future. It has been pointed out, for example, that the legend of the patriarchs was removed from the center of religious interest by the new Prophetic self-consciousness and consciousness of God. Now all true consciousness of time becomes a consciousness of the future. "Remember ye not the former things, neither consider the things of old," cried Isaiah.[53] "Time," says Hermann Cohen, who of all modern thinkers has felt this fundamental idea of the Prophetic religion most deeply and renewed it in the greatest purity,

> Time becomes future and only future. Past and present are submerged in this time of the future. This return to time is the purest idealization. Before this idea, all existence vanishes. The existence of man is transcended in this future being. . . . What Greek intellectualism could not create, Prophetic monotheism succeeded in creating. History in the Greek consciousness is synonymous with knowledge as such. Hence for the Greeks history is oriented solely toward the past. The Prophet, however, is a seer, not a scholar. . . . The Prophets are the idealists of history. Their seerdom created the concept of history as the being of the future.[54]

The whole present, that of man as well as of things, must be reborn out of this idea of the future. Nature, as it is and endures, can offer no support to the Prophetic consciousness. Just as a new heart is required of man, so there must also be a "new heaven and a new earth"—a natural substratum as it were of the new spirit in which all time and change are seen. The theogony and cosmogony of myth and of the mere nature religions are thus surpassed by a spiritual principle of an entirely different form and origin. And the idea of the Creation disappears almost entirely, at least in the pre-exilic Prophets.[55] Their God stands not so much at the

53. Isaiah 43:18.
54. Hermann Cohen, *Die Religion der Vernunft aus den Quellen des Judentums,* Grundriss der Gesamtwissenschaft des Judentums, Vol. *8* (Leipzig, 1919), pp. 293 ff., 308.
55. Cf. Gunkel, p. 160.

beginning of time as at its end; he is not so much the origin of all history as its ethical-religious fulfillment.

The temporal consciousness of the Persian religion also stands under the sign of this pure religious idea of the future. Here dualism, the conflict between the powers of good and evil, forms the basic ethical-religious theme; but this dualism is not ultimate, insofar as it is expressly limited to a definite span of time, to the "prevailing time of the long period. "At the end of this epoch the power of Ahriman is broken and the spirit of the good is alone victorious. Here again religious feeling is not rooted in the intuition of the given but is entirely oriented toward the accomplishment of a new reality and a new time. Yet compared with the prophetic idea of the "end of time," the striving toward the future in Persian religion seems at first sight more limited, more earthbound. It is the striving toward culture and an optimistic cultural consciousness which have here attained their full religious sanction. He who tills and waters the fields, plants a tree, destroys harmful animals, and provides for the preservation and increase of useful animals is fulfilling the will of God. These "good deeds of the countryman" are praised over and over again in the Avesta.[56] The man of right, the preserver and helper of the Asha, is he who brings forth the grain, the source of life from the earth: he who cultivates the grain observes the law of Ahura Mazda. It is this religion that Goethe described in the "Legacy of Old-Persian Faith" in his *West-östlicher Divan:* "Daily observance of hard labor; apart from this no revelation is needed." For mankind as a whole and man in particular do not stand aside from the great cosmic struggle, they do not experience it as a mere outward fate, but are destined to intervene in it by their own action. Only by their constant collaboration can the Asha, the order of the good and right, be victorious. Only in common with the will and action of right-thinking men, the men of the Asha, does Ormazd ultimately succeed in his work of liberation and redemption. Every good deed, every good thought of man increases the power of the good spirit, just as every evil thought multiplies the realm of the evil one. Thus despite the orientation toward an outward building of culture, it is ultimately from the "universe within" that the idea of God draws its true force. The accent of religious feeling rests on the aim of action—on its *telos,* in which the mere process of time is surpassed by being concentrated in a single supreme summit.

56. See Yasna, XII, LI, etc. Eng. trans. by L. H. Mills, *The Zend-Avesta.* The Sacred Books of the East, ed. F. Max Müller, Vol. *31* (Oxford, the Clarendon Press, 1887).

Again all light falls on the final act in the great cosmic drama, on the end of time, in which the spirit of light will have conquered the spirit of darkness. Then redemption is accomplished not only through God but also through man and with his help. All men with one accord sing loud praises to Ormazd. "The renovation arises in the universe by *his* will, *and* the world is immortal for ever and everlasting." [57]

If to this fundamental view we compare the picture of time and change prevailing in the philosophical and religious speculation of India, the contrast is immediately discernible. Here again an annulment of time and change is sought. However, it is not the energy of the will which ultimately concentrates all contingent action upon a single, supreme goal; it is from the clarity and depth of thought that this annulment of time is expected. Once the first natural form of the early Vedic religions was overcome, religion more and more assumed the color of thought. When reflection penetrates behind the illusion of the multiplicity of things, when it acquires the certainty of the absolute One beyond all multiplicity, then the form of time, along with the form of the world, vanishes for it. Perhaps we can best perceive the contrast between the Indian and the Iranian attitudes in one characteristic point, the religious position and evaluation of sleep. In the Avesta sleep appears as a mere demon because it paralyzes the activity of man. Here waking and sleeping are opposed, like light and darkness, good and evil.[58] Even in the older Upanishads, however, Indian thinking is drawn as though by a mysterious enchantment toward the idea of the deep, dreamless sleep, which it fashions more and more into a religious ideal. Here, where all the limits of being merge, all torments of the heart are overcome. Here the mortal becomes immortal and attains to the Brahman. "As a man, when in the embrace of a beloved wife, knows nothing within or without, so this person, when in the embrace of the intelligent Soul, knows nothing within or without. Verily, that is his . . . form, in which his desire is satisfied, in which . . . he is without desire and without sorrow." [59] Here lies the germ of that characteristic feeling of time which emerges in full clarity and extreme intensity in the

57. Bundahish, xxx, 23, 32. Eng. trans. by E. W. West, *Pahlavi Texts,* The Sacred Books of the East, ed. F. Max Müller, Vol. 5 (Oxford, the Clarendon Press, 1880), pp. 126, 129.

58. Cf. Yasna, xliv, 5. For details concerning the demon of sleep (Busyansta) see A. W. Jackson, "Die iranische Religion," in *Grundriss der iranischen Philologie unter Mitwirkung,* ed. Wilhelm Geiger (3 vols. Strassburg, 1895–1904), 2, 660.

59. Brihadaranyaka Upanishad, iv, 3, 21 ff. Eng. trans. by Robert E. Hume, *The Thirteen Principal Upanishads* (2d ed. Madras; Geoffrey Cumberlege, 1949), p. 136.

Buddhist source. The only aspect of time retained in the teachings of Buddha is that of coming into being and passing away; but the essence thereof is pain. The source of suffering is the threefold thirst: the thirst for pleasure, the thirst for growth, and the thirst for cessation of being. Here it is the endlessness of change as embodied in the temporal form of all empirical history, which at one stroke reveals all its senselessness and hopelessness. In change itself there can be no conclusion, hence no aim, no *telos*. As long as we are fastened to the wheel of change, it spins us around unremittingly and inexorably, without rest and purpose. In the "Questions of Milinda," King Milinda asks Saint Nâgasena for a metaphor for the transmigration of souls. Nâgasena draws a circle on the ground and asks, "Has this circle an end, great king?" "No, my lord, it has not." "So moves the cycle of births." "Is there then no end to this chain?" "No, there is none, my lord." [60] The religious and philosophical method of Buddhism may actually be characterized by the observation that wherever the common empirical world view sees being, existence, and permanence, Buddhism detects the factor of birth and death in this apparent being and experiences this mere *form* of succession, quite aside from what moves and shapes itself in it as suffering. For Buddhism all knowledge and all ignorance are rooted in this one point. As Buddha instructs a monk:

> "The untaught manyfolk know not as it really is that 'the nature of body is to come to pass!' . . . They know not as it really is that 'the nature of body is to pass away!' . . . So with feeling, perception, the activities, and consciousness—they know not as it really is that 'the nature of consciousness is to come to pass and to pass away!' . . . This, brother, is called ignorance, and thus far is one ignorant." [61]

Thus, in sharp contrast with the active feeling of time and the future in the Prophetic religion, Buddhism looks on all activity, *sankhara,* and particularly our own actions, as the source and root of suffering. Our acts as well as our sufferings obstruct the course of the true, the inward life, by enmeshing it in the form of time. Since all actions move in time and possess reality only in it and through it, action is no different from

60. Cf. Hermann Oldenberg, *Aus Indien und Iran* (Berlin, W. Hertz, 1899), p. 91.

61. Samyutta-Nikaya, xxii, 126. Eng. trans. by F. L. Woodward, *The Book of the Kindred Sayings,* Pali Text Society, Translation Series, Vol. *13* (London, Oxford Univ. Press, 1925), p. 146. On the doctrine of the Sankhara cf. Oldenberg, *Buddha. Sein Leben, seine Lehre, seine Gemeinde* (Berlin, 1881), 4th ed. pp. 279 ff. Eng. trans. by William Hoey, *Buddha: His Life, His Doctrine, His Order* (London and Edinburgh, 1882).

suffering. Both are redeemed if we can annul their temporal foundation, this substratum of all suffering and action, by perceiving its nonessentiality. Suffering as well as action is destroyed by the destruction of time, after which the spirit enters into the true eternity of Nirvana. Here the aim consists not in the "end of time," as for Zoroaster and the Jewish prophets, but in the disappearance for the religious view of time as a whole, with everything that is in it and everything that acquires "shape and name" in it. For the pure gaze of knowledge the flame of life is extinguished. "He has cut the round and won desirelessness; dried utterly, the flood flows no more; cut off, the round revolves not. That's Ill's ending." [62]

And another, no less significant, view of time is disclosed when we survey the Chinese religion. Despite the countless threads connecting China with India, despite the close relation between certain forms of Chinese and Indian mysticism, the two cultures seem far apart in their characteristic feeling of time and in their intellectual and emotional attitude toward temporal existence. The Taoist ethic also culminates in a doctrine of immobility and inactivity: for immobility and silence are the fundamental attributes of the Tao itself. If man is to participate in the Tao, the fixed course and permanent order of the heavens, he must above all generate the "emptiness" of the Tao in himself. The Tao engenders all creatures and yet abjures possession of them; it makes them and yet renounces them. That is its mysterious virtue: to create, yet renounce. Thus, inactivity becomes a principle of Chinese mysticism: "Practice inaction, busy thyself with inaction" is its supreme rule. Yet as soon as we penetrate to the heart and meaning of this mysticism, we find a direct antithesis to the religious tendency prevailing in Buddhism. While in the doctrine of Buddha the true goal consists in *redemption* from life, from the endless cycle of births, Taoist mysticism characteristically seeks and promises the *prolongation* of life. "The refinement which the Tao of the highest order confers," says a sage to the Emperor Huang, "is deepest mysteriousness and darkest darkness; its ultimate point is unconsciousness and silence. Be without seeing, without hearing, and your body will spontaneously remain in the correct condition; be still, and you are sure to become pure; do not subject your body to toil, do not dis-

62. Udana, VII, 2. Eng. trans. by F. L. Woodward, *The Minor Anthologies of the Pali Canon*. Sacred Books of the Buddhists, Vol. 8 (London, Humphrey Milford, 1935), p. 90.

turb your refinement, and you may live long." [63] Whereas Buddhist nothingness, Nirvana, purports to efface time, the inactivity of Taoist mysticism aims to preserve it, to perpetuate not only being in general, but ultimately the individual body as well. "When thine eyes see nothing more, when thine ears hear nothing more, when thy heart feels nothing more, then thy soul will preserve thy body and thy body will live forever." What this mysticism strives to negate, to overcome, is not, as we see, time as such, but rather change in time. By this negation of change it hopes to achieve pure duration, endless and identical survival, an unlimited repetition of sameness. Being is viewed as a simple, immutable survival in time; for Chinese speculation, in sharp contrast to Indian thought, precisely this survival becomes the aim of religious striving, the expression of a positive religious value. "Time, in which all changes of phenomena are to be thought," Kant once said, "endures and never changes; because it is that in which succession and coexistence can only be represented as attributes of the phenomena themselves." This unchanging time which forms the substratum of all change is apprehended by Chinese thought and concretely viewed in the image of the heavens and their eternally recurrent configurations. The heavens govern but do not act; they determine all being without departing from themselves, from their always identical forms and rule. All earthly power and government should copy them. "Because Heaven does not operate actively. . . the formation and development of all that exists takes place thereby; because the ruler does not work actively . . . the myriads of works and occupations of mankind are properly accomplished." [64] Thus instead of the factor of variability, instead of genesis and passing away, it is the factor of pure substantiality that is here ascribed to time and to the heavens and made into the supreme ethical-religious norm. Pure, uniform permanence is the rule which time and the heavens prescribe for man. Just as the heavens and time are not created but have been from all eternity and will endure for all eternity, so man in his actions must renounce the illusion of action and creation and seek to preserve the existing order.

It need scarcely be pointed out that a very definite and specific cultural sense is expressed in this religious formation of the concept of time. The

63. See De Groot, *Universismus*, p. 104; cf. pp. 43 ff., 128 ff.

64. De Groot, *Universismus*, p. 49. Cf. Wilhelm Grube, *Religion und Kultus der Chinesen* (Leipzig, 1910), pp. 86 ff.

ethics of Confucius is permeated with this feeling, for what it stresses
above all is the "imperturbable" character of the celestial and the human
Tao. Thus ethics becomes the doctrine of man's four immutable attributes
which are the same as those of the heavens, which are as eternal and unchanging as the heavens themselves. This fundamental presupposition
enables us to understand the strict traditionalism that is characteristic of
this ethic. Confucius called himself not a creator but a transmitter, who
believed in and loved antiquity, and in the Tao te' King it is written
that one dominates present reality by holding to the Tao of antiquity.
"To be able to recognize the beginnings of antiquity, that is called parting the threads of the Tao." [65] Here there is no call for a "new heaven"
and a "new earth." The future has religious justification only insofar as it
can legitimize itself as a simple continuation, an exact and faithful copy
of the past. The speculative thinking of the Upanishads and of Buddhism seeks a being transcending all multiplicity, all change and all
time; in the Messianic religions the pure *will* toward the future determines the form of faith; here, on the other hand, the given order of things,
just as it is, is perpetuated and sanctified. And this sanctification extends
even to the merest particulars of the *spatial* order and arrangement of
things.[66] In the contemplation of the One unmoved order of the universe
the spirit attains to silence and time itself seems to achieve immobility,
for now the remotest future seems bound to the past by unbreakable
threads. The cult and reverence of ancestors are accordingly the principal
requirements of Chinese morality and the foundation of Chinese religion.
"While the family constantly obtains new members by childbirth," writes
de Groot in describing the Chinese ancestor cult,

> it gradually dies out at its summit. However, the dead do not separate
> from it. Even in the other world, they continue to exert their dominion

65. Tao te' King, XIV.

66. Cf., e.g., the account of the Fung-shui system in De Groot, *The Religious System of China*, 3, 1041:

> The repairing of a house, the building of a wall or dwelling . . . the planting of a pole
> or cutting down of a tree, in short, any change in the ordinary position of objects may
> disturb the Fung-shui of the houses and temples in the vicinity and of the whole quarter,
> and cause the people to be visited by disasters, misery and death. Should anyone suddenly
> fall ill or die, his kindred are immediately ready to impute the cause to somebody who
> has ventured to make a change in the established order of things, or has made an
> improvement in his own property. . . . Instances are by no means rare of their having
> stormed his house, demolished his furniture, assailed his person.

and their beatific will. . . . Their souls, made present by wooden tablets with their names inscribed on them, find their place on the house altar and in the temple of the ancestors, where they are faithfully worshiped and consulted for advice, and respectfully nourished with sacrifices of food. Thus the living and the dead form together a larger family. . . . As in their lifetime, the ancestors are the natural guardians of their descendants, whom they protect against the harmful influences of evil spirits and thus assure them of happiness, prosperity, and rich progeny.[67]

In this form of ancestor cult we have again a clear example of a feeling of time in which the religious-ethical accent is neither on the future nor on the present in its pure immediacy, but above all on the past, and in which the succession of the particular moments of time is transformed into a perpetual coexistence and interpenetration.

This religious tendency toward permanence assumes still a different aspect in the fundamental views of the Egyptian religion. Here again religious feeling and thought cling fast to the world; here again there is no passing beyond given existence to its metaphysical source, nor is there any thought of another, ethical order beyond it which it strives always to approach and by which it aspires to gain new form. What is sought and yearned for is rather simple survival—a survival which refers above all to the individual existence and form of man. Immortality, the survival of this form, is entirely bound up with the preservation of the physical substratum of life, of the human body in all its particularity. It is as though the pure idea of the future could assert itself only through the immediate presence and concrete intuition of this substratum. Accordingly, the greatest care must be taken to protect from destruction the body as a whole as well as every single part of it. Every part of the body, every organ, must be removed from its perishable state by embalming and magic spells and made eternal and indestructible, for thus alone can the perpetual survival of the soul be guaranteed.[68] Here "life after death" is a simple prolongation of empirical existence, every particular of which the Egyptians strive to preserve in immediate physical concretion. Similarly in ethical life there prevails the idea of an order which is not only governed by the gods, but in which man himself must unremittingly

67. De Groot, *Universismus*, pp. 128 ff.
68. Concerning these methods see, e.g., Budge, *Egyptian Magic*, pp. 190 ff.

participate. Here, however, there is concern not, as in the Iranian religion, with a new life in the future, but only with the conservation of what is. The spirit of evil is never definitively conquered; since the beginning of the world there has been the same balance of forces and the same periodic ups and downs in the phases of the struggle.[69] In this fundamental view all temporal dynamics is ultimately transformed into a kind of spatial statics. This transformation has found its clearest expression in Egyptian art, where this tendency toward stabilization is most magnificently and consistently represented—where all reality, all life, and all movement seem to be confined within rigid geometric forms. The negation of mere temporality, sought in India by methods of speculative thought and in China through a political-religious ordering of life, is here achieved by immersion in the purely intuitive, plastic, and architectonic *form* of things. In its clarity, concreteness, and eternity this form triumphs over all mere succession, over the ceaseless flux and transience of all temporal configurations. The Egyptian pyramid is the visible sign of this triumph, hence the symbol of the fundamental aesthetic and religious intuition of Egyptian culture.

In all the typical attitudes toward time that we have considered up to now, pure thought, and feeling and intuition as well, master time only by abstracting or *negating* it in some way. There remains still another approach to time, quite apart from this mere abstraction and negation. Fundamentally, time and fate can be truly dominated only where the characteristic factors of temporality are not disregarded but are posited and affirmed. Only such an affirmation makes it possible to surpass time, not outwardly but inwardly, not transcendently but immanently. Once this path is taken, the consciousness and feeling of time enter upon a new phase of development. Now the intuition of time and fate begins to break loose from its primordial mythical source: the concept of time enters into a new form, the form of philosophical thought. It was the philosophy of the Greeks which prepared the ground and created the fundamental presuppositions for this great transformation—perhaps one of the most important in the history of human culture. In its beginnings Greek thought reveals close ties with speculative-religious doctrines of time emanating from the orient. Regardless of whether a direct historical connection can be demonstrated between Zruvanite speculation and the Orphic cosmogo-

69. Cf. the remarks of George B. Foucart, *Histoire des religions et méthode comparative* (Paris, 1912), pp. 363 ff.

nies and cosmologies,[70] the factual similarity between certain fundamental motifs is unmistakable. In the theogony of Pherecydes of Syros, which is now assigned roughly to the middle of the sixth century B.C., the threshold of the great creations of Greek philosophy, Time, Zeus, and Chthonia are the primal gods, from which all being is descended: Ζὰς μὲν καὶ χρόνος ἦσαν ἀεὶ καὶ χθενίη—ὁ δὲ χρόνος ἐποίησε ἐκ τοῦ γόνου ἑαυτοῦ πῦρ καὶ πνεῦμα καὶ ὕδωρ.[71] Here creation with everything contained in it is the product of time, while in other Orphic poems it originates in night and chaos. And much later, at the summit of Greek speculation, we sometimes perceive echoes of such fundamental mythical ideas and attitudes. In Empedocles' doctrine of metempsychosis and redemption, time and fate, χρόνος and ἀνάγκη, are again seen as one.

> There is an oracle of Necessity, an ancient decree of the gods, eternal, sealed fast with broad oaths, that when one of the divine spirits whose portion is long life sinfully stains his own limbs with bloodshed and following Hate has sworn a false oath—these must wander for thrice ten thousand seasons far from the company of the blessed, being born throughout the period into all kinds of mortal shapes, which exchange one hard way of life for another.[72]

Here objective change and the oppositions that develop within the one world order, within the *sphairos,* are subject to inviolable laws and measures of time; to each antagonism a definite "epoch" is assigned, in which it is completed. But when time has been fulfilled τελειομένοιο χρόνοιο), one antithesis must cede to the other, love to hate or hate to love (Fragment 30, ed. Diels). And yet in Empedocles this old concept of time and fate seems merely to echo a remote world that had vanished for philosophical thinking. For where Empedocles speaks not as a seer and priest of atonement but as a philosopher and scientist, his doctrine is based on that of Parmenides. And in Parmenides Greek thought gained an entirely new position in regard to the problem of time. It is his great achievement that for the first time in the history of thought he made the logos the measure of being, from which the final decision, the κρίσις, concerning

---

70 A direct connection is assumed by Robert Eisler particularly, who sees in Zruvanism the direct prototype of the Indian doctrine of Kala and the Orphic doctrines of Χρόνος ἀγήρατος. See Eisler's *Weltenmantel und Himmelszelt* (Munich, 1910), 2, 411 ff., 499 ff. Cf. the above-cited lecture of Junker.

71. Pherecydes, Fragment 1, ed. Diels. Cf. Damascus, 1246, Diels 71A, 8.

72. Fragment 30, ed. Diels; in Freeman, p. 65.

being and nonbeing is expected. And for him the power of time and change becomes mere illusion. Only for myth is there a temporal origin, a "genesis" of being—for the logos the very question of an origin loses its meaning.

There is only one other description of the way remaining, namely that What Is Is. To this way there are very many sign-posts: that being has no coming-into-being and no destruction, for it is whole of limb, without motion and without end. And it never Was, nor Will Be, because it Is now, a Whole all together, One, continuous; for what creation of it will you look for? How, whence (could it have) sprung? . . . what necessity impelled it, if it did spring from Nothing, to be produced later or earlier? Thus it must be absolutely, or not at all. . . . Justice has never released Being in its fetters and set it free either to come into being or to perish, but holds it fast.

(τοῦ εἵνεκεν οὔτε γενέσθαι οὔτ' ὄλλυσθαι ἀνῆκε δίκη χαλάσασα πέδησεν, ἀλλ' ἔχει.) (Fragment 8, ed. Diels). Thus in the mythical language which Parmenides' didactic poem still speaks throughout, the permanence of being is again linked to the commandment and order of fate, of Δίκη. But this fate, which is the expression no longer of an outside power but rather of the necessity of thought itself, has now become timeless—timeless as the truth in whose name Parmenides pronounces his verdict on the world of change as a world of illusion. It is in this exclusion of all temporal determinations that the mythical concept of fate for the first time passes into the logical concept of necessity, that for the first time Δίκη becomes ἀνάγκη. The solemn rigidity of the archaic style in which Parmenides' poem is written prevents any expression of a subjective, personal feeling; yet in the verses of this poem we sometimes seem to hear the triumph of the logos over the mythical powers of fate, the triumph of pure thought and its unassailable permanence over the temporal world of illusion.

Thus coming-into-being is quenched and destruction also into the unseen. . . . But (Being) is motionless in the limits of mighty bonds, without beginning, without cease, since Becoming and Destruction have been driven far away, and true conviction has rejected them. And remaining the same in the same place, it rests by itself and thus remains there fixed; for a powerful Necessity holds it in the bonds of

a Limit, which constrains it round about . . . therefore all things that
mortals have established, believing in their truth, are just a name:
Becoming and Perishing, Being and Not-Being, and Change of position, and alteration of bright color.

(Fragment 8, ed. Diels; Freeman, pp. 21 ff.) Here it is directly stated that
the power of the philosophical idea of true conviction rejects change both
as a mythical power and in its empirical-sensuous form. (ἐπεὶ γένεσις καὶ
ὄλεθρος τῆλε μαλ' ἐπλάχθησαν, ἀπῶσε δὲ πίστις αληθής.) The power of
time is broken, since time, seen from the standpoint of philosophical
thought, negates itself dialectically, reveals its own inner contradiction.
For religious feeling, particularly in India, time signifies above all the
burden of *suffering;* but for philosophical thinking, here where it first
appears in full independence and consciousness, time is annihilated by
the burden of *contradiction.*

As Greek philosophy developed, this fundamental idea underwent many
transformations but was confirmed as an enduring force. Both Democritus
and Plato took the path which Parmenides had indicated as the only path
of "true conviction"—the path of the logos, which for them, too, became
the highest authority in the decision concerning being and nonbeing. But
while Parmenides thought he had destroyed change by thought, they
demanded that thought should penetrate it. They called for a *theory* of
change itself. They did not deny the world of change; rather, they set out
to rescue it; but this can be done only if a solid intellectual substratum is
provided for the world of sensuous phenomena. It was in answer to this
need that Democritus conceived the world of atoms and Plato the world
of ideas. To temporal coming-into-being and passing-away the one opposed the permanence of immutable natural laws which govern all physical events, the other opposed a realm of pure timeless forms, in which
all temporal existence participates. Democritus was the first to state the
concept of natural law in clear and universal form, and thanks to the new
standard thus established to disparage all mythical thinking as merely
subjective and anthropomorphic. "Men have fashioned an image of
Chance as an excuse for their own stupidity" (Fragment 119, ed. Diels).
To this human idol he opposed the eternal necessity of the logos, which
knows no chance, no exception to the universal rule of the world process.
(οὐδὲν χρῆμα μάτην γίνεται ἀλλὰ πάντα ἐκ λόγου τε καὶ ἀνάγκης.)
And side by side with this new *logical* concept of *ananke,* a new *ethical*

concept of necessity arose more and more clearly and consciously. It is true that this concept developed primarily in Greek poetry, that a new meaning and power of the individual, of the ethical self as opposed to an all-powerful fate were for the first time discovered in tragedy; yet Greek thinking not only accompanied this process, this gradual breaking away from the mythical-religious source in which tragedy is originally rooted, but gave it its true foundation. Like the oriental religions, Greek philosophy in its beginnings saw the temporal order as at once physical and ethical. It looked upon time as the fulfillment of an ethical law. "The source from which existing things derive their existence," says Anaximander, "is also that to which they return at their destruction, according to necessity; for they give justice and make reparation to one another for their injustice, according to the arrangement of Time." Theophrastus, who handed down these words, was well aware of their mythical, poetic sound.[73] But, more and more, a new ethical depth and inwardness were given to the mythical concept of time as fate. In as early a writer as Heraclitus we find the profound saying that a man's character is his fate and his demon: ἦθος ἀνθρώπῳ δαίμων (Fragment 119, ed. Diels). And in Plato this idea is completed in that picture of the judgment of the dead which, perhaps deriving from motifs of Iranian mortuary belief, gave new form and significance to these motifs. In the tenth book of the *Republic* we find the image of the "spindle of necessity" ('Ανάγκης ἄτρακτον) by which all the spheres are set in motion.

> These are the Fates, daughters of Necessity, who are clothed in white robes and have chaplets on their heads, Lachesis and Clotho and Atropos, who accompany with their voices the harmony of the sirens— Lachesis singing of the past, Clotho of the present, Atropos of the future. . . . When Er and the spirits arrived, their duty was to go at once to Lachesis; but first of all there came a prophet who arranged them in order; then he took from the knees of Lachesis lots and samples of lives, and having mounted a high pulpit, spoke as follows: "Hear the word of Lachesis, the daughter of Necessity. Mortal souls, behold a new cycle of life and mortality. Your genius will not be allotted to you, but you will choose your genius. . . . Virtue is free,

73. Theophrastus, *Phys. Opin.*, Fragment 2D, 476, ed. Diels, 2, 9: ἐξ ὧν δὲ ἡ γένεσίς ἐστι τοῖς οἶσι, καὶ τὴν φθορὰν εἰς ταῦτα γίνεσθαι κατὰ τὸ χρεὼν διδόναι γὰρ αὐτὰ δίκην καὶ τίσιν αλλήλοις τῆς ἀδικίας κατὰ τὴν τοῦ χρόνου τάξιν, ποιητικωτέροις οὕτως ὀνόμασιν αὐτὰ λέγων.

and as a man honours or dishonours her he will have more or less of her; the responsibility is with the chooser—God is justified." [74]

In this magnificent vision which once again epitomizes the whole spirit of mythical creation peculiar to the Greeks and particularly to Plato, we have nevertheless departed from the sphere of myth. For here we find the fundamental Socratic idea of man's moral responsibility for himself as opposed to the idea of mythical guilt and fate. The meaning and center of man's life, his true destiny, is placed within him; whereas for Parmenides time and fate were conquered by pure thought, here they are overcome by the ethical will.

It is this inner process of spiritual liberation that accounts for the characteristic feeling of time which attained its first true maturity among the Greeks. We might say that here for the first time thought and feeling became free to gain a pure and full consciousness of the temporal present. Only the Being of Parmenides can be conceived as "present": it never was and never will be, because the whole of it, one and indivisible, exists only in the now. (οὐδέ ποτ᾽ ἦν, οὐδ᾽ ἔσται, ἐπεὶ νῦν ἔστιν ὁμοῦ πᾶν ἕν, συνεχές.) The Platonic Idea is purely present, for only as something that always is and never becomes can it satisfy thought with its postulate of identity, of a never-changing determinacy. And for Plato, the philosopher is the man who by virtue of his reason is always oriented toward being.[75] Even that thinker who is commonly regarded as the true "philosopher of becoming" is only a seeming exception to this basic character of Greek philosophical thought. For it is a misunderstanding to impute a solely negative meaning to Heraclitus' thesis of the "flux of things." [76] It is true that he spoke in unforgettable images of the "stream of time" — that stream which irresistibly carries all being along with it and in which no man can step twice. But his attention is by no means focused on this mere fact of flowing and passing but is directed toward the eternal measures which he apprehends in it. These measures are the truly one and immutable logos of the world. "This ordered universe which is the same for all," he declares, "was not created by any one of the gods or of mankind, but it was ever

74. Plato, *Republic*, 616C ff. Eng. trans. by Benjamin Jowett (3d ed. New York, Scribner's, 1928).

75. Plato, *The Sophist*, 254A.

76. In this opinion I agree particularly with Karl Reinhardt, *Parmenides und die Geschichte der griechischen Philosophie* (Bonn, 1916), pp. 206 ff. I refer the reader to his arguments.

and is and shall be ever-living Fire, kindled in measure and quenched in measure" (Fragment 30, ed. Diels). And again it is the figure of Dike as Justice and Fate who personifies this idea of the measure immanent in all events. "The sun will not transgress his measures; otherwise the Furies, ministers of Justice, will find him out" (Fragment 94). On this certainty of a *metron,* a sure and necessary rhythm which is maintained in all change, rests the certainty "of a hidden harmony that is better than the visible harmony." It is only in order to assure himself of this hidden harmony that Heraclitus turns back again and again to the contemplation of change. What captivates him is not the naked fact of change, but its meaning. "That which is wise is one; to understand the purpose which steers all things through all things" (Fragment 41). This twofold attitude—this attachment to temporal intuition and this striving to surpass it by the thought of a unity of law, indwelling and immediately grasped in it—most precisely expresses Heraclitus' distinction as a Greek thinker. Oldenberg has pointed to numerous parallels between the Heraclitean doctrine and the Buddhist doctrines of change and the soul. "The creations of the West and the East," he writes,

> show in many respects an amazing correspondence in fundamentals as in secondary matters, even down to the form of the maxims to which the religious consciousness is so devoted, or of the metaphors intended to bring the great orders of the world process close to the imagination. . . . It is obviously no accident that at precisely the phase of development of which we are speaking the correspondences between the ideas of two peoples far removed from each other both outwardly and inwardly are stronger in many respects than in the preceding period. The myth-creating imagination which dominated in the earlier period goes its ways without plan or aim; it is driven by chance which links things far apart according to its whims, which playfully shakes ingenious baroque figures from its cornucopia. But as soon as reflection, rapidly growing into inquiring thought, begins to devote itself more and more purposively to the problems of the world and of human existence, the area of possibility is reduced. What almost inevitably appears as reality to the attentive but still inexperienced eye of those days confines the stream of ideas in a set channel and thus imprints the most diverse and striking traits of similarity upon the analogous thought processes of Greek and Indian minds.[77]

77. Oldenberg, *Aus Indien und Iran,* pp. 75 ff.

And yet, precisely when we look into these similarities, the typical antithesis between the modes of thought and general intellectual attitudes becomes all the clearer and more meaningful. In Buddhism the finite form to which all existence is bound must above all be shattered, the illusion of the intrinsically limited figure must be negated, before the religious meaning of events can be disclosed. Form (*rupa*) is the first of the five elements of existence which bear within them the source and foundation of all suffering. "I will teach you the burden, brethren," says Buddha in one of his sermons, "the taking hold of the burden, the lifting of it up and the laying of it down. . . . What, brethren, is the burden? It is the mass of the five factors of grasping, should be the reply. What five? The mass of the body factors of grasping, of the feeling factors, the perception, activities and consciousness factors of grasping." For "Body, friends, is impermanent, that is woe. What is woe, has ceased, been destroyed."[78] No one stressed more sharply than Heraclitus the changeable character of what is commonly called the "form" of things; but from this fact he draws the opposite consequence to that drawn in Buddha's sermon. It leads him not to a rejection but to a passionate affirmation of existence. While, in the Buddhist legend, Siddhattha the king's son flees from his first sight of old age, sickness, and death to become an ascetic and penitent, Heraclitus *seeks* all this and dwells on it, because he needs it as a means of grasping the secret of the logos which *is* only by virtue of the fact that it is perpetually splitting into opposites. While the mystic feels in temporal change only the torment of impermanence, Heraclitus delights in the intuition of the great One, which must split in two in order to find itself again. "That which is in opposition is in concert, and from things that differ comes the most beautiful harmony; harmony consists of opposing tension, like that of the bow and the lyre" (Fragment 8, ed. Diels; Freeman, p. 51). For Heraclitus the intuition of this harmony of opposing tension solves the riddle of form and takes from us the burden of change. Now, the temporal no longer appears as a deficiency pure and simple, as limitation and suffering; in it, rather, is disclosed the innermost life of the divine. There is no peace and beatitude in the negation of change, in perfection without tension; rather, "disease makes health pleasant and good, hunger satisfaction, weariness rest" (Fragment 111). Now, even the oppo-

---

78. Samyutta-Nikaya, xxii, 22, 85. Eng. trans. by Woodward, *Sayings*, pp. 24–25, 96. Cf. Karl E. Neumann, trans., *Die Reden Gotamo Buddhas aus der mittleren Sammlung* (2d ed. Munich, 1921), *3*, 384.

sition of life and death becomes relative. "And what is in us is the same thing: living and dead, awake and sleeping, as well as young and old; for the latter having changed becomes the former" (Fragment 88). As with Buddha, Heraclitus likes to use the image of the circle to express his doctrine. In the circumference of the circle, he declares in one fragment (Fragment 103), beginning and end are one. But while for Buddha the circle serves as a symbol of the endlessness and hence aimlessness and meaninglessness of change, for Heraclitus it is a symbol of perfection. The line returning to itself suggests self-contained form as the determining law of the universe. And similarly Plato and Aristotle made use of the circle to shape and round out their intellectual picture of the cosmos.

Thus, while Indian thinking is oriented essentially toward the transience of the temporal world and Chinese thinking toward its permanence; while Indian thinking one-sidedly stresses the factor of change and Chinese thinking that of permanence—Greek thought establishes a pure inner balance between the two factors. The ideas of variability and substantiality fuse into one. And from this fusion arises a new feeling, which might be called the purely speculative feeling of time and presence. Here there is no longer, as in myth, a return to the temporal *beginning* of things, or as in the religious-ethical mood of the Prophets an orientation toward its *ultimate goal;* here thought dwells on the eternally unchanging fundamental law of the universe. In this feeling of the present the I gives itself to the moment but is not confined within it: it seems to hover free in the moment, untouched by its pain. In this speculative "now" the distinctions of the empirical form of time are thus absorbed. In a fragment preserved by Seneca Heraclitus says that one day is like another, *unus dies par omni est* (Fragment 106). This does not signify any equivalence in the content of events, which on the contrary changes from day to day, from hour to hour, from moment to moment, but refers to the always identical form of the world process, which is manifested just as definitely in little things as in big, in the simplest point of the present and in the infinite duration of time. Among the moderns it is Goethe who has been deeply sensitive to this truly Greek feeling of time and life, who has revived it with the greatest intensity: "Heut ist heute, morgen morgen—und was folgt und was vergangen, reisst nicht hin und bleibt nicht hangen." Indeed, the speculative view of time reveals a tendency which would seem to relate it closely to the artistic view. For in both we are relieved of the *burden* of change which finds so moving an expression in the doctrine of Buddha. For him who, in his intuition of time, no longer clings to the content of events but apprehends their pure form—for him this content is ultimately raised to the level of form; the substance of being and becoming is transformed into pure play. It is in this light perhaps that we should understand the strangely profound saying of Heraclitus: αἰὼν παῖς ἐστι παίζων, πεττεύων παιδὸς ἡ βασιληίη, "Time is a child playing a game of draughts; the kingship is in the hands of the child" (Fragment 52).

Here we cannot go on to describe how the speculative view of time, the foundations of which were here laid, continued to develop and how it ultimately came to play a crucial role in empirical-scientific knowledge, but in this area too the philosophy of the Greeks, particularly of Plato, forms the connecting link. For sharply as he distinguished the pure being of the idea from the world of change, he did not content himself with a negative evaluation of time and change. In the works of Plato's old age the concept of motion even enters into his exposition of the realm of pure ideas—there is a motion of the pure forms themselves, a κίνησις τῶν εἰδῶν. And the new significance of the concept of time for the general structure of Plato's doctrine becomes clearer in the formulation of his natural philosophy. In the *Timaeus*, Time becomes the intermediary between the worlds of the visible and the invisible; it explains how the visible world can participate in the eternity of the pure forms. The physical, corporeal world begins with the creation of time. The demiurge looked upon eternal being, upon the ideas as the eternal prototypes, and strove to make the sensuous world as much like them as possible. But the nature of the eternal prototypes could not be wholly transferred to the world of becoming, and so the demiurge decided to create a moving image of eternity. This moving image of eternity with its perpetual unity is what we call "time"—and thus days and nights, months and years appeared, linked with the structure of the whole by the will of the demiurge. Thus time, since it moves in a circle according to number, is the first and most complete imitation of the eternal insofar as such an imitation is possible in the world of change.[79] With this, time—which hitherto had seemed, as an expression of that which merely becomes and never is, to constitute a fundamental barrier to thought—has become a basic concept for the knowledge of the cosmos. It is this intermediary concept of a temporal order which within the Platonic system effects what

79. *Timaeus*, 37D ff.

might be called a "cosmodicy," since it warrants the investing of the world with soul and its elevation into a spiritual totality.[80] Here Plato still consciously speaks the language of myth; and yet he points out a path which has led, in strict historical continuity, to the foundation of the modern scientific view of the world. Kepler shows himself to be thoroughly imbued with the central ideas of the *Timaeus*: they guided him unremittingly from his first work, the *Mysterium cosmographicum de stella nova* (1596) to the mature exposition of the *Harmonices mundi* (1619). And here for the first time a new concept of time appears in full clarity: the time concept of mathematical natural science. In the formulation of Kepler's three laws time appears as the fundamental variable—that uniformly changing magnitude to which all un-uniform change and motion are referred and by which they are measured. This henceforth is its ideal, purely logical significance, as Leibniz, from the standpoint of the new mathematical physics, was soon to state in universal philosophical terms.[81] The concept of time has thus been imbued with the concept of function; it now appears as one of the most important applications and expressions of functional thinking; and thereby it is raised to an entirely new level of signification. The Platonic concept of time has now been confirmed: only by being ordered in the continuum of time, only by being related to this "moving image of eternity," have phenomena become ripe for knowledge, have gained their share in the idea.

But the fact that his insight was reached through the problem of planetary motion points to a very significant historical connection. The planets, "the moving, wandering stars," have from the earliest times aroused mythical and religious interest. Along with the sun and moon they are worshiped as gods. In the astral religion of the Babylonians it is above all Venus, the

---

80. Cf. my account of the Platonic philosophy in Dessoir, *Lehrbuch, 1*, 111 ff.

81. Une suite de perceptions réveille en nous l'idée de la durée, mais elle ne la fait point. Nos perceptions n'ont jamais une suite assez constante et régulière pour répondre à celle du temps qui est un continu uniforme et simple, comme une ligne droite. Le changement des perceptions nous donne occasion de penser au temps, et on le mesure par des changements uniformes: mais quand il n'y auroit rien d'uniforme dans la nature, le temps ne laisseroit pas d'être déterminé, comme le lieu ne laisseroit pas d'être déterminé, aussi quand il n'y auroit aucun corps fixe ou immobile. C'est que connoissant les règles des mouvements on peut toujours les rapporter à des mouvements uniformes intelligibles et prévoir par ce moyen ce qui arrivera par des différents mouvements joints ensemble. Et dans ce sens le temps est la mesure du mouvement, c'est-à-dire le mouvement uniforme est la mesure du mouvement difforme. G. W. Leibniz, *Nouveaux Essais*, Bk. 2, ch. 14, sec. 16.

morning and evening star, which was thus worshiped and which, in the image of the goddess Ishtar, became a leading figure in the pantheon. And we find this cult of the planets in far distant cultures, as for example, among the Aztecs. In the subsequent religious development, particularly in the transition to monotheism, belief in these old gods long remained alive, but now they were degraded into hostile demons which troubled the lawful order of the universe. In the Iranian religion the planets are looked upon as evil powers who resist the Asha, the cosmic order of the good. As servants of Ahriman, they invade the celestial sphere and disturb its regular course with their unfettered movements.[82] This demonization of the planets recurs later, particularly in Gnosticism. The demonic planetary powers are the true enemies of the Gnostic; in them is embodied the power of destiny, εἱμαρμένη, from which he seeks redemption.[83] And down to the beginning of modern philosophy, down to the Renaissance speculations on the philosophy of nature, this notion of the irregularity of the planets is echoed. In antiquity Eudoxus of Cnidos, the mathematician and astronomer of the Platonic Academy, drew up a strictly mathematical theory of planetary motion, in which he furnished proof that the planets were not "errant stars" but moved according to fixed laws. Yet Kepler was still confronted by the arguments of Patrizzi, who declared that any attempt on the part of mathematical astronomy to determine the course of the planets by interlocking orbits, cycles, and epicycles was vain because in reality the planets were nothing other than animate beings, endowed with reason, who, just as appearance indicates, describe the most diverse, strangely tortuous paths through the liquid ether. It is characteristic of Kepler's manner of thinking that he countered this conception primarily by a methodological argument—an argument which he himself characterized as "philosophical." To resolve all seeming disorder into order, in every seeming irregularity to seek the hidden rule: precisely this—he stressed in opposing Patrizzi—is the basic principle of "philosophical astronomy."

Among the adherents of a sound philosophy there is none who is not of this opinion, who would not congratulate himself and astronomy if he succeeded in disclosing the causes of error and distinguishing the

82. Bundahish, ɪɪ, xxv. Eng. trans. by West, pp. 10 ff., 91 ff. Cf. Jackson in *Grundriss der iranischen Philologie, 2,* 666, 672; Darmesteter, p. 277.

83. Cf. Wilhelm Bousset, *Hauptprobleme der Gnosis* (Göttingen, 1907), pp. 38 ff.; idem, *Kyrios Christos* (Göttingen, 1926), pp. 185 ff.

true movements of the planets from their accidental orbits which rest only on sensory illusion, and in thus proving the simplicity and ordered regularity of their orbits.[84]

In these simple and profound words from Kepler's pamphlet in defense of Tycho Brahe, and in the concrete confirmation which they soon received through Kepler's treatise on the movements of Mars, the planets were dethroned as the ancient gods of time and fate, and the general view of time and of the temporal process was transferred from the image-world of the mythical-religious imagination to the *exact* conceptual world of scientific cognition.

5. Mythical Number and the System of Sacred Numbers

Besides space and time, the third great formal motif dominating the structure of the mythical world is number. And here again, if we would understand the mythical function of number as such, we must sharply distinguish it from the theoretical meaning and function of number. In the system of theoretical knowledge number signifies the great connecting link which can embrace the most dissimilar contents and transform them into the unity of the concept. Through this resolution of all multiplicity and diversity into the unity of knowledge, number appears as an expression of the fundamental theoretical aim of knowledge itself, as an expression of "truth" as such. Since its first philosophical-scientific definition, this fundamental character has been imputed to it. "The nature of number," we read in the fragments of Philolaus,

> is the cause of recognition, able to give guidance and teaching to every man in what is puzzling and unknown. For none of existing things would be clear to anyone, either in themselves or in their relationship to one another, unless there existed Number and its essence. But in fact, Number, fitting all things into the soul through sense-perception, makes them recognizable and comparable with one another . . . in that number gives them body and divides the different relationships of things, whether they be Non-Limited or Limiting, into their separate groups.[85]

In this connection and separation, in this fixing of set limits and relations, the strictly logical power of number is contained. By it the sensuous world

---

84. Johann Kepler, *Apologia Tychonis contra Ursum,* in *Joannis Kepleri astronomi opera omnia,* ed. C. Frisch (8 vols. Frankfurt, Heyder and Zimmer, 1858–71), *1,* 247.

85. Philolaus, Fragment 11, ed. Diels, 32B, 11; Freeman, p. 75.

itself, the "matter" of perception, is more and more divested of its specific nature and recast in a universal intellectual form. Measured by the "true" nature of reality the immediate sensuous character of the impression—its visibility, audibility, tactility etc.—appears only as a "secondary quality," whose true source, whose primary ground, is to be sought in pure specifications of magnitude, that is to say, ultimately in purely numerical relations. The development of modern theoretical science has carried this ideal of knowledge toward its fulfillment by reducing not only the specific character of sense perception, but also the specific nature of the pure forms of intuition, the nature of space and time, to that of pure number.[86] And just as number here serves as the true logical instrument for creating a homogeneity of the contents of consciousness, so number itself develops more and more into an absolutely homogeneous and uniform entity. The particular numbers disclose no differences over against one another, other than those arising from their position in the system as a whole. They have no other being, no other character and nature, than that which comes to them through this position, in other words through the relations within an ideal aggregate. Accordingly, it is possible to "define," i.e. constructively produce, specific numbers which, though they directly correspond to no assignable sensuous or intuitive substratum, are unequivocally characterized by these relations: as, for example, in the explanation of irrational numbers that has become dominant since Dedekind, where the irrational numbers appear as "cuts" within the system of rational numbers (i.e. as complete divisions of this system into two classes, effected by a definite logical rule). Fundamentally the pure thinking of mathematics can apprehend "individual" number only in this form: for mathematical thought numbers are nothing but an expression of conceptual relations; only in their totality do they represent the self-enclosed and unitary structure of number as such and of the realm of number.

But number takes on a very different character as soon as we pass from the modality of thought and pure theoretical knowledge to other fields of cultural development. Our inquiry into language has already shown that there is a phase of number formation in which every particular number, instead of signifying merely a link in a system, bears a very individual imprint, a phase in which the representation of number does not possess abstract universality but is always grounded in some concrete individual intuition from which it cannot be detached. Here numbers are not yet

86. Cf. my *Zur Einstein'schen Relativitätstheorie* (Berlin, 1921), pp. 119 ff.

universal specifications applicable to any content whatever; there are no numbers "as such"; rather, the notion and appellation of number grow out of a particular numerable thing and remain confined to the intuition of this thing. And because of the material diversity of numerable things, because of the particular intuitive content and the particular feeling tone attaching to specific quantities, the diverse numbers do not seem absolutely uniform but rather take on the appearance of highly differentiated entities, each having in a sense its own tonality.[87] This affective tonality of number, contrasting with the purely conceptual, abstract-logical determination, becomes still more evident when we turn to the sphere of mythical ideas. As we have seen, nothing in myth is *merely* ideal; for myth similarity of contents is not a mere relation between them but a real bond which attaches them to one another—and this is particularly true of numerical similarity. Whenever two quantities appear as equal in number, i.e. wherever it is evident that they can be coordinated member for member, myth "explains" this possibility of a coordination, which in cognition appears as a purely ideal relationship, by imputing a common mythical "nature" to the two quantities. However they may differ in sensuous appearance, things bearing the same number are mythically "the same": it is *one* essence which merely cloaks and conceals itself under different manifestations. This elevation of number to an independent substance and power is only a particularly important and characteristic example of the fundamental form of mythical hypostatization.[88] And from this it follows that the mythical view of number—as of space and time—contains at the same time a factor of universality and a factor of thoroughgoing particularity. Here number is never a mere ordinal, a mere designation of position within a comprehensive general system: rather, each number has its own essence, its own individual nature and power.[89] But this individual nature is itself universal insofar as it can permeate entities which are utterly heterogeneous for mere empirical conception and by so doing cause them to partake of one another. Thus, in mythical thinking as elsewhere, number serves as a primary and fundamental form of relation. Here, however, this relation is never taken merely as such, but appears as something immediately real and efficacious, as a mythical object with

87. Cf. *1*, 233 ff.

88. Cf. above, pp. 53 ff.

89. Cf. examples of this "individual physiognomy" of numbers in mythical thinking in Lévy-Bruhl, *Das Denken der Naturvölker*, pp. 178 ff.

attributes and powers of its own. Whereas for logical thinking number possesses a universal function and signification, for mythical thinking it appears always as an original "entity," which imparts its essence and power to everything subsumed under it.

Thus we see that in theoretical and mythical thinking the concept of number does not develop in the same direction. In both, it is true, the concept spreads over ever wider spheres of sensation, intuition, and thinking, and finally draws almost the whole realm of consciousness into its orbit. But in the two spheres we encounter two entirely different aims and two entirely different fundamental attitudes. In the system of pure cognition, number, like space and time, serves primarily and essentially the purpose of reducing the concrete diversity of phenomena to the abstract and ideal unity of their "grounds." It is through the unity of number that the sensuous world first assumes intellectual form, that it is composed into a self-contained cosmos, into the unity of a purely logical conception. All phenomenal being is referred to number and expressed in it, because this reduction to number proves to be the only way to establish a thoroughgoing and unequivocal relation of *law* among phenomena. Ultimately, everything which knowledge, which science, considers under the name of "nature" is built up out of purely numerical elements and determinations which serve as the actual instruments by which to recast all merely accidental existence into the form of thought, law, and necessity. Likewise in mythical thinking number appears as such a medium of spiritualization—but here the process takes another direction. While in scientific thinking number appears as the great instrument of *explanation,* in mythical thinking it appears as a vehicle of religious *signification.* In the one case it serves to prepare all empirical existence for acceptance in a world of purely ideal relationships and laws; in the other it serves to draw all existing things, all immediate data, everything that is merely "profane" into the mythical-religious process of sanctification. For whatever partakes of number in any way, whatever reveals in itself the form and power of a definite number, no longer leads a mere irrelevant existence for the mythical-religious consciousness but has precisely thereby gained an entirely new significance. Not only number as a whole but every particular number is, as it were, surrounded by an aura of magic, which communicates itself to everything connected with it, however seemingly irrelevant. Down to the lowest sphere of mythical thinking, down to the sphere of the magical world view and the most primitive magical practice, we feel this sacred awe surrounding number, for all magic is in large part number magic. In the development of theoretical science the transition from the magical to the mathematical view of number was effected only gradually. Just as astronomy goes back to astrology and chemistry to alchemy, so arithmetic and algebra go back to an older magical form of number theory, to a science of almacabala.[90] And not only do the founders of actual theoretical mathematics, the Pythagoreans, stand between the two views of number; even in the transition to modern times, in the era of the Renaissance, we encounter the same mixed, intermediary forms. Side by side with Fermat and Descartes stand Giordano Bruno and Reuchlin, who devoted special works to the miraculous magical-mythical power of number. Often the two tendencies are united in a single individual: Cardanus, for example, represents a highly characteristic and historically interesting example of this twofold type of thought. But in all these cases such a historical mixture of forms would not have been possible if the forms did not agree, in both content and systematic significance, in at least one characteristic motif, one fundamental tendency. Mythical number stands then at a spiritual turning point—it too strives to escape from the narrowness and confinement of the immediate sensuous-material world view to a freer, more universal view. However, the mind cannot apprehend and penetrate this new universality as its own creation but sees it as a foreign, demonic power. Thus Philolaus still seeks "the nature of number and its power" not only in all human works and words, not only in every kind of artistic production and in music, but also in "supernatural and divine existences" [91]—so that it becomes, like Plato's Eros, the great intermediary, by which the earthly and divine, the mortal and immortal, communicate with each other and are composed into the unity of a world order.

To explore this process of the deification and sanctification of number in detail and seek out its particular intellectual and religious motives would seem, to be sure, a vain undertaking. For at first sight we find only the free play of the mythical fantasy that mocks every fixed rule. It would seem futile to inquire further after a principle of selection, after the cause to which the *individual* numbers owe their special character of "holiness," for every number without distinction can become an object

90. Cf. the remarks of W. J. McGee, "Primitive Numbers," *Nineteenth Annual Report of the [U.S.] Bureau of American Ethnology*, 1897–98 (Washington, 1900), pp. 825–851.

91. Philolaus, Fragment 11.

of mythical interpretation and worship. When we run through the series of elementary numbers, we encounter such mythical-religious hypostases at every step. For one, two, and three we everywhere find examples of such hypostases, not only in the thinking of primitive peoples but also in the great cultural religions. The problem of the unity, which emerges from itself, which becomes "another" second entity and is ultimately reunited with itself in a third—this problem belongs to the common cultural heritage of mankind. Although it takes this purely intellectual formulation only in the speculative philosophy of religion, the universal distribution of the idea of a "triune God" shows that this idea must be based on some ultimate and concrete foundations in feeling, to which it points back and from which it continually arises anew.[92] Next comes the number four, whose universal religious-cosmic significance is attested above all in the religions of North America.[93] The same dignity is accorded in still higher degree to the number seven, which emanates in all directions from the oldest human culture sites in Mesopotamia but which appears as a specifically sacred number even where no Babylonian-Assyrian influence is demonstrable or probable.[94] This mystical-religious character still adheres to it in Greek philosophy; in a fragment attributed to Philolaus it is likened to the motherless, virgin Athene, "for it is ruler and teacher of all things; it is God, One ever-existing, stable, unmoving, itself like to itself, different from the rest." [95] In the Christian Middle Ages the Church Fathers speak of seven as the number of fullness and perfection, as the universal and absolute number: "septenarius numerus est perfectionis." [96] But from an early period the number nine vied with it; in the myths and cults of the Greeks and in Germanic beliefs as well, enneadic intervals occupy a place similar to that of the hebdomadic periods.[97] And

92. That the idea of triunity is found at very primitive levels of religious development is emphasized by Brinton, pp. 118 ff. However, he offers too abstract an explanation of this phenomenon, seeking to reduce it to purely logical facts, to the form and special character of the fundamental laws of thought. Cf. below, pp. 150 ff.

93. See below, p. 150.

94. On the significance and distribution of seven as a sacred number cf. Franz Boll, "Hebdomas," in *Paulys Real-Encyclopädie der classischen Altertumswissenschaft* (Stuttgart, 1912), 7, 2547–2578. See also Ferdinand von Andrian-Werburg, "Die Siebenzahl im Geistesleben der Völker," *Mittheilungen der anthropologischen Gesellschaft, 31* (1901), 225–274.

95. *Philolaus,* Fragment 20, ed. Diels, 32B.

96. Examples in Sauer, *Symbolik des Kirchengebäudes,* p. 76; Boll, *Die Lebensalter,* pp. 24 ff.

97. See Wilhelm H. Roscher, *Die enneadischen und hebdomadischen Fristen und Wochen der ältesten Griechen,* Abh. der phil.-hist. Klasse der kön. Sächs. Ges. der Wiss., Vol. *21* (Leip-

since this sacred character of the simple numbers is extended to the composite numbers, since not only three, seven, nine, twelve, etc. but their products as well have special mythical-religious powers, there remains in the end hardly any numerical term which cannot be drawn into this sphere of intuition and this process of sanctification. Here the mythical creative drive has before it an unlimited area in which to move freely, undeterred by any fixed logical norm or by any regard for the laws of objective experience. While for science number becomes a criterion of truth, a condition and preparation for all strictly rational knowledge, here it imprints on everything that enters its sphere and is touched and permeated by it a character of mystery—a mystery inaccessible to reason.

And yet, as in other fields of mythical thinking, a very definite spiritual direction can be discerned in the seemingly impenetrable maze of the mythical-mystical doctrines of number. Here too, though mere "association" holds free sway, the main paths of development can be distinguished; here too we can gradually discern certain typical guiding lines which determine this process of the sanctification of number and thus of the world. We shall find a sound basis for a knowledge of these if we review the development of the concept of number in linguistic thinking. Here we have seen that all representation and designation of numerical relations goes back to a concrete-intuitive base; spatial, temporal, and "personal" intuition prove to be the principal spheres in which consciousness of number and its significance developed.[98] We may presume a similar articulation in the growth of the mythical representations of number. If we attempt to trace the affective value attached to the various sacred numbers back to its origins, we almost always find it to be grounded in the particularity of the mythical feeling of space, time, or the I. As far as space is concerned, not only are the various zones and directions as such imbued in the mythical view, with very definite religious accents, but such an accent adheres also to the totality of these directions, to the whole to which they are conceived to belong. Where north, south, east, and west are distinguished as the cardinal points of the world, this specific distinction usually serves as a model and prototype for all articulation of the world and the world

zig, 1903); and *Die Sieben- und Neunzahl im Kultus und Mythus der Griechen*, op. cit., Vol. 24 (1904). For the Germanic religions see Weinhold, *Die mystiche Neunzahl bei den Deutschen*. Regarding seven- and nine-day periods in astrology see Auguste Bouché-Leclercq, *L'astrologie grecque* (Paris, 1899), pp. 458 ff., 476 ff.

98. See *1*, 229 ff., 241 ff.

process. Four now becomes the sacred number par excellence, for in it is expressed precisely this relation between every particular reality and the fundamental form of the universe. Anything which shows an actual four-fold organization—whether as an immediately known "reality" imposing itself upon sensory observation, or whether conditioned in a purely ideal way by a specific mode of mythical apperception—seems attached, as though by inner magical ties, to certain parts of space. Here mythical thinking does not see a mere mediated *transference;* rather, it sees with intuitive evidence the one in the other: in every particular fourness it apprehends the universal form of the cosmic fourness. We encounter the number four in this function not only in most of the North American religions [99] but also in Chinese thinking. In the Chinese system, a particular season, color, element, animal species, organ of the human body, etc. corresponds to each one of the principal directions, west, south, east, and north, so that ultimately, by virtue of this relation, the entire diversity of existence is in some way distributed and, as it were, fixated and established in a particular intuitive sphere.[100] We find this symbolism of the number four among the Cherokees, where similarly a particular color or institution, or a particular state of fortune such as victory or defeat, sickness or death, is assigned to each of the cardinal points.[101] And, in accordance with its peculiar nature, mythical thinking cannot content itself with apprehending all these relations and articulations as such, with viewing them *in abstracto* as it were, but must, in order to make certain of their truth, concretize them in an intuitive form and set them before us in a sensuous image. Thus, the veneration of the number four is expressed in the worship of the form of the cross, which is attested as one of the oldest religious symbols. We can follow a fundamental trend common to all religious thought from the swastika, the earliest form of the four-pronged cross, down to the medieval speculation which infuses the whole content of the Christian doctrine into the intuition of the cross. When in the Middle Ages the four ends of the Cross were identified with

99. For examples see A. W. Buckland, "Four as a Sacred Number," *Journal of the Anthropological Institute of Great Britain and Ireland,* 25 (1896), 96–102; McGee, "Primitive Numbers," p. 834.

100. Cf. De Groot, *Universismus,* p. 119; idem, *The Religious System of China, 1,* 316 ff.; and my *Die Begriffsform im mythischen Denken,* pp. 26, 60 ff.

101. Cf. James Mooney, "Sacred Formulas of the Cherokees," *Seventh Annual Report of the [U.S.] Bureau of [American] Ethnology,* 1885–86 (Washington, 1890), p. 342.

the four zones of Heaven, when the East, West, North, and South were equated with certain phases of the Christian story of salvation, it was a revival of certain primeval cosmic-religious motifs.[102]

Like the veneration of the number four, that of the numbers five and seven can develop from the cult of the cardinal points: along with the four principal directions, east, west, north, and south, the middle of the world is counted as the place in which the tribe or nation has its appointed seat and the above and below, the zenith and nadir, are also accorded a special mythical-religious distinction. It is such spatial-numerical articulation that gives rise, among the Zuñis for example, to that form of septuarchy which determines their sole theoretical and practical, intellectual and sociological view of the world.[103] And elsewhere as well the magical-mythical significance of the number seven reveals a connection with certain fundamental cosmic phenomena and ideas. But here it is immediately evident that the mythical feeling of space is inseparably bound up with the mythical feeling of time and that the two together form the starting point for the mythical view of number. It is, as we have seen, one fundamental characteristic of the mythical feeling of time that in it the factors of "subjective" and "objective" still lie undifferentiated side by side and merge with each other. Here change is not split into two different halves, an inside and outside; there is only a peculiar "feeling of phases," a feeling for the punctuation of change as such. Hence, mythical time is always conceived as the time both of natural processes and of the events of human life: it is a biological-cosmic time.[104] And this twofold character is imparted to the mythical view of number. Every mythical number points back to a definite sphere of objective intuition, in which it is rooted and from which it continuously draws new power.

However, this objective world itself is never *only* material; it is filled with an inner life of its own, which moves in very definite rhythms. This periodicity is perpetuated in all particular change, however disparate the forms it may assume and whatever its situation in mythical space. It is above all the phases of the moon in which this universal period of the cosmic process is represented. The moon—as its very name in most Indo-

102. Cf. the sec. "Symbolik der Himmelsrichtungen" in Sauer, *Symbolik des Kirchenge-bäudes*, pp. 87 ff. With regard to the meaning and distribution of the swastika cf. Thomas Wilson, "The Swastika," *Report of the U.S. National Museum*, 1894 (Washington, 1896), pp. 757–1030.

103. See Cushing, *Outlines of Zuñi Creation Myths*. Cf. above, p. 92.

104. Cf. above, pp. 107 ff.

Germanic languages and in the Semitic and Hamitic languages indicates [105]—appears everywhere as the true divider and measurer of time. But it is still more than this, for all change in nature and in human existence is not only coordinated with it in some way but goes back to it as its origin, its qualitative source. This primeval mythical intuition has found a place even in modern biological theories, so that the number seven has regained its significance as the ruler over all life.[106] It is only in relatively late times, in the era of Greco-Roman astrology, that the veneration of the number seven appears linked with the cult of the seven planets; originally, the seven-day periods and weeks showed no such relation but followed from the natural and one might almost say spontaneous division of the twenty-eight day month into four parts.[107] The foundation for the hallowing of the number seven and for viewing it as a "perfect number," as the number of "fullness and wholeness," proves to be a very definite intuitive sphere—which, however, becomes truly *effective* only when, by virtue of the form and special character of mythical, "structural" thinking, it is progressively broadened until it ultimately embraces all being and all change. It is in this sense, for example, that we encounter the number seven as the true member of cosmic structure in the pseudo-Hippocratic book on the number seven; it acts and moves in the seven spheres of the universe, it determines the number of the winds, the seasons, and the ages of life; upon it is based the natural articulation of the organs of the human body and the distribution of faculties in the human soul.[108] From Greek medicine the belief in the "vital force" of the number seven passed into medieval and modern medicine: every seventh year used to be regarded as a "climacteric" year which brings with it a decisive turn in the mixture of the vital humors, in the temperament of body and soul.[109]

105. On the designation of the moon as the "measurer" of time in Indo-Germanic languages and Egyptian cf. Roscher, *Die enneadischen und hebdomadischen Fristen*, p. 5. For the Semitic languages see Johannes Hehn, *Siebenzahl und Sabbat bei den Babyloniern und im alten Testament* (Leipzig, 1907), pp. 59 ff.

106. Cf. Wilhelm Fliess, *Der Ablauf des Lebens* (Vienna, 1906); Hermann Swoboda, *Das Siebenjahr. Untersuchungen über die zeitliche Gesetzmässigkeit des Menschenlebens* (Leipzig and Vienna, 1917).

107. The material for a decision on this question is completely compiled in Boll, "Hebdomas." See also Roscher, *Die enneadischen und hebdomadischen Fristen*, pp. 71 ff.; Hehn, pp. 44 ff.

108. Cf. Roscher, *Die Hippokratische Schrift*, pp. 43 ff.

109. On the theory of "climacteric years" in ancient medicine and its subsequent development see Boll, *Die Lebensalter*, pp. 29 ff. Cf. Bouché-Leclercq, p. 526. It should be mentioned that the peculiar mythical "phase feeling" which we have recognized as a basic component

But while in the cases thus far considered a particular sphere of objective intuition has determined the hallowing of certain numbers, a glance back at the linguistic expression of numerical relations reminds us that this objective factor is not the sole determinant. It is not exclusively through the perception of outward things or processes that the consciousness of number matures. One of its strongest roots is rather to be sought in the fundamental distinctions arising from subjective-personal existence, from the relation between I, thou, and he. In the example of the dual and trial, as well as the forms of the "inclusive" and "exclusive" plural, language shows how the numbers two and three in particular refer back to this sphere and are thereby determined in their expression (cf. *I* 241 ff.). And our observations in the field of mythical thinking are analogous. In Usener's book on the number three, in which he seeks to lay the foundation of a mythical theory of number, he argues that there are two groups of typical numbers, one of which goes back to the intuition and articulation of time, while the other, to which particularly two and three belong, has a different origin. He goes on to explain the sanctity of the number three and its specifically mystical character by the supposition that in times of primitive culture three constituted the end of the numerical series and thus became an expression of perfection, of absolute totality as such. Even from an ethnological standpoint grave objections can of course be raised against this theory, for in the last analysis the relation it assumes between the concept of the trial and that of infinity is purely logical and speculative.[110] Nevertheless, the distinction betwen two different groups of sacred numbers and the indication of their different spiritual and religious sources remain valid. Particularly in connection with the number three the history of religious ideas suggests that the purely "intelligible" significance which

---

of the mythical intuition of time does not limit itself to an articulation of life into characteristic, sharply distinct segments but often carries it back to the time *preceding* birth. Even the growth of the foetus is governed by the same rhythmic rule which follows man, once born, through the whole of his life. Such views on the development of the foetus in the womb seem, e.g., to be the basis for the veneration accorded to the number 40, particularly in the Semitic religions. Roscher makes it seem likely that this number owes its significance to the division of the period of pregnancy, set at 280 days, into seven equal segments of 40 days, to each of which is attributed a special characteristic function in the total process of foetal growth. Cf. Wilhelm H. Roscher, *Die Zahl 40 im Glauben, Brauch und Schrifttum der Semiten*, Abh. der phil.-hist. Klasse der kön. Säch. Ges. der Wiss., Vol. 27 (Leipzig, 1909), pp. 100 ff.

110. See Hermann K. Usener, "Dreiheit," *Rheinisches Museum für Philologie*, 3d ser., *58* (1903), 1–47, 161–208, 321–362. For the ethnological critique of Usener's theory see, e.g., Lévy-Bruhl, *Das Denken der Naturvölker*, pp. 180 ff.

it almost everywhere achieves in highly developed religious speculation is only a late and derivative consequence following from a relationship of a different kind, which one might call "naive." While the *philosophy* of religion immerses itself in the mysteries of the divine triunity, while it determines this unity by the triad of Father, Son, and Holy Spirit, the *history* of religion teaches that this triad itself was originally understood and felt very concretely, that very definite "natural" forms of human life find their expression in it. Often the natural triad of father, mother, and child is still easily discernible beneath the speculative triad of Father, Son, and Spirit. Particularly in the form taken by the divine triad in the Semitic religions this basic intuition is still plainly discernible.[111]

All these examples confirm that peculiar magic of number which makes it appear as a fundamental power in the realm of the spirit and in the structure of the human self-consciousness. It proves itself to be the bond which joins the diverse powers of consciousness into a mesh, which gathers the spheres of sensation, intuition, and feeling into a unity. Number thus fulfills the function which the Pythagoreans impute to harmony. It is "a Unity of many mixed elements and an agreement between disagreeing elements" ($\pi o\lambda\upsilon\mu\iota\gamma\acute{e}o\nu$ $\acute{e}\nu\omega\sigma\iota\varsigma$ $\kappa\alpha\grave{\iota}$ $\delta\acute{\iota}\chi\alpha$ $\phi\rho o\nu\epsilon\acute{o}\nu\tau\omega\nu$ $\sigma\upsilon\mu\phi\eta\rho\acute{o}\nu\sigma\iota\varsigma$) (Philolaus, Fragment 10); it acts as the magic tie which not so much links things together as brings them into harmony within the soul.

111. Documentation of this thesis has been compiled in Ditlef Nielsen's monograph, *Der dreieinige Gott in religionshistorischer Beleuchtung* (Copenhagen, 1922), Vol. *1*.

PART III

Myth as a Life Form. Discovery and Determination of the Subjective in the Mythical Consciousness

Chapter 1

The I and the Soul

It would not be possible to speak of a discovery of the subjective in myth if the widespread view that the concepts of the I and the soul were the *beginning* of all mythical thinking were justified. Ever since Tylor in his fundamental work advocated this theory of the animistic origin of myth formation, it seems to have been accepted more and more as the secure empirical core and empirical rule of research in mythology. Wundt's approach to myth from the standpoint of ethnic psychology is entirely built on this theory; he, too, sees all mythical concepts and ideas essentially as variants of the idea of the soul, which thus becomes the empirical *presupposition* rather than the specific *aim* of the mythical world view. And even the reaction embodied in the so-called pre-animistic theories, merely attempted to add certain features that had been disregarded in the animistic interpretation, to the factual content of the mythological world, but did not alter the principle of explanation as such. For even though the concept of the soul and of personality is not regarded as the necessary condition and true constituent of certain original strata of mythical thinking, particularly of the most primitive magical usages, the importance of this concept is in general recognized for all later contents and forms of mythical thinking. Even if we should accept the pre-animistic variations of Tylor's theory, myth would remain, in its general structure and total function, nothing other than an attempt to twist the world of objective change back into the subjective world and interpret it according to the categories of the subjective world.

But against this assumption, which still remains generally unopposed among ethnologists and ethnic psychologists, a grave objection arises as soon as we consider it in the context of our general problem. For a glance at the development of the various symbolic forms shows us that their essential achievement is not that they copy the outward world in the inward world or that they simply project a finished inner world outward, but rather that the two factors of "inside" and "outside," of "I" and "reality" are *determined* and delimited from one another only in these symbolic forms and through their mediation. If each of these forms embraces a spiritual coming-to-grips of the I with reality, it does not imply that the two, the I and reality, are to be taken as given quantities, as finished, self-enclosed halves of being, which are only subsequently composed into a whole. On the contrary, the crucial achievement of every symbolic form lies precisely in the fact that it does not *have* the limit between I and reality as pre-existent and established for all time but must itself create this limit—and that each fundamental form creates it *in a different way*. These general systematic considerations in themselves lead us to suppose that myth, too, does not start from a finished concept of the I or the soul, from a finished picture of objective reality and change, but must *achieve* this concept and this picture, must form them from out of itself.[1] And the phenomenology of the mythical consciousness actually provides thoroughgoing confirmation of this systematic assumption. The more widely we extend the scope of this phenomenology, the more deeply we penetrate its primal and fundamental strata, the more evident it becomes that for myth the concept of the soul is no stereotype into which it forces everything that comes within its grasp but is rather a fluid, plastic element which changes in its hands. Whereas metaphysics and "rational psychology" treat the concept of the soul as a given possession, taking it as a substance with definite immutable attributes, the mythical consciousness operates in an exactly opposite way. For myth none of the attributes and properties which metaphysics tends to regard as analytical characteristics of the concept of soul, neither its unity nor its indivisibility, neither its immateriality nor its permanence, proves to be linked with it from the very beginning; all merely designate certain factors which must be acquired very gradually in the process of mythical imagination and thinking and the acquisition of which passes through very different phases. In this sense the concept of the soul may just as well be called the end as the beginning of mythical thinking. The meaning and spiritual scope of this concept lie precisely in the fact that it is a beginning and an end. It leads us in a continuous progress, in an uninterrupted series of creations from one extreme of the mythical consciousness to the other: it appears simultaneously as

1. Cf. *1*, 249 ff.

that which is most immediate and that which is most mediated. In the beginnings of mythical thinking the soul may appear as a "thinghood," as familiar and tangible as any physical substance. But in this thing a change is effected through which it gradually acquires spiritual meaning, until at last the soul becomes the peculiar principle of spirituality as such. Not immediately but only gradually and by all manner of detours does the new category of the I, the idea of the person and the personality, grow from the mythical category of the soul; and the peculiar meaning of this idea is fully revealed only through the resistance which it must overcome.

Yet this is no mere process of reflection, no product of pure meditation. It is not mere meditation but action which constitutes the center from which man undertakes the spiritual organization of reality. It is here that a separation begins to take place between the spheres of the objective and subjective, between the world of the I and the world of things. The farther the consciousness of action progresses, the more sharply this division is expressed, the more clearly the limits between I and not-I are drawn. Accordingly, the world of mythical ideas, precisely in its first and most immediate forms, appears closely bound up with the world of efficacy. Here lies the core of the magical world view, which is saturated with this atmosphere of efficacy, which is indeed nothing more than a translation and transposition of the world of subjective emotions and drives into a sensuous, objective existence. The first energy by which man places himself as an independent being in opposition to things is that of desire. In desire he no longer simply accepts the world and the reality of things but builds them up for himself. This is man's first and most primitive consciousness of his ability to give form to reality. And since this consciousness permeates all inward as well as outward intuition, all reality seems subject to it. There is no existing thing and no occurrence which must not ultimately submit to the omnipotence of thought and the omnipotence of desire.[2] Thus, in the magical world view the I exerts almost unlimited sway over reality: it takes all reality back into itself. But precisely this immediate identification of I and reality involves a peculiar dialectic in which the original relationship is

2. This term, the "omnipotence of thought" (*die Allmacht des Gedankens*), was first used, in characterizing the magical world view, by Sigmund Freud, to whose remarks I refer the reader. See "Animismus, Magie und Allmacht der Gedanken," in *Totem und Taboo* (2d ed. Vienna, 1920), pp. 100 ff. Eng. trans. of 1st ed. by A. A. Brill, *Totem und Taboo* (New York, 1918).

reversed. The enhanced feeling of self which seems to express itself in the magical world view indicates actually that at this stage there is as yet no true self. Through the magical omnipotence of the will the I seeks to seize upon all things and bend them to its purpose; but precisely in this attempt it shows itself still totally dominated, totally "possessed," by things. Even its supposed doing amounts to undergoing; indeed, all its ideal powers, the power of words and language for example, are at this stage seen in the form of demonic beings and projected outward as something alien to the I. Thus the expression of the I that is here achieved, and also the first magical-mythical concept of the soul, are totally confined within this intuition. The soul itself appears as a demonic power which acts upon man's body from outside and possesses it—and hence possesses the man himself with all his vital functions. Thus precisely the increased intensity of the I-feeling and the resulting hypertrophy of action produce a mere illusion of activity. For all true freedom of action presupposes an inner limitation, a recognition of certain objective limits of action. The I comes to itself only by positing these limits, by successively restricting the unconditional causality with respect to the world of things, which it initially imputed to itself. Only when emotion and will no longer seek to grasp the object immediately and draw it into their sphere, only when more and more clearly apprehended intermediary links are interpolated between the mere wish and its goal, do objects and the I acquire independent values: the two worlds are determined only by this form of mediation.

Wherever this mediation is lacking a peculiar indifference continues to adhere to the representation of action itself. All reality and change, both as units and as a whole, appear shot through with magical-mythical action; but in the intuition of this action there is as yet no separation between fundamentally different factors, between "material" and "spiritual," between "physical" and "psychic." There is only a single undivided sphere of efficacy, within which a continuous exchange takes place between the two spheres that we usually distinguish as the world of the soul and the world of matter. Precisely at the point where the idea of efficacy becomes an all-embracing category in man's understanding and explanation of the world does this indifference appear most plainly. The mana of the Polynesians, the manitou of the Algonquin tribes, the orenda of the Iroquois, etc. have as their common factor the concept and intuition of an increased *efficacy as such,* transcending all mere "natural" bounds; no sharp distinction is made between the particular potencies of this efficacy, between its modes and forms. Mana is attributed equally to mere things and to persons, to "spiritual" and "material," to "animate" and "inanimate" entities. Thus, when the adherents of pure animism as well as their opponents the pre-animists invoked the notion of mana in support of their conception, it was rightly argued against them that the word *mana* "in itself is neither a pre-animistic nor an animistic term, but utterly neutral toward these theories." Mana is the powerful, effective, productive; the specific determination—conscious, "psychic," or personal in the restricted sense—does not enter into this efficacy.[3]

Elsewhere as well we find that as we go back to the more primitive levels of mythical thinking, the sharpness, clarity, and definiteness of subjective and personal existence diminish. Primitive thinking is actually characterized by the peculiarly fluid and fugitive character of its intuition and concept of personal existence. Here there is as yet no soul as an independent unitary substance separate from the body; the soul is nothing other than life itself, which is immanent in the body and necessarily attached to it. And in accordance with the peculiarity of complex mythical thinking this immanence reveals no sharp spatial determination and delimitation. Life as an undivided whole dwells in the whole of the body and also in each of its parts. Not only are certain vital organs such as the heart, the diaphragm, and the kidneys regarded in this sense as the "seat" of life, but any component whatsoever of the body, even if it no longer stands in any organic connection with the body as a whole, can be thought of as a vehicle of the life inherent in it. A man's spittle, his excrement, his nails, cuttings of his hair, are and remain in this sense vehicles of life and the soul[4]: any action exerted upon them immediately affects and endangers the life of the body as a whole. Here again we see the reversal by which the soul, seemingly endowed with all power over physical reality and change, is in truth only confined the more securely to the sphere of material existence and its destinies. Even the phenomenon of death does not dissolve this bond. In original mythical thinking death by no means signifies a sharp divi-

3. Cf. Friedrich Lehmann, *Mana,* pp. 35, 54, 76, etc. (see above, p. 57). Similarly, for the orenda of the Iroquois Hewitt showed that it is solely an expression for "power in general" and that this power is not yet defined "as a . . . biotic or psychic faculty." Cf. "Orenda and a Definition of Religion," pp. 44 ff.

4. Cf. Preuss, "Ursprung der Religion und Kunst," pp. 355 ff. Cf. above, pp. 52 ff.

sion, a parting, of the soul from the body. We have seen above that such a distinction, such a definite contrast of the conditions governing life and death, is contrary to the mythical mode of thought, that for myth the boundary between the two remains fluid.[5] Thus for myth death is never an annihilation of existence but only a passage into another form of existence, and at the basic and original levels of mythical thinking this form itself can be conceived only in thoroughgoing sensuous concretion. The deceased still "is," and this being can be seen and described only in physical terms. Even if, unlike the living, he appears as a powerless shadow, this shadow itself still has full reality; it resembles him not only in form and feature but also in its sensory and physical needs. In the Iliad the shade of Patroclus appears to Achilles as "his very image in stature and wearing clothes like his, with his voice and those lovely eyes." In Egyptian monuments a man's *ka,* which survives him at his death, is depicted as his physical double.[6] Thus, though the soul as an "image," an εἴδωλον, seems on the one hand to have cast off all coarse materiality, though it seems woven of more delicate stuff than the world of material things, on the other hand, from the standpoint of mythical thinking the image itself is never purely ideal but is endowed with a definite sensuous being and with "real" powers of action.[7] Hence even the shadow has a kind of physical reality and physical form. According to the Hurons the soul has a head and body, arms and legs, in short it is in every way an exact imitation of the "real" body and its members. Often it preserves all physical relations, merely reducing them to a smaller space as in a miniature. Among the Malays the soul is conceived in the form of a little man living inside the body, and this sensuous, naive conception is sometimes carried over into spheres which in other respects have progressed to a totally different, purely spiritual intuition of the I. In the midst of the speculations of the Upanishads on the pure essence of the self, the *atman,* the soul, is once again designated as the *purusha,* the man the size of a thumb:

> A Person of the measure of a thumb
> Stands in the midst of one's self (*ātman*),

5. See above, pp. 36 ff.

6. Cf., e.g., the bas-relief from the temple of Luxor reproduced in E. A. T. W. Budge, *Osiris and the Egyptian Resurrection* (London, 1911), 2, 119. See also Adolf Erman, *Die ägyptische Religion* (2d ed. Berlin), p. 102.

7. See above, pp. 42 ff.

> Lord of what has been and of what is to be.
> One does not shrink away from Him.[8]

In all this we see the same tendency to situate the soul as image and shadow in another dimension of being as it were, while on the other hand precisely because it remains an image and a shadow it possesses no independent features of its own but borrows everything it is and has from the material properties of the body. Even the form of life extending beyond the bodily existence which is attributed to it is nothing more than a simple prolongation of its sensuous, earthly life. The soul with its whole being, with its impulsions and needs, remains oriented toward and confined within the material world. For its survival and well being it requires its physical possessions, which are sent along with it in the form of food and drink, clothes and weapons, household implements and ornaments. Though in later forms of the soul cult such gifts appear as purely symbolic,[9] originally no doubt they were conceived as real and destined for the practical use of the dead. Thus, likewise in this respect, the other world first appears as a mere duplication, a simple sensuous copy, of this world. And even where an attempt is made to distinguish the two by accentuating their material differences, this picture of contrast shows no less than those of similarity that in this view the "here" and "hereafter" are looked upon precisely as different aspects of one and the same homogeneous form of sensuous existence.[10] And as a rule the social order of this life continues into the realm of the dead: each man occupies the same rank and performs the same occupation and function as in earthly existence.[11]

8. Katha Upanishad, iv, 12. Eng. trans. by Hume, p. 355. On the ethnological material see Frazer, *Golden Bough*, Vol. *3*, Pt. II, pp. 27, 80, etc.

9. Thus, e.g., in the Chinese sacrifices to the dead great quantities of paper clothes or imitations of clothes were burned along with real clothing and thus sent to the deceased in the other world. See De Groot, *The Religious System of China*, *2*, 474 ff.

10. The religion of the Bataks of Sumatra and their picture of the realm of the dead may serve as a characteristic example of this. "The ways of the *begu* (the spirits of the dead)," Warneck writes, "are the opposite of those of the living. When they go downstairs, they climb head foremost. When several carry a burden, they look forward but walk backward. They also hold markets but only at night. Their council meetings and all their activities take place at night." *Die Religion der Batak*, p. 74.

11. This conception seems to find its sharpest expression in China and Egypt. Cf. De Groot, *The Religious System of China*, *1*, 348 ff.; James H. Breasted, *Development of Religion and Thought in Ancient Egypt* (New York, Scribner's, 1912), pp. 49 ff. According to the texts of the Egyptian Book of the Dead the deceased retains the use of his limbs; he eats the food prepared for him by the gods; he possesses lands and fields which he himself cultivates. Ovid describes in a well-known passage how the shades move about without blood,

Thus, precisely where it seems to surpass the world of given, sensuous-empirical existence, to transcend it in principle, myth clings fast to this world. According to the Egyptian texts the soul can survive only if its sensory functions and organs are restored by magical means. The ceremony of the opening of the mouth, ear, nose, etc., which is believed to give back the senses of sight, hearing, smell, and taste to the dead, are described and prescribed down to their smallest details.[12] It has been said that these regulations are not so much a picture of the realm of the dead as a passionate protest against it.[13] Thus in Egyptian mortuary inscriptions the departed is generally designated as "he who lives," while the Chinese speak of coffins as "living coffins," of the bodies of the dead as "corpses buried alive." [14]

Thus at this level the I of man, the unity of his self-consciousness and feeling of self, are by no means constituted by the soul as an independent principle separate from the body. As long as a man lives, as long as he is present in concrete corporeity and sensuous efficacy, his personality is included in the totality of this existence. His material existence and his psychic functions and accomplishments, his feeling, his sensation, and his will form one and the same undifferentiated whole. Accordingly, even after a visible separation seems to have taken place between the two, even after life, sensation, and perception have fled the body, man's "self" remains, as it were, split between the two elements which formerly made up this whole. In Homer when a man's psyche has left him, the man *himself,* i.e. his corpse, remains to be eaten by the dogs; but we also encounter another conception and another linguistic usage, according to which his "self" lives on as a shade in Hades. And the Vedic texts show the same characteristic vacillation: sometimes it is the body and sometimes the soul of

bodies, or bones; some gather in the forum, others go about their affairs, each imitating the previous form of his life. *Metamorphoses,* Bk. IV, lines 443 ff. Recent penetrating investigations have shown that Roman mortuary beliefs were astonishingly close to those of "primitive" peoples, not only in details but also in the general intuition underlying them. Cf. Walter F. Otto, *Die Manen;* Franz V. M. Cumont, *After Life in Roman Paganism* (New Haven, 1922), pp. 3 ff., 45 ff., etc.

12. Cf. Budge, *Osiris, 1,* 74, 101 ff., etc.

13. Cf. Breasted, p. 91, on the oldest Pyramid Texts: "The chief and dominant note throughout is insistent, even passionate, protest against death. They may be said to be the record of humanity's earliest supreme revolt against the great darkness and silence from which none returns. The word death never occurs in the Pyramid Texts except in the negative or applied to a foe. Over and over again we hear the indomitable assurance that the dead lives."

14. Cf. De Groot, *The Religious System of China, 3,* 924 ff.

the deceased that is conceived as the true "himself," the vehicle of his personality.[15] Attached to different but equally sensuous forms of existence, this "himself" cannot yet develop its purely ideal, functional unity.[16]

Thus while in the theoretical development of the concept of soul the unity and simplicity of the soul becomes its essential, truly constitutive characteristics, for myth, originally, the opposite was true. Even in the history of speculative thought we can see how this unity and simplicity were achieved only gradually: even in Plato the logical-metaphysical motif of ἔν τι ψυχῆς had to assert itself against its counter-motif, the multiplicity of the "parts of the soul." But in myth—and not only in its elementary forms but often in relatively advanced configurations—the motif of the soul's division far overbalances that of its unity. According to Ellis the Tshis believe in two souls; according to Mary Kingsley the West Africans believe in four; and according to Skeat the Malays assume the existence of seven independent souls. Among the Yorubas each individual possesses three souls, one dwelling in the head, one in the stomach, and the third in the big toe.[17] But the same intuition can also express itself in a far subtler form, which almost reveals logical differentiation and system. This systematic differentiation of individual souls and their functions seems to be most sharply developed in the Egyptian religion. Side by side with the elements which make up the body—the flesh, bones, blood, muscles—there are others subtler but also conceived as material, from which the different souls of man are composed. Besides the *ka*, which during a man's life-

15. Cf. Oldenberg, *Religion des Veda* (2d ed.), pp. 585 ff., 530, n. 2; cf. Rohde, *Psyche*, *1*, 5 ff.

16. Mythical thinking finds this division of a man's "self" between the corpse and the shadow all the more natural since the fluid and indeterminate character of the mythical concept of personality makes possible an analogous division during life. Here, too, one and the same man can at the same time be in different bodies which he regards as "belonging" to him. Thus, e.g., in the totemic systems of the Australian aborigines the belief prevails that certain objects of wood or stone, the so-called *tjurungas*, into which the bodies of the totemic ancestors have been transformed, "belong" in this way to the members of the corresponding totem. "The relation between man and *tjurunga*," Strehlow reports, "is expressed in the sentence: *nana unta mburka nama*—this (i.e. the *tjurunga*) this your body is. Thus, every man has two bodies, that of flesh and blood and that of stone or wood." Cf. Carl Strehlow, *Die Aranda- und Loritja-Stämme in Zentral-Australien* (5 vols. Frankfurt, Städtischen Völker-Museum, 1907–20), Vol. *1*, No. 2, pp. 77 ff.

17. Cf. Alfred B. Ellis, *The Yoruba-speaking Peoples of the Slave Coast of West Africa* (London, 1894), pp. 124 ff.; Skeat, *Malay Magic*, p. 50. Further data is in Frazer, *Golden Bough*, Pt. I, p. 528; Pt. II, p. 27. The same belief in a multiplicity of souls is found also among the aborigines of Australia, according to Spencer and Gillen, *The Native Tribes of Central Australia*, pp. 512 ff.; idem, *The Northern Tribes of Central Australia*, pp. 448 ff.

time lives in his body as his spiritual double and which does not leave him after his death but remains with his corpse as a kind of guardian ghost, there is a second "soul," the *ba,* different in significance and in existential form, which flies at the moment of death from his body in the shape of a bird, which then wanders about freely in space, and only from time to time visits the ka and the corpse in the tomb. And the texts also speak of a third "soul," the *khu,* which is described as immutable, indestructible, and immortal, whose meaning seems consequently to come closest to our concept of spirit.[18] Here an attempt is made to define the particularity of psychic as opposed to bodily being in three different ways. But this very diversity of approach proves that a specific principle of personality had not yet been worked out.[19] And it was not only a negative factor but also a highly important positive one which for a long time impeded the discovery of this principle: not only an intellectual incapacity of the mythical consciousness, but also a principle deeply rooted in the special nature of the mythical life feeling itself. We have seen that this life feeling is primarily manifested in a "phase feeling," so that it takes life as a whole—not as an absolutely unitary and unbroken process but as interrupted by very definite caesuras, by critical points and intervals. And these interruptions which divide the continuum of life into sharply delimited segments also divide the unity of the self. Here the ideal "unity of self-consciousness" does not work as an abstract principle which encompasses the manifold of contents to constitute itself the pure form of the I; rather, this formal synthesis finds in the contents themselves and in their concrete make-up quite definite barriers. Where the diversity of contents becomes so extreme as to turn into a complete contrariety, the discrepancy negates the coherence of life and with it the unity of the self. It is a new self which begins with every characteristically new phase of life. Precisely in the primitive strata

18. On the three Egyptian "souls," their function and significance, see Budge, *Osiris,* Vol. 2, ch. 19, in which the ethnological parallels from other African religions also are treated in detail. Cf. Foucart in Hastings' *Encyclopaedia of Religion and Ethics,* Vol. 2, s.v. "Body (Egyptian)"; Adolf Erman, *Ägypten und ägyptisches Leben im Altertum* (2 vols. Tübingen, 1923), 2, 414 ff.

19. Breasted, p. 56, remarks in his account of the Egyptian beliefs regarding the soul: "It is necessary to remember in dealing with such terms as soul among so early a people that they had no clearly defined notion of the exact nature of such an element of personality. It is evident that the Egyptian never wholly dissociated a person from the body as an instrument or vehicle of sensation, and they resorted to elaborate devices to restore to the body its various channels of sensibility after the *ba,* which comprehended these very things, had detached itself from the body."

of the mythical consciousness we encounter this fundamental intuition over and over again. Here the transition from boyhood to manhood, which is generally regarded as a mythical event of a special character and which is singled out from life as a whole by particular magical-mythical usages, does not take place in the form of development, of evolution, but signifies the acquisition of a new I, a new soul. A tribe in the hinterland of Liberia is reported to believe that once a boy enters the sacred grove where the initiation takes place he is killed by a wood spirit but then awakened to new life and re-animated.[20] Among the Kurnais of Southeastern Australia the boy in the initiation rite is cast into a kind of magical sleep, unlike ordinary sleep, from which he awakens as another, as an image and reincarnation of the totemic tribal ancestor.[21] In both these cases we see that at this level the I as a purely functional unity has not yet the power to embrace and compose the phases which appear separated by certain critical turning points. Here the concrete, immediate life feeling triumphs over the abstract feeling of I and the self, as it does not only in the mythical imagination but often in purely intuitive artistic natures. It is no accident that Dante calls the experience of his love for Beatrice, through which he grew from youth to manhood, a "vita nuova." Goethe, too, throughout his life looked back upon the most significant phases of his development as "a sloughing off of passing and past states." He felt his own works to be nothing more than a "castoff snake skin abandoned along the way."[22] For mythical thinking the same splitting process can be successive as well as coexistent: just as very different "souls" can live peacefully side by side in one and the same man, so the empirical sequence of the events of life can be distributed among wholly different "subjects," each of which is not only *thought* in the form of a separate being, but also *felt* and *intuited* as a living demonic power which takes possession of the man.[23]

20. See Heinrich Schurtz, *Altersklassen und Männerbunde* (Berlin, 1902), pp. 102 ff.; Boll, *Die Lebensalter,* pp. 36 ff.

21. See Howitt, *The Native Tribes of South-East Australia;* Wilhelm Schmidt, *Die geheime Jugendweihe eines australischen Urstamms* (Paderborn, 1923), pp. 26 ff.

22. See Goethe to Reimer, June 23, 1809; to Eckermann, January 12, 1827. *Goethes Gespräche,* ed. Flodoard W. von Biedermann (2d ed. Leipzig, 1909–11), 2, 42; 3, 316.

23. It might appear at first sight as though the split which occurs again and again in the mythical feeling of the I and concept of the soul was incompatible with what has been designated above as the "complex," nonanalytical character of mythical thinking (cf. above, pp. 45 ff.). On closer scrutiny it becomes evident, however, that we have to do with two factors which correspond to and complement one another. Whereas, as theoretical thinking progresses, it increasingly develops the form of "synthetic unity" as a unity of *different*

If the intuition of the I is to be freed from this confinement, if the I is to be apprehended in ideal freedom as an ideal unity, a new approach is needed. The decisive turn occurs when the accent of the soul concept shifts —when the soul ceases to be considered as the mere vehicle or cause of vital phenomena and is taken rather as the subject of the ethical consciousness. Only when man's vision passes beyond the sphere of life to that of ethical action, beyond the biological to the ethical sphere, does the unity of the I gain primacy over the substantial or semisubstantial notion of the soul. This transformation can already be seen in mythical thinking. The oldest historical record of it would seem to be provided by the Egyptian Pyramid Texts, in which we can clearly follow the gradual development of a new ethical self through a series of preliminary stages characterized by a wholly sensuous view of the self. It is the first, self-evident presupposition of Egyptian religious doctrine that any survival of the soul after death requires a survival of its material substratum. Any concern for a dead man's soul must therefore primarily imply the preservation of the mummy. But the soul itself is not a corporeal soul; it is also an image soul and a shadow soul, and this circumstance is reflected in the form of the cult. From the material, concrete corporeity with which the cult is originally concerned religious thought and intuition rise more and more to the pure image form. Now the statue comes to be regarded as the main assurance that the self will endure and takes its place beside the mummy as an equally effective instrument of immortality. It is this fundamental religious intuition that gives rise to the plastic arts of the Egyptians, particularly sculpture and architecture. The tombs of the Pharaohs, the pyramids, become the mightiest symbol of this spiritual trend, which aims at the temporal eternity, the unlimited duration of the I and which can

---

things, whereas it thus posits a correlative relation between the one and the many, original mythical thinking sees only an *alternative* relation between the two. Thus it must either negate the differences—by identifying the particular elements which it places in a spatial, temporal, or causal relation to one another, making them concresce in a single configuration (cf. above, pp. 62 ff.)—or, where this negation can no longer be effected, where the mere difference grows into an antithesis and as such forces itself directly upon consciousness, it must distribute the diverse *determinations* among a multiplicity of separate *beings*. Here, then, the difference is either not posited or is hypostatized at the same time as it is posited. The *functional* unity of consciousness, toward which theoretical thinking strives, posits difference in order to bridge it, in order to dissolve it in the pure form of thought. The *substantial*, mythical mode of thought either makes the many into one or the one into many. Here there is only concrescence or divergence; there is not that characteristic union of different things which is effected in the purely intellectual syntheses of consciousness and in its specific logical form of unity, in the "transcendental unity of apperception."

achieve this aim only in architectural and plastic embodiment, only in the intuitive visibility of space. But one can only advance beyond this whole phase of intuition and representation when the ethical motif of the self becomes more sharply defined. The survival and fate of the soul no longer depend exclusively on the material aids that are put into the tomb with it or on the performance of certain ritual acts which lend it magic support; they now depend on its ethical being and ethical action. In early Egyptian texts the favor of Osiris, the god of the dead, is gained by magical usages; in later texts, the emphasis is on the *judgment* of Osiris regarding good and evil. In the Book of Gates the dead man appears before Osiris to confess his sins and justify himself. Only after his heart has been weighed in the scales that stand before the god and has been found guiltless, can he enter the realm of the blessed. It is not his power and rank on earth, not his magical art, but his righteousness and freedom from guilt that now decide whether he will triumph in death. "Thou awakenest in beauty at daybreak," runs one of the texts. "All evil has fallen away from thee. Thou passest joyously through eternity with the praise of the god who is in thee. Thy heart is with thee; it does not leave thee." Here the heart, the ethical self of man, has become one with the god in him: "the heart of man is his very god" (Book of the Dead).

Thus we see in typical clarity the progress from the mythical to the ethical self. Man rises from magic to religion, from the fear of demons to the worship of gods, and this apotheosis is not so much outward as inward. Now man apprehends not only the world but above all himself, in a new spiritual form. In the Persian belief the soul remains by the corpse for three days after its separation from the body; but on the fourth day it goes to the place of judgment, to the Bridge of Chinvat that passes over hell. From here the soul of the righteous man rises through the abodes of good thoughts, good words, and good deeds to the realm of light, while the soul of the unrighteous man descends through the abodes of evil thoughts, evil words, and evil deeds into the "house of the lie." [24] Here the mythical image appears as scarcely more than a transparent veil,

24. On the Persian beliefs on death and the other world cf. Richard Reitzenstein, *Das iranische Erlösungsmysterium. Religionsgeschichtliche Untersuchungen* (Bonn, 1921). See also Jackson in *Grundriss der iranischen Philologie*, 2, 684 ff. For the Egyptian view of the judgment of the dead cf. the account and texts in Erman, *Ägyptische Religion*, pp. 117 ff.; Alfred Wiedemann, *Die Religion der alten Ägypter* (Münster, 1890), pp. 47 ff., 132 ff. Eng. trans., *Religion of the Ancient Egyptians* (New York, 1897). Cf. also Budge, *Osiris*, pp. 305 ff., 331 ff.

behind which certain basic forms of the ethical self-consciousness are clearly discernible.

In this way the transformation from mythos to ethos has its prehistory within the phenomenology of the mythical consciousness itself. At the lowest level of primitive belief psychic being confronts man as a mere thing; it is an outward, alien force that is manifested in him as a demonic power, to which he succumbs unless he can ward it off by magical means. But once the soul is taken not as a spirit of nature but as a *tutelary* spirit, we have the beginning of a new relation. For the tutelary spirit stands in a closer, more intimate relation to the person with whom it is associated. It not only dominates that person but guards and guides him; it is no longer something purely outward and alien but something belonging specifically to the individual, something familiar and close to him. Thus in the Roman belief the *lares* are distinguished from the *larvae:* the latter are wandering phantoms that spread terror and evil, while the former are friendly spirits which bear a certain individual stamp, which are bound up with a particular person or place, house or field, and protect it from harmful influences.[25] The conception of such personal tutelary spirits seems to recur in the mythology of almost all peoples. It has been found in the religions of the American Indians as well as among the Greeks and Romans, the Finns, and the Old Celts.[26] True, the tutelary spirit is not for the most part thought of as the man's I, as the "subject" of his inner life, but as something objective, which dwells in man, which is spatially connected with him and hence can also be spatially separated from him. Among the Uitotos the tutelary spirits seem to be the souls of various objects, of captured animals, for example; they not only remain with their possessor but can also be sent out on errands.[27] And even where the closest possible relation exists between the tutelary spirit and the man in whom it dwells, even where the tutelary spirit governs his whole being and destiny, it nevertheless appears as something existing for itself, something separate and strange. Thus the Bataks, for example, believe that a man before his birth, before his sensuous corporeal existence, is chosen by his soul, his *tondi,* and that everything connected with his life, all his weal or woe, depends on this choice. Anything that

25. Cf. Cumont, *After Life in Roman Paganism,* pp. 61 ff. See also Georg Wissowa, "Die Anfänge des römischen Larenkultes," *Archiv für Religionswissenschaft,* 7 (1904), 42–57.
26. Cf. Brinton.
27. Cf. Preuss, *Religion und Mythologie der Uitoto, 1,* 43 ff.

happens to the man happens because his tondi so wished it. His physical health, his temperament, his fate, and his character are wholly determined by the special nature of his tutelary spirit. This spirit is "a kind of man within the man, but does not coincide with his personality and is often in conflict with his I; it is a special being within the man, having its own will and its own desires, which it is able to gratify against the man's will and to the man's discomfiture." [28] Here man's fear of his demon still outweighs his feeling of intimacy with the demon, his feeling that the demon belongs to him by an inner necessity.

However, from this first demonic form the soul gradually begins to assume another more spiritual signification. Usener has followed this latter change through the gradual change in linguistic signification undergone by the terms δαίμων and genius in Greek and Latin. The demon is at first a typical example of what Usener designates as a "momentary or special god." Any perceptual content, any object, insofar as it arouses mythical-religious interest, be it ever so fleetingly, can be raised to the level of an independent god, a demon.[29] But there is another movement which tends to transform the outward demons into inward demons, and the accidental gods of the moment into gods of destiny. It is not what outwardly befalls a man but what he fundamentally *is* that constitutes his demon. It is given to him from birth, to accompany him through life and to guide his desires and his actions. In the sharper form which this basic intuition assumes in the Italic concept of genius it becomes, as the name itself indicates, the actual creator of the man, and not only his physical but also his spiritual creator, the origin and expression of his personal particularity. Thus everything that possesses a true spiritual form has a genius of this sort. It is attributed to the individual and to the family and the household, the state, the people, and in general to every form of human community. Similarly, in Germanic belief the individual as well as the family and the whole tribe possesses his tutelary spirit: in the Nordic saga the *kynfylgja,* guardians of the tribe, are differentiated from the *mannsfylgja,* guardians of the individual.[30] And this notion seems to take

28. Warneck, p. 8.

29. Usener, *Götternamen,* pp. 291 ff. On the history of the word δαίμων see also Albrecht Dieterich, *Nekyia. Beiträge zur Erklärung der neuendeckten Petrusapokalypse* (2d ed. Leipzig and Berlin, 1913), p. 59.

30. See Golther, pp. 98 ff. For Roman linguistic usage and concepts see in addition to Usener (op. cit. p. 297) Wissowa, *Religion und Kultus der Römer,* pp. 175 ff. Cf. Walter F. Otto, "Genius," in *Paulys Real-Encyclopädie.*

on sharper outlines and assume a more significant role as mythical-religious thinking advances from the purely natural sphere of intuition to the intuition of a spiritual "realm of purposes." Thus, for example, in the Persian religion, which is oriented entirely toward the one fundamental opposition of good and evil, the *fravashi,* the tutelary spirits, assume a central position in the hierarchical ordering of the world. It is they who aided the supreme ruler Ahura Mazda in the creation of the world and who in the end will decide in his favor the battle which he is waging against the spirit of darkness and lies. "Through their brightness and glory," Ahura Mazda proclaims to Zoroaster,

> "I maintain that sky, there above, shining and seen afar, and encompassing this earth all around. . . . Through their brightness and glory, O Zarathustra! I maintain the wide earth made by Ahura, the large and broad earth, that bears so much that is fine, that bears all the bodily world, the live and the dead, and the high mountains, rich in pastures and waters. . . . Had not the awful Fravashis of the faithful given help unto me, those animals and men of mine, of which there are such excellent kinds, would not subsist; strength would belong to the Drug, the dominion would belong to the Drug, the material world would belong to the Drug." [31]

Thus even the supreme ruler, the true creator god, requires sustenance; for according to the fundamental view of the Mazdean religion as a prophetic-ethical religion, he is what he is not so much through his own overwhelming physical might as by virtue of the sacred order whose executor he is. This eternal order of justice and truth is embodied in the fravashi and by their mediation descends from the world of the invisible to the world of the visible. According to a passage in the Bundahish, Ormazd gave the fravashi, when they were still pure, bodiless spirits, the choice of remaining in this state of pure bliss or of being provided with bodies and supporting him in his battle against Ahriman. Choosing the latter course, they entered into the material world to free it from the power of the hostile principle, the power of evil. In its basic trend this conception almost recalls the summits of speculative religious idealism, for here the sensuous, material world appears as a barrier to the "intelligible" world. Yet this

31. Yasht, XIII, 1. Eng. trans. by James Darmesteter, *The Zend-Avesta,* Pt. II; The Sacred Books of the East, ed. F. Max Müller, Vol. 23 (Oxford, the Clarendon Press, 1883), pp. 180, 182, 183.

barrier is necessary, for only through it, only by progressively overcoming it, can the power of the spiritual be confirmed and visibly manifested. Thus the sphere of the "spiritual" here coincides with the sphere of the "good": evil has no fravashi. We see in this development how the mythical concept of the soul has narrowed by taking on an ethical accent, but how this very narrowing implies a wholly new concentration on a specifically spiritual meaning, for the soul as a merely biological principle of movement and life no longer coincides with the spiritual principle in man. "Although the concept of the fravashi," writes an authority on Persian religion,

> most probably grew out of the ancestor cult that is so pronounced among the Indo-European peoples, it is noticeably distinguished from the cult of the Manes by its increased spiritualization; the Hindu or Roman worships the soul of the departed ancestors, the Mazdean reveres his own fravashi and that of all other men, whether dead or alive or to be born in the future.[32]

Indeed, the new feeling of personality that is here emerging is connected with the new feeling of time that prevails in the religion of Zoroaster. Out of the ethical-prophetic idea of the future grows a true discovery of man's individuality, of his personal self. Primitive mythical conceptions of the soul serve as a foundation for the discovery, but on this material an entirely new form is ultimately imprinted.

Thus the mythical consciousness undergoes at this point a development which is destined to surpass its limits. In the history of Greek philosophy we can still follow in detail this gradual release of the *speculative* idea of the self from its native mythical soil. The Pythagorean doctrine of the soul is still shot through with primordial mythical conceptions: Rohde has said that its central notions merely reflect phantasms of archaic popular psychology—in the accentuated form given them by theologians and lustratory priests and finally by the Orphics.[33] And yet these notions do not exhaust the essential particularity of the Pythagorean psychology, which is rooted in the same factor that gives the Pythagorean concept of the world its specific stamp. The soul is neither something material nor, despite the mythical migration of souls, a mere breath or shadow; rather,

32. Victor Henry, *Le Parsisme* (Paris, Dujarric, 1905), pp. 53 ff. On the Fravashi cf. Nathan Söderblom, *Les Fravashis* (Paris, 1899); Darmesteter, pp. 118, 130 ff.

33. Rohde, *Psyche*, 2, 167.

it is defined, in its deepest being and ultimate foundation, as harmony and number. In Plato's *Phaedo* this view of the soul as the "harmony of the body" is developed by Simmias and Cebes, the pupils of Philolaus. And with this for the first time the soul gains a share in the idea of measure as an expression of limit and form as such, of the logical as well as the ethical order. Thus, number becomes the ruler both over all cosmic being and over all things divine and demonic.[34] And this *theoretical* conquest of the mythical-demonic world, this subordination of it to a definite law which is expressed in number, now finds its completion in the corresponding development of ethics in Greek philosophy. From the saying of Heraclitus that man's character is his demon this development continues to Democritus and Socrates.[35] Perhaps it is only in this connection that we can fully appreciate the particular meaning and resonance of the Socratic concept of *eudaemonia*. Eudaemonia is based upon this new form of knowledge discovered by Socrates. It is achieved when the soul ceases to be a mere natural potency and apprehends itself as an ethical subject. Only now is man free from fear of the unknown, from the fear of demons, because he no longer feels that his self, his innermost being, is dominated by a dark mythical power but knows himself capable of molding this self from clear insight, through a principle of knowledge and will. Thus there arises in opposition to myth a new consciousness of inner freedom. At primitive levels of animism we encounter even today the view that a man is chosen by his soul demon. Among the Bataks of Sumatra diverse life destinies are offered to the soul before its embodiment by the primal father of gods and men, and the choice it makes determines the destiny of the man into which it will enter: his particularity, his character, and the whole course of his life.[36] This fundamental mythical motif is taken up by Plato in the tenth book of the *Republic,* but the consequence he derives from it is opposed to the mythical manner of thinking and feeling. "Your genius will not be allotted to you, but you will choose your genius," says Lachesis to the souls. "Virtue is free, and as a man honours or dishonours her he will have more or less of her; the responsibility is with the chooser—God is justified" (*Republic,* 617D). These words are spoken to the souls in the name of necessity, Ananke, as whose daughter Lachesis is represented, but since mythical necessity is replaced by ethical necessity, its law coincides

---

34. Philolaus, Fragment 11, ed. Diels, 32B; Freeman, p. 75.
35. For Democritus see especially Fragments 170, 171, ed. Diels.
36. Cf. the very characteristic myths communicated by Warneck, pp. 46 ff.

with that of the highest ethical freedom. Man now achieves his true self through self-responsibility. And yet the subsequent development of the concept of the soul in Greek philosophy shows how hard it was even for the philosophical consciousness to preserve the new meaning of this concept in its specific particularity. If we follow this motif from Plato to the Stoics and thence to the Neoplatonists, we see how the old mythical intuition of the soul demon gradually recovered its preponderance: among the works of Plotinus there is a treatise which again speaks expressly "of the demon that is allotted to us." [37]

But there is still another aspect of subjectivity, no longer ethical but purely theoretical, which was discovered in myth before it was discovered in philosophical thought. The mythical consciousness conceives of an I which is no longer material and which can be defined by no analogy to things, an I for which, rather, the objective world exists as mere appearance. The classical example of such a version of the I-concept, hovering on the borderline between mythical intuition and speculative contemplation, is to be found in the development of Indian thought. In the speculation of the Upanishads the separate stages of the road that had to be traveled are most clearly distinguished. We see here how religious thought seeks ever new images for the self, for the intangible and incomprehensible subject, and how in the end it can only define this self by dropping all these images as inadequate and unsuitable. The I is what is smallest and what is largest: the atman in the heart is smaller than a grain of rice or millet and yet greater than the air, greater than the heavens, greater than all these worlds. It is bound neither to spatial barriers, to a "here" and "there," nor to the law of temporality, to a coming into being and passing away, to an acting and being acted upon; it is all-embracing and all-governing. For to everything that is and everything that happens it stands as a mere onlooker, who is himself not involved in what he sees. In this act of pure contemplation it differs from everything that has objective form, that has "shape and name." To it applies only the simple determination "it is," without any closer specification and qualification. Thus, the self is opposed to everything that is intelligible and yet at the same time it is the heart of the intelligible world. Only he who does not know it, knows it—he who knows it, knows it not. It is not known by the knower,

---

37. *Enneades,* Treatise III, sec. 4. For the position of the "personal tutelary demon" among the Stoics and Neoplatonists cf. Theodor Hopfner, *Griechischägyptischer Offenbarungszauber* (2 vols. Leipzig, 1921–24), pp. 10 ff., 27 ff.

known by the nonknower.[38] With all its intensity the drive to knowledge is directed toward it, but at the same time, the problematic nature of all knowledge is contained in it. The aim of knowledge is not to manifest things; it is the self that one should see, hear, understand—and he who has seen it, heard it, understood it, and known it knows the whole world. And yet precisely this all-knowing entity is itself unknowable.

> "From where there is a duality . . . there one sees another; there one smells another; there one hears another; there one speaks to another; there one thinks of another; there one understands another. . . . [But] whereby would one understand him by whom one understands this All? Lo, whereby would one understand the understander?" [39]

It could not be stated more clearly that here a new certainty has opened up to the human spirit, but that this certainty, as a principle of knowledge, is comparable to none of the objects or images of knowledge, and accordingly remains inaccessible to all those modes of knowledge which are suitable precisely for these objects. And yet it would be premature to find an inner kinship, not to mention an identity, between the I-concept of the Upanishads and that of modern philosophical idealism.[40] For the *method* by which religious mysticism seeks to apprehend pure subjectivity and determine its content is clearly distinguished from the critical analysis of knowledge and its content. Yet the general direction of the movement itself, the direction from the objective to the subjective, remains, despite all differences in the ultimate aims of this movement, a common factor. Great as is the gulf dividing the self of the mythical-religious consciousness from the I of transcendental apperception, it is no greater than the distance within consciousness itself between the first primitive intuitions of the soul demon and the advanced conception in which the I is apprehended with a new form of "spirituality" as the subject of willing and knowing.

38. See Kena Upanishad, 11 (3); Katha Upanishad, vi. Eng. trans. by Hume, pp. 337, 358–361.

39. Brihadaranyaka Upanishad, 11, 4 (5), (14). Eng. trans. by Hume, pp. 101–102.

40. Cf. the critical remarks of Oldenberg, *Die Lehre der Upanishaden*, pp. 73 ff., 196 ff., with Deussen's conception and exposition.

Chapter 2

The Development of the Feeling of Self from the Mythical Feeling Of Unity and Life

1. The Community of All Life and Mythical Class Formation. Totemism

THE opposition of subject and object, the differentiation of the I from all given, determinate things, is not the only form in which progress is made from a general, still undifferentiated life feeling to the consciousness of the self. In the sphere of pure knowledge, it is true, progress consists above all in the differentiation of the principle of knowledge from its content, of the knower from the known; but mythical consciousness and religious feeling embrace a still more fundamental contrast. Here the I is oriented not immediately toward the outside world but rather toward a personal existence and life that are similar to it in kind. Subjectivity has as its correlate not some outward thing but rather a "thou" or "he," from which on the one hand it distinguishes itself, but with which on the other hand it groups itself. This thou or he forms the true antithesis which the I requires in order to find and define itself. For here again the individual feeling and consciousness of self stand not at the beginning but at the end of the process of development. In the earliest stages to which we can trace back this development we find the feeling of *self* immediately fused with a definite mythical-religious feeling of *community*. The I feels and knows itself only insofar as it takes itself as a member of a community, insofar as it sees itself grouped with others into the unity of a family, a tribe, a social organism. Only in and through this social organism does it possess itself; every manifestation of its own personal existence and life is linked, as though by invisible magic ties, with the life of the totality around it. This bond can relax only very gradually; only gradually can there develop an I independent of the surrounding spheres of life. And here again myth not only *accompanies* the process but *mediates* and *conditions* it, constituting one of its most significant and effective motifs. Since every new attitude of the I toward the community finds its expression in the mythical consciousness, since it is mythically objectified primarily in the form of the soul concept, the development of the soul concept not only represents but becomes a spiritual instrument for the act of "subjectivization," by which the individual self is achieved and apprehended.

A consideration of the mere contents of the mythical consciousness indicates that they are far from pertaining exclusively or even predominantly to the immediate intuition of nature. Even if we do not, in line with the "manistic" theory developed principally by Herbert Spencer, regard ancestor worship as the actual source of mythical thinking, it would seem possible to demonstrate that it has played an important part wherever we find a clear concept of the soul and a definite mythical theory of the home and origin of the soul. Of the great religions it is chiefly that of the Chinese which is rooted in ancestor worship and which seems to have preserved its original features with the greatest purity. Where this ancestor cult prevails, the individual not only feels himself bound to his ancestors by the continuous process of generation but knows himself to be identical with them. The souls of his ancestors are not dead: they exist and are; they will be embodied in his grandchildren, and they will forever be renewed in the generations to come. And even when this primary circle of mythical-social intuition broadens, when the intuition of the family progresses to that of the tribe and the nation, every single phase of this progress proves, as it were, to possess its mythical exponent. Every change in the social consciousness is imprinted upon the form and character of the gods. Among the Greeks the family gods, the θεοὶ πατρῷοι, are subordinated to the gods of the phratry and clan, the θεοὶ φράτριοι and φύλιοι, and these in turn to the gods of the city state and the universal national deities. Thus the "state of the gods" becomes a faithful copy of the organization of social life.[1] Yet Schelling by anticipation raised a decisive argument against any attempt to derive the form and the content of the mythical consciousness from the empirical conditions of human society and so to make social reality the foundation of religion, sociology the basis of a science of religion. "It seems to me," he remarks in his lectures on the philosophy of mythology,

1. As early a work as Aristotle's *Politics* traces the idea of the "state of the gods" back to the social organism: καὶ τοὺς θεοὺς διὰ τοῦτο πάντες, φασί βασιλεύεσθαι, ὅτι καὶ αὐτοὶ οἱ μὲν ἔτι καὶ νῦν οἱ δὲ τὸ ἀρχαῖον ἐβασιλεύοντο. *Politics*, Bk. I, sec. 2, line 1252b.

that precisely this notion that no one has ever questioned up to now is very much in need of investigation: namely, whether it is possible for mythology to have *originated* from or in a nation. For first of all, what is a nation, or what makes it a nation? Certainly it is not the mere spatial coexistence of a greater or lesser number of similar individuals, but rather a community of consciousness among them. This community has its immediate expression only in a common language; but wherein shall we seek this community itself or its foundation except in a common world view, and wherein can this common world view in turn be originally contained and given to a people except in its mythology? Hence it would seem impossible that mythology should come to an already existing nation unless it arises through the invention of individuals within this nation or by a common instinctive production. This, too, seems impossible, because it is inconceivable that a *nation* should exist without mythology. One might conceivably reply that a nation is held together by the common performance of some occupation—e.g. agriculture or trade—or by common customs, legislation, authority, etc. True, all this belongs to the concept of a nation, but it seems almost superfluous to recall how intimately authority, legislation, customs, even occupations are, among all nations, bound up with representations of the gods. The question is precisely whether all these things that are presupposed in the concept "nation" and assuredly given *with* it can be conceived without religious ideas, which are never wholly free from mythology.[2]

Methodologically speaking, these words of Schelling remain in force even if we replace "nation" with some more primitive social organism and attempt to derive the ideal form of religious consciousness from it as a basic objective form. For here again we are compelled to reverse our orientation: the mythical-religious consciousness does not simply *follow* from the empirical content of the social form but is rather one of the most important *factors* of the feeling of community and social life. Myth itself is one of those spiritual syntheses through which a bond between "I" and "thou" is made possible, through which a definite unity and a definite contrast, a relation of kinship and a relation of tension, are created between the individual and the community. Indeed, we cannot understand the mythical and religious world in its true depth if we see in it only an expression, i.e.

2. Schelling, *Philosophie der Mythologie*, pp. 62 ff.

a mere copy, of any pre-existing divisions pertaining either to natural or to social reality. In it we must rather see an instrument of the "crisis" itself, an instrument of the great process of spiritual differentiation through which basic determinate forms of social and individual consciousness arise from the chaos of the first indeterminate life feeling. In this process the elements of social existence and physical existence provide merely the raw material, which acquires its form only through certain fundamental spiritual categories not situated in it and not to be derived from it. Here above all it is characteristic of the direction of myth that the dividing lines which it draws between "inside" and "outside" are of an entirely different character and quite differently placed from those drawn by empirical-causal cognition. Here the relation between the two factors of objective intuition and subjective feeling of the self and of life is different from the structure of theoretical knowledge, and this shift in spiritual accent modifies all the basic measures of being and change; the various spheres and dimensions of reality merge and diverge according to criteria entirely different from those which apply to the purely empirical order and articulation of the world of perception, to the structure of pure existence and its object.

It is the task of the sociology of religion, which today has become a special science with its own problems and methods, to describe in detail the relations between religious form and social form. We, for our part, are concerned only with disclosing those universal religious categories which prove effective not so much in this or that particular form of social organization as in the establishment of the fundamental forms of the social consciousness in general. The apriority of these categories may be asserted in no other sense than that which critical idealism assumes and allows for the fundamental forms of knowledge. Here again there can be no question of isolating a fixed group of religious conceptions, which recur always and everywhere and produce a similar effect upon the structure of the social consciousness. We can only establish a certain direction, a certain unity of perspective, in which the mythical-religious view articulates both the world and the community. This perspective can be more closely determined only by attention to the special conditions of life under which the particular concrete community stands and develops; but this does not prevent us from recognizing that here again certain universal spiritual motifs of formation are at work. First of all, the development of myth shows one thing very clearly: even the most universal form of the human consciousness of kind, even the manner in which man differentiates himself from the totality of biological forms and groups himself with his fellow men into a natural species, is not given from the beginning as a *starting point* of the mythical-religious world view but should be understood rather as a mediated product, a *result* of this very world view. For the mythical-religious consciousness the limits of the species "man" are not rigid but thoroughly fluid. Only by a progressive concentration, only by a gradual narrowing of that universal life feeling in which myth originates, does it gradually arrive at the specifically human feeling of community. In the early stages of the mythical world view there is as yet no sharp boundary separating man from the totality of living things, from the world of animals and plants; particularly in totemism the kinship between man and animal, and above all the relation between a clan and its totem animal or plant, is taken by no means in a figurative but in a strictly literal sense. In his actions and institutions, in his whole form and manner of life, man feels himself to be one with the animal. It is reported that even today the Bushmen, when asked, cannot define a single point of difference between man and animal.[3] Among the Malays there is a belief that the tigers and elephants have a city of their own in the jungle, where they live in houses and behave in every respect like human beings.[4] Regardless of what specific explanation is offered for the significance and origin of totemism, this intermingling of the biological species, this fluidity of their natural and spiritual limits in the primitive-mythical consciousness—which in other respects is positively characterized by the sharpness with which it apprehends all sensuous-concrete distinctions, all nuances of perceptible form—must be rooted in some universal tendency in the "logic" of mythical thinking, in the general form and direction of its concept and class formation.

Mythical class formation is primarily distinguished from that prevailing in our empirical-theoretical view of the world by its lack of the strictly logical instrument which the latter possesses and of which it constantly makes use. When empirical and rational knowledge divides the world of things into species and classes, it employs the form of causal inference as its vehicle and guide. Objects are grouped into genera and species, on the basis not so much of their purely sensuous similarities or differences as of their causal dependency. We do not classify them according to the manner in which they appear to outward or inward perception but according to

3. Report of Campbell, quoted in Leo Frobenius, *Die Weltanschauung der Naturvölker* (Weimar, 1898), p. 394.
4. Skeat, p. 157.

groupings which follow from the rules of our causal thinking. Thus, for example, the whole articulation of our empirical, perceptual space is determined by these rules: the manner in which we single out the particular objects from this space and set them off against one another, the way in which we determine their position and distance from one another—all this derives not from simple sensation, from the material content of our visual and tactile impressions, but from the form of their causal coordination and connection, hence from acts of causal inference. And our classification of the morphological forms, of the biological genera and species, follows the same principle, since it is essentially based on criteria which derive from the rules of heredity, and from our insight into the order and causal relationship of generation and birth. When we speak of a particular genus of living creatures, the underlying assumption is that it is engendered according to certain natural laws: the idea of the unity of the genus arises from the way in which we think of it as perpetuated in a continuous reproductive sequence. "In the animal kingdom," says Kant in his treatise *On the Different Races of Men,*

> the natural classification into genera and species is based on the common law of reproduction, and the unity of the genera is nothing other than a unity of the generative power, valid for a certain number of animals. . . . The scholastic classification seeks to arrive at classes and is based on similarities; the natural classification seeks to arrive at roots and classifies the animals according to kinships in respect to generation. The former creates a school system for the memory; the latter a natural system for the understanding; the former aims merely to subsume the creatures under rubrics, the second strives to subordinate them to laws.

Such a "natural system for the understanding," such a reduction of the species to roots and to the physiological laws of generation, is utterly alien to mythical thinking. For mythical thinking generation and birth are not purely "natural" processes subject to universal and fixed rules; they are essentially magical occurrences. The act of mating and the act of birth are not related to one another as cause and effect; they are not two temporally separated phases of a unitary causal relationship.[5] Among the Australian

---

5. Cf. W. Foy, "Australien 1903/04," *Archiv für Religionswissenschaft,* 8 (1905), quoted in Albrecht Dieterich, *Mutter Erde* (Leipzig, B. G. Teubner, 1905), p. 32: "In the whole northeastern region (of Australia) as in Central Australia, motherhood has nothing to do with sexual intercourse. . . . The finished human embryos are introduced into the womb by a higher being." Cf. Strehlow, pp. 52 ff.

aborigines, who seem to have preserved certain basic forms of totemism in the greatest purity, the belief prevails that conception is connected with certain places, certain totemic centers, where the spirits of the ancestors reside; when a woman visits these places, the ancestral spirit enters into her body in order to be reborn.[6] Frazer has attempted to explain the whole totemic system on the basis of this notion.[7] But regardless of whether such an explanation is admissible and adequate, the idea as such throws a bright light on the way in which mythical concepts of genus and species are formed. The mythical consciousness does not form species by composing certain elements into a unity on the basis of immediate sensuous similarity or of a mediated causal relation between them; the unity of mythical species is rather of a fundamentally magical origin. Those elements which belong to one and the same field of magical efficacy, which fulfill a certain magical *function* in common, always show a tendency to fuse, to become mere manifestations of an underlying mythical identity. In our previous analysis of the mythical form of thought we attempted to explain the fusion by reference to the nature of the mythical form of thought itself. Whereas the members of a synthetic combination effected by theoretical thinking are preserved as independent elements within this very combination, whereas theoretical thinking keeps them distinct even while bringing them into relation with one another, mythical thinking causes those things which are related to one another, which are united as though by a magical bond, to merge into *one* undifferentiated form.[8] Thus, things which are totally dissimilar from the standpoint of immediate perception or from the standpoint of our "rational" concepts, may appear similar or alike provided they enter into one and the same magical complex.[9] The category of sameness is not based on agreement in any sensuous characteristics or abstract-

6. Cf. Spencer and Gillen, *The Native Tribes of Central Australia*, p. 265; idem, *The Northern Tribes of Central Australia*, p. 170; Strehlow, pp. 51 ff.

7. On James G. Frazer's theory of "conceptional totemism" cf. *Totemism and Exogamy* (4 vols. London, 1910), *4*, 57 ff.

8. Cf. above, pp. 62 ff.

9. Here, even the relation between the soul and the body is not organic and causal but purely magical. Consequently, the soul does not have a single body which belongs to it and which it animates; rather any lifeless thing is taken as its body, provided it belongs to the same totemic class. The tjurunga, an object of wood or stone into which a totemic ancestor has transformed himself, is regarded as the *body* of an individual named after the totem in question. A grandfather shows his grandchild the tjurunga with the words: "This thou body art; this thou the same. Thou place to other shouldst not take, thou pain"—i.e. "This is thy body, this is thy second I. If thou takest this tjurunga to another place, thou wilt feel pain." See Strehlow, p. 81. Cf. above, p. 163, n. 16.

conceptual factors, but is conditioned by the law of magical connections, of magical "sympathy." All things that are united by this sympathy, all things that "correspond" to one another or support one another magically coalesce into the unity of a magical genus.[10]

If we apply this principle of mythical concept formation to the relation between man and animal, a path opens by which we may arrive at an understanding of at least the *fundamental form* of totemism, if not of its special variants and ramifications. For in this relationship we find at the outset an essential factor, a central condition of mythical unity. The original relation between man and animal in primitive thinking is neither exclusively practical nor empirical-causal; it is a purely magical relation. For the primitive view, animals seem more than any other beings to be endowed with magical powers. Even Mohammedanism, it is reported, has been unable to eradicate the Malays' deep-rooted awe and reverence of animals. Supernatural, demonic powers are ascribed particularly to the larger ones, to the elephant, the tiger, the rhinoceros.[11] It is well known that most primitive peoples regard the animals that appear at a certain season as the makers, the bringers of this season: in mythical thinking it is truly the swallow that "makes" the spring.[12] The effect of the animal upon nature and man is wholly understood in this magical sense, and the same is true of man's practical activity in relation to the animal. Hunting is no mere technique for tracking and killing game; its success does not depend merely on the observance of certain practical rules but rather presupposes a magical relation which the man creates between himself and his quarry. It has been observed among all North American Indians that the "real" hunt must be preceded by a magical hunt which sometimes lasts whole days and weeks and which is bound up with very definite precautionary

10. Highly characteristic examples of this process of magical fusion may be found in Lumholtz' account of the "symbolism" of the Huichol Indians. In this "Symbolism," which obviously amounts to more than mere symbolism, the deer, e.g., is considered to be essentially the same as a certain species of cactus, the peyote, because both have the same magical history and because they occupy the same place in practical magic. These varieties which "inherently"—i.e. according to the laws of our empirical and rational concept formation— are utterly different here appear the same, because they correspond to one another in the magical-mythical ritual of the Huichols, which dominates and determines their whole world view. Cf. Carl Lumholtz, *Symbolism of the Huichol Indians*, Memoirs of the American Museum of Natural History, Vol. 3 (New York, 1900), pp. 17 ff.; Preuss, *Die geistige Kultur der Naturvölker*, pp. 12 ff.

11. See Skeat, pp. 149 ff.

12. Cf. above, p. 44

measures, with all sorts of taboo regulations. Thus, the bison hunt is preceded by the bison dance, in which the capture and slaying of the beast are mimetically represented in every detail.[13] And this mythical ritual is not a mere game or masquerade but an integral part of the "real" hunt, whose success depends essentially on its observance. And a similar ritual is attendant on the preparation and enjoyment of the meal. In all this it is evident that in the primitive view man and animal are united in a magical context and that their magical energy flows continuously from one to the other.[14] But from the standpoint of mythical thinking this unity of action would not be possible without an underlying unity of *essence*. Thus, the relationship governing our theoretical breakdown of the biological world into definite and distinct forms of life, into species and classes, is here reversed. The mythical species are not determined on the basis of empirical-causal rules of reproduction; the idea of the genus does not depend on the empirical relationship between the begetting and the begotten; here the primary consideration is rather the belief in the identity of the genus, growing out of the reciprocal magical relation between man and animal, and the idea of common descent is only a secondary appendage.[15] This identity is by no means merely "derived"; it is mythically believed, because it is magically experienced and felt.[16] Wherever totemic conceptions retain

13. See the description of this dance in George Catlin, *Illustration of the Manners, Customs, and Conditions of the North American Indians* (8th ed. London, 1851), *1*, 128, 144 ff. A compilation of further ethnographic material on the magical usages connected with hunting or fishing is to be found in Lévy-Bruhl, *Das Denken der Naturvölker*, pp. 200 ff.

14. Here it might be recalled that wherever the inhibitions created by conscious reflection, by our causal analysis and analytical classification, fall away, the intuition of this essential identity between man and animal tends to reappear. Psychiatric case reports are full of examples of this sort, as Schilder emphasizes in *Wahn und Erkenntnis*, p. 109.

15. This is particularly evident where "conceptional totemism" prevails, for here again the unity of a particular totemic group does not rest on the way in which the members of the group are reproduced; rather, the process of generation presupposes this unity of the group. For the totemic spirits enter into such women as they have recognized as essentially akin to them. "If a woman passes by a place where the body of a kindred ancestor is standing [writes Strehlow, p. 53] a *ratapa* who has been on the lookout for her *and has recognized in her a mother of his class*, enters into her body through her hip . . . . when the child is born, it belongs to the totem of the respective *altjirangamitjina.*"

16. It seems that this foundation in pure feeling of the totemic "systems" can be demonstrated even where the ideational components of totemism have been repressed and are recognizable only in isolated vestiges. Highly instructive material on this is presented in a dissertation by Bruno Gutmann, "Die Ehrerbietung der Dschagganeger gegen ihre Nutzpflanzen und Haustiere," *Archiv für die gesamte Psychologie, 48* (1924), 123–146. Here, as it were, the "life form" of totemism underlying its "thought form" is shown very vividly and concretely. In Gutmann's treatise we gain an insight into a stratum of ideas where the

their full intensity, we still find the belief that the members of the different clans not only are descended from different animal ancestors, but really *are* these varieties of animals,—aquatic creatures or jaguars or red parrots, for example.[17]

But although one of the fundamental assumptions of totemism is made understandable by the general tendency of mythical thinking, although we now understand why myth must classify the species very differently than do empirical perception and empirical-causal inquiry, this does not yet solve the central problem presented by totemism. For the specific peculiarity of the phenomena which we tend to subsume under the general concept of totemism is not that certain bonds, certain mythical identities, are here assumed to exist between man *in general* and certain animal species, but rather that each separate group possesses its *particular* totem animal to which it stands in a special relation, to which it appears "related," to which it seems strictly speaking to "belong." It is this differentiation with its social consequences and companion phenomena—above all the principle of exogamy, the prohibition of marriage between members of the same totemic group—which constitutes the basic form of totemism.

We would seem to move closer to an understanding of this differentiation when we hold fast to our view that the mode of man's intuition and "classification" of objective reality goes back ultimately to differences in the mode and direction of his action. How this principle dominates the whole structure of the world of mythical intuition, how the world of mythical objects proves almost everywhere to be a mere objective projection of human action, will later be considered in detail.[18] Here it suffices to consider that the first germ of such a development is given even at the lowest levels of mythical thinking, even within the magical world view,

---

"identity" between man and animal and between man and plant is not postulated as a concept and logically thought but is rather mythically experienced as an immediate unity and equivalence. "The fundamental power . . . is the feeling of vital unity with animal and plant and the desire to shape them into a community which is dominated by man, which rounds them into a circle in which everything is fully completed and sealed off from outside" (p. 124). Thus, even today, the Jagga "identifies his life stages with the banana and molds them in its image. . . . In the rituals of adolescence and of marriage, the banana stalk plays a leading role. . . . Although the cult in it present form, which is determined by ancestor worship, conceals a good deal and lends their actions with the banana a purely symbolic character, it has not been able to conceal entirely the original immediate connection between the banana and the new human life" (pp. 133 ff.).

17. Cf. Von Steinen's account of the Bororos, above, p. 66.

18. See below, pp. 199 ff.

since the magical powers on which all occurrences depend do not extend equally to all spheres of reality but may be distributed in very different ways. Even where the intuition of subjective action has been so little individualized that the whole world seems filled with an indeterminate magic force, that the atmosphere seems charged as it were with spirit electricity, the particular subjects share very unequally in this universally distributed, inherently impersonal force. In many individuals and in certain classes and callings the magical potency that permeates and dominates the universe seems to be present in a particularly intense and concentrated form; the power as such, the universal mana, is broken apart into the special forms of mana: the mana of the warriors, the mana of the chieftains, the mana of priests or doctors.[19] But to this quantitative division, in which the magical power still appears as a common and transferable possession, which is merely stored up as it were in certain places and certain persons, a qualitative division can and must be added at an early stage. For it is impossible to conceive of any community, however primitive, as a mere collectivity in which there is only an intuition of the being and action of the whole but no consciousness of the action of the parts. Very early there must be at least the beginnings of an individual or social differentiation; there must develop a multiple division and stratification of human action which will in some way be expressed at once and reflected in the mythical consciousness. Not every individual, group, or society can do everything; to each, rather, is reserved a certain sphere of action in which it must prove itself and beyond which it becomes powerless. Starting from these limits of ability, the mythical intuition gradually determines the limits of reality and its different classes and kinds. Whereas in pure cognition, in pure "theory," the sphere of vision is characteristically broader than the sphere of action, mythical intuition first opens up in the sphere to which it is practically and magically oriented and which it practically and magically dominates. To it the words of Goethe's Prometheus apply: for it only the sphere that it fills with its efficacy exists; there is nothing above it and nothing below it. But from this it directly follows that to each particular variety and mode of action a particular aspect of reality and type of relation between the elements of reality must correspond. With these elements of reality man forms an essential unity, which affects him immediately and which he immediately acts upon. His attitude toward the animal must

19. Cf. the exposition and documentation in Friedrich Lehmann, *Mana*, pp. 8 ff., 12 ff., 27 ff.

also be determined and differentiated according to this view. The hunter, the shepherd, the farmer—all feel a bond with the animal in their immediate activity; they feel dependent on the animal and thus, in accordance with a fundamental rule which dominates all mythical concept formation, akin to it; but in each of them this community applies to entirely different spheres of life, to different animal genera and species. On this basis, perhaps, we can understand how the original, inherently indeterminate unity of the life feeling, through which man feels an equal bond with all living things, gradually grows into that more specialized relation which links particular groups of men with particular animal classes. And indeed, those totemic systems that have been most accurately observed and studied offer numerous indications that originally the choice of a totem animal was by no means purely outward and accidental, that the totem is no mere "heraldry" but rather that a specific life attitude and spiritual attitude is represented and objectified in it. Even certain present-day societies which are far from primitive and in which the original picture of totemism has been so overlaid by accidental traits as to become unrecognizable often reveal this basic tendency quite clearly. In the mythical-sociological world view of the Zuñis the totemic organization largely coincides with the caste organization, so that warriors, hunters, farmers, and medicine men all belong to a particular group designated by specific totem animals.[20] And sometimes the relationship between the clan itself and its totem animal is so close that it is hard to decide whether the clan chooses a particular totem animal according to its own character or whether it has not rather molded itself according to the character of the animal; warlike clans and occupations correspond to wild, powerful animals and peaceful clans and occupations to tame animals.[21] It would seem as though the clan saw itself objectively in its totem animal, as though it recognized its nature, its particularity, its basic trend of action in the animal. And since in the highly developed totemic systems the articulation is not limited to any particular social groups but extends concentrically to all reality and all activity,[22] the entire

---

20. Cushing, *Outlines of Zuñi Creation Myths*, pp. 367 ff.

21. Cf. the report in *The Cambridge Expedition to Torres Straits*, 5, 184 ff., quoted in Lévy-Bruhl, *Das Denken der Naturvölker*, pp. 217 ff. Cf. Thurnwald, "Das Problem des Totemismus."

22. This concentric spread is particularly evident in the totemic system of the Marind-anim, which has been described in detail by P. Wirz, *Die religiösen Vorstellungen und Mythen der Marind-anim und die Herausbildung der totemistischen Gruppierungen* (Hamburg, 1922). Cf. my *Die Begriffsform im mythischen Denken*, pp. 19 ff., 56 ff.

universe is divided according to such "affinities" into sharply distinguished mythical genera and species.[23]

But sharp as these differentiations may gradually become for mythical feeling and consciousness, the idea of the *unity of life* persists in them undiminished. Life is felt to have a single dynamic and rhythm throughout the innumerable objective forms in which it may be manifested. Not only man and beast have this rhythm in common, but also man and the plant world. And in the development of totemism animal and plant are never sharply differentiated. A clan reveres its totem plant as much as its totem animal; the same taboos which prohibit the killing of the totem animal, or permit it only if certain conditions, certain magic ceremonies, are observed, apply to the eating of the totem plant.[24] Man's descent from a certain plant variety as well as the transformations of men into plants and plants into men are an everywhere recurring motif of myth and the mythical tale. Here again outward form and physical character can so easily be regarded as a mere mask, because from the outset the feeling of the community of all living things effaces all visible distinctions and all distinctions which can be postulated in analytical-causal thinking, or acknowledges them as mere accidents. This feeling finds its strongest support in the

23. To what extent this division is conditioned by a general trend of mythical "structural thinking" becomes evident when we compare in this respect the totemic systems with other mythical classifications of totally different *content*, particularly the systems of astrology. Here again the "genera" of reality, the coordination of its particular elements, is arrived at first of all by the differentiation of definite spheres of magical efficacy, each governed by one of the planets. The mythical principle of σύμπνοια πάντα is thus differentiated: one element of reality cannot act directly upon every other but can act only on those elements that are essentially related to it, which stand within the same magical-astrological chain of things and events. Thus, to single out one of these chains, Mars, according to the exposition in the *Picatrix*, is the source of attractive forces. It has under its protection natural science, veterinary medicine, surgery, tooth pulling, bleeding, and circumcision. Of languages, it is Persian that belongs to it; of the outer organs, the right nostril; within the body, the red gall; of materials, half-silk and the fur of rabbits, panthers, and dogs; of the trades, blacksmithing; of tastes, hot and dry bitterness; of jewels, the carnelian; of metals, sulpharsenite, sulphur, naphtha, glass, and copper; of colors, dark-red, etc. Cf. Hellmut Ritter, *Picatrix, ein arabisches Handbuch hellenistischer Magie* (Leipzig, 1921–22), pp. 104 ff. And here again the magical genus which embraces the most diverse contents of reality and composes them into a unity implies the idea of generation, of the begetter and the begotten; for whatever stands under a certain planet, whatever belongs to its magical sphere of action, has this planet as its ancestor and is descended from it. Cf. the well-known pictorial representations of the "children of the planets": Fritz Saxl, "Beiträge zu einer Geschichte der Planetendarstellungen im Orient und im Okzident," *Der Islam, 3* (1912), 151–177.

24. See, e.g., the table of the totem plants of the Arandas and Loritjas in Strehlow, pp. 68 ff.

mythical intuition of time, for which all life is marked off in very definite *phases* which are always and everywhere similar.[25] These phases are not mere measures, according to which we artificially and arbitrarily punctuate change; rather, they represent the essence and fundamental character of life itself as a *qualitative* unity. Thus it is not a merely mediated and re-flected expression of his own being that man finds in the plant world, par-ticularly in sprouting and growth, in passing away and decay; in it he ap-prehends himself immediately and with full certainty; in it he experiences his own destiny. "From the winter, verily," runs a Vedic saying, "the renascent spring arises. For from the former the latter returns to existence. Thus, verily, he who knows this returns to existence in this world."[26] Of all the great religions it is that of the Phoenicians which preserved this fundamental mythical feeling in the greatest purity and developed it most intensively. The "idea of life" has indeed been designated as the center of this religion, from which everything else emanates. Whereas the Baalim seem to be relative latecomers in the Phoenician pantheon, whereas they seem to be not so much personifications of natural forces as the lords of the nation and rulers of the soil, no such national tie pertained originally to the goddess Astarte. She rather represents the mother goddess pure and simple, who brings forth all life from her womb, who continuously bears anew and not only the nation but all physical and natural existence. And beside her as the eternal genetrix, as the image of inexhaustible fertility, stands the image of the youthful god, her son, who though subject to death frees himself from it over and over again and is resurrected into a new form of existence.[27] Not only does this image of the dying and resurrected god run through most of the historical religions; it recurs in many variants, yet essentially the same, in the religious experience of the primitive peoples. And everywhere a great religious force flows from it. If we compare the vegetation cults of primitive peoples with the Babylonian cult of Tammuz, the Phrygian cult of Attis, and the Thracian cult of Dionysus, we find in them all the same fundamental line of development and the same source of specifically religious emotion. In none of these cults does man stop at the mere contemplation of the natural process; he is impelled to burst through the barrier that separates him from the universe of living things, to intensify the life feeling in himself to the point of liberating himself

25. Cf. above, pp. 107 ff.
26. See Oldenberg, *Die Lehre der Upanishaden*, p. 29.
27. Cf. Wolf W. F. von Baudissin, *Adonis und Esmun* (Leipzig, 1911).

from his generic or individual *particularity*. This liberation is achieved in wild, orgiastic dances which restore man's identity with the original source of life. Here we have no mere mythical-religious interpretation of the natural process but an immediate union with it, an authentic drama which the religious subject experiences in himself.[28] The mythical narrative is for the most part merely an outward reflection of this inner process, a light veil behind which this drama is apparent. Thus in the cult of Dionysus it is the form of the cult that gives rise to the story of Dionysus-Zagreus, who is overpowered by the Titans, torn to pieces and devoured, so that the One divine being is broken into the multiplicity of the forms of this world and of men: for from the ashes of the Titans whom Zeus shatters with his thunderbolt arises the human race.[29] The Egyptian Osiris cult is also grounded in the identity assumed between god and man. Here the dead man himself becomes Osiris: "As true as Osiris lives, he too will live; as true as Osiris did not die, he too will not die; as true as Osiris has not been destroyed, he too will not be destroyed." [30] For the highly developed *metaphysical* consciousness the certainty of immortality rests above all on a sharp analytical distinction between body and soul, between the physical-natural world and the spiritual world. But the original mythical consciousness knows nothing of any such division or dualism. Here the certainty of survival is rooted in the reverse view: here it is continuously reinforced by the intuition of nature as a cycle of new births. For all things that grow are interrelated and magically intertwined. In the festive rituals with which man accompanies certain decisive phases of the year, above all the descent of the sun from the autumnal equinox or its rising and the return of light and life, it is everywhere evident that this is no mere reflection, no analogical copy of an outward event, but that human action and the cosmic process

28. For the cults of Adonis, Attis, and Osiris and their "primitive" parallels cf. the comprehensive treatment of Frazier, "Adonis, Attis, *Osiris*," *Golden Bough*, Vols. *5–6*, Pt. IV. For the vegetation cults see also Konrad T. Preuss, "Phallische Fruchtbarkeits-Dämonen als Träger des altmexikanischen Dramas," *Archiv für Anthropologie*, n.s., *1* (1903), 158 ff., 171 ff. Recently, Gustav Neckel, *Die Überlieferungen vom Gotte Balder* (Dortmund, 1920), has made it appear likely that the Germanic Balder myth belongs to the same sphere of intuition and, in fact, that there is a direct genetic connection between Balder and Adonis-Tammuz.

29. On the origin and significance of the legend of Dionysus-Zagreus see Rohde, *Psyche*, 116 ff., 132.

30. See Erman, *Ägyptische Religion* (2d ed.), pp. 111 ff.; Renouf, *Lectures on the Origin and Growth of Religion*, pp. 184 ff. The same fundamental intuition and the same mythical formula occur in the Phrygian cult of Attis (θαρρεῖτε, Μίσται, τοῦ θεοῦ σεσωσμένου. ἔσται γὰρ ἡμῖν ἐκ πόνων σωτηρία). Cf. Reitzenstein, *Die hellenistischen Mysterienreligionen* (1st ed. 1910), pp. 205 ff.

are here directly interwoven. No more than the complex mythical intuition originally dissects being into a multiplicity of sharply differentiated biological varieties does it differentiate the various life-giving and generative powers of nature. It is one and the same vital force which brings about the growth of plants and the birth and growth of man. In the magical world view and in magical activity the one can therefore always replace the other. Just as, in the well-known custom of the "marriage bed in the field," the practice or representation of the sexual act results directly in the impregnation and fruitfulness of the earth, so, conversely, it is the mimetic representation of the fertilization of the earth that enables souls to be reborn after death. The rain that fructifies the earth has its corresponding magical counterpart in the male member, the furrow in the woman's womb: the one is given with the other.[31]

Accordingly, the conception of Mother Earth, or the corresponding conception of the earth as father, represents a central and original idea which has shown its power again and again, from the beliefs of primitive peoples down to the highest productions of the religious consciousness. The Uitotos believe that during the season when there is no grain the grain goes down to the father under the earth: the "soul" of the grain and of all plants goes to the dwelling place of the father.[32] The Greeks held that the earth is the common mother who brings the sons of man to light and to whom they are given back after death to be resurrected to new life in the cycle of becoming; Electra's prayer at the tomb of Agamemnon [33] in the *Choephoroi* of Aeschylus directly expresses this view, which is fundamental to the Greek faith. Even in Plato's *Menexenos,* we still find it said that it is not the earth which imitates women in conceiving and giving birth but women who imitate the earth. But for the original mythical intuition there is here no before or after, no first or second, only the complete and indissoluble involvement of the two processes. The mystery cults translate this universal belief into individual terms. Through the practice of sacramental acts representing the primordial secret of growth, death, and rebirth the initiate seeks to obtain assurance of rebirth. In the Isis cult Isis, the creator of the

31. On all this see Mannhardt, *Wald- und Feldkulte,* especially chs. 4–6; idem, *Mythologische Forschungen* (Strassburg and London, 1884), ch. 6, pp. 351 ff.

32. Preuss, *Religion und Mythologie der Uitoto, 1,* 29. Cf. idem, "Religionen der Naturvölker," *Archiv für Religionswissenschaft,* 7 (1904), 234.

33. *Choephoroi,* verses 127 ff. Cf. Ulrich von Wilamowitz-Moellendorff, "Einleitung zur Übersetzung der Eumeniden des Äschylos," in *Griechische Tragödien* (4 vols. Berlin, 1906–23), 2, 212.

green seeds, is to her worshipers the Mother of God, the Great Mother, the Queen, who gives life to all men.[34] And here, as in other mystery cults, it is expressly taught that the initiate, before achieving his new *spiritual* being, his spiritual "transfiguration," must have gone through all the spheres of nature and of physical life, that he must have been in all the elements and forms of life—in the earth, the water, the air, in the animals and the plants —that he must have accomplished a journey and metamorphosis through the zones of heaven and all the animal forms.[35] Thus, even where there is a strong tendency toward separation of the spiritual from the physical, toward a dualism between body and soul, the original mythical feeling of unity continuously breaks through. At first the fundamental categories of man's social life are taken both as "natural" and as "spiritual." Particularly the primordial form of the human family, the triad of father, mother, and child, is both ascribed to and read out of nature. In the Vedic as in the Germanic religion, "Mother Earth" is opposed to "Father Heaven." [36] Among the Polynesians the lineage of man is traced back to heaven and earth as his first parents.[37] The triad of father, mother, son is represented in Egyptian mythology in the figures of Osiris, Isis, and Horus; it is found among almost all Semitic peoples, and its presence has been demonstrated among the Germanic peoples,[38] the Italic tribes, the Scythians, and the Mongols. Usener holds that this divine triad represents a fundamental category of the mythical-religious consciousness, "a deep-rooted form of intuition, endowed with the force of a natural drive." [39] In the development of Christianity, too, the religious-ethical conception of divine filiation developed only very gradually from definite concrete-physical intuitions of this relationship; here, too, the hope of resurrection rests

34. Cf. Dieterich, *Nekyia*, pp. 63 ff.; idem, *Eine Mithrasliturgie* (2d ed. Leipzig and Berlin, 1910), pp. 134 ff.; idem, *Mutter Erde*, pp. 82 ff. On the conception of Mother Earth in the Semitic sphere see Theodor Nöldeke, "Mutter Erde und Verwandtes bei den Semiten," *Archiv für Religionswissenschaft*, 8 (1905), 161–166; Baudissin, *Adonis und Esmun*, pp. 18 ff.

35. Cf. Reitzenstein (1st ed., 1910), pp. 33 ff.

36. Cf. Oldenberg, *Religion des Veda* (2d ed.), pp. 244 ff., 284; Schröder, *Arische Religion*, *1*, 295 ff., 445 ff.

37. See the legend reported by George Grey, *Polynesian Mythology* (2d ed. Auckland, 1885), pp. 1 ff., under the title "The Children of Heaven and Earth."

38. For the Germanic triad of gods, Balder, Frigg, and Odin, see Neckel, *Die Überlieferungen vom Gotte Balder*, pp. 199 ff.

39. See Usener, "Dreiheit." For the triad of father, son, and mother in the Semitic sphere see Nielsen, *Der dreieinige Gott*, pp. 68 ff. For Egypt, Babylonia, and Syria see Wilhelm Bousset, "Gnosis," in *Paulys Real-Encyclopädie*.

chiefly on the notion, fundamental to the old primitive religion, that the pious man is physically akin to God the Father, is flesh of His flesh.[40]

Thus myth expresses all natural reality in the language of human, social reality and expresses all human, social reality in the language of nature. Here no reduction of the one factor to the other is possible; it is rather the two together, in complete correlation, that determine the peculiar structure and complexion of the mythical consciousness. Hence it is hardly less one-sided to "explain" mythology in purely sociological terms than to explain it in purely naturalistic terms. The most incisive and consistent attempt at such an explanation has been undertaken by the modern French school of sociologists, particularly by their founder, Émile Durkheim, who starts by saying that neither animism nor naturism can be the true root of religion; for if they were, this would simply mean that all religious life is without solid foundation, an aggregate of mere delusions, a sum of phantasms. Religion cannot rest on such shaky ground, for if it is to claim any kind of inner truth, it must express some objective reality. This reality is not nature but society; it is not of a physical but of a social nature. The true object of religion, the sole and original object to which all religious forms and expressions can be traced back, is the social group to which the in-dividual indissolubly belongs, which wholly conditions his being and his consciousness. It is this social group which not only determines the form of mythology and religion but also provides the basic schema and model for all theoretical understanding, for all knowledge of reality. All the cat-egories in which we apprehend this reality—the concepts of space, time, substance, and causality—are products not of individual but of social think-ing and accordingly have their religious-social prehistory. To trace them back to this prehistory, to derive their seemingly purely logical structure from definite social structures: that is to explain these concepts and under-stand them in their true apriority. To the individual everything must seem a priori, universally valid and necessary, a fact which arises not from his own activity but from the activity of the species. The real bond which links the individual with his tribe, his clan, and his family is therefore the ultimate demonstrable foundation for the ideal unity of his world-con-sciousness, for the religious and intellectual structure of the cosmos. Here we shall not take up at any length Durkheim's epistemological grounding of his attempt to replace the "transcendental" deduction of the categories by

40. Documentation in Nielsen, pp. 217 ff. Cf. the historical analysis of the term "living God" in Baudissin, pp. 498 ff.

a social deduction. It is true that we might ask whether the categories which
Durkheim seeks to derive from social reality are not rather the *conditions*
of this reality: whether it is not the pure forms of thought and intuition
which make possible and constitute both the content of society and that
empirical regularity of phenomena which we call nature. But even if we
exclude this question, even if we limit ourselves to the phenomena of the
mythical-religious consciousness, it develops on closer scrutiny that even
here Durkheim's theory amounts to a ὕστερον πρότερον. For the form of
society is not absolutely and immediately *given* any more than is the objective form of nature, the regularity of our world of perception. Just as
nature comes into being through a theoretical interpretation and elaboration of sensory contents, so the structure of society is a mediated and ideally
conditioned reality. It is not the ultimate, ontologically real cause of the
spiritual and particularly the religious categories, but rather is decisively
determined by them. If we seek to explain these categories as mere repeti-
tions and, as it were, copies of the empirical form of society, we forget that
the processes and the function of mythical-religious formation have entered
precisely into this real form. We know of no form of society, however
primitive, which does not disclose some kind of religious imprint; and
society itself can be regarded as a determinate form only if we tacitly presuppose the mode and direction of this imprint.[41] Durkheim's explanation
of totemism, which he regards as the true test of his fundamental view,
indirectly confirms this relationship. For Durkheim totemism is merely
an outward projection of certain inner social relations. Because individuals
know their own life only within an encompassing society, and because
within this society they single out special groups which they set off one
against the other as characteristic unities, objective existence can be intel-
lectually apprehended only through this fundamental form of experience;
it can only be interpreted through a detailed articulation of all being and all
change into species and classes. Totemism does nothing more than transfer
the relationships and kinships which man immediately experiences as a

41. If we wish to find concrete historical examples for this process of "imprinting"—the
manner in which the religious consciousness forms society in its image—we need only read
Max Weber's fundamental works on the sociology of religion. Here the specific form of the
religious consciousness is shown to be not so much the product of a definite social structure
as its condition; in other words, the same primacy of religion that we have seen expressed
in Schelling (see above, pp. 176 ff.) is stated in modern formulation and terminology. Cf.
Weber's own remarks on his approach to the sociology of religion, *Gesammelte Aufsätze zur
Religionssoziologie* (Tübingen, 1920), *I*, 240 ff.

member of the social body to nature as a whole; it copies the social microcosm in the macrocosm. Thus here again Durkheim sees society as the actual object of religion, whereas the totem is regarded only as a sensuous sign by which anything whatsoever can be stamped as socially significant and hence raised to the religious sphere.[42] But this nominalistic theory, which regards the totem only as a kind of accidental, more or less arbitrary sign behind which stands an entirely different, mediated object of worship, passes by the central problem of totemism. Admittedly myth and religion everywhere require such images, such sensuous signs, but the *particularity* of the various mythical-religious symbols remains a question which cannot be answered on the basis of the *universal* function of symbolism. The relating of all forms of reality to certain animal or plant forms would seem to remain unexplained unless we can account for its specific character by a definite trend in mythical thinking and in the mythical life feeling and so give to totemism not, it is true, a fixed correlate in the world of things, a *fundamentum in re,* but a foundation in the mythical-religious *consciousness.* The very existence and form of human society itself requires such a foundation; for even where we suppose that we have society before us in its empirically earliest and most primitive form, it is not something originally given but something spiritually conditioned and mediated. All social existence is rooted in concrete forms of community and of the feeling of community. And the more we succeed in laying bare this root, the more evident it becomes that the primary feeling of community never stops at the dividing lines which we posit in our highly developed biological class concepts but goes beyond them toward the totality of living things. Long before man had knowledge of himself as a separate species distinguished by some specific power and singled out from nature as a whole by a specific primacy of value he knew himself to be a link in the chain of life as a whole, within which each individual creature and thing is magically connected with the whole, so that a continuous transition, a metamorphosis of one being into another, appears not only as possible but as necessary, as the "natural" form of life itself.[43]

42. See Émile Durkheim, *Les formes élémentaires de la vie religieuse* (Paris, 1912), pp. 50 ff., 201 ff., 623 ff. Eng. trans. by Joseph W. Swain, *The Elementary Forms of the Religious Life* (London and New York, 1915). Cf. Durkheim and Marcel, Mauss, "De quelques formes primitives de classification," *Année sociologique,* 6 (1901–2), 47 ff.

43. Although one is often tempted to regard totemism as the original and fundamental phenomenon of mythical thinking, the ethnographical facts would seem to lead us to the opposite inference. Totemism seems everywhere embedded in a universal mythical view,

From this it becomes understandable that even in the images which are
the original life and being of myth and which immediately and concretely
embody its special character, god, man, and beast are never sharply distinguished. Only gradually does a transformation occur, which is the unmistakable symptom of a spiritual transformation, of a *crisis* in the development of the human self-consciousness. In the Egyptian religion the gods
generally take the form of animals, the heavens are represented as a cow,
the sun as a sparrow-hawk, the moon as an ibis, the god of the dead as a
jackal, the water god as a crocodile; and in the Vedas we find side by side
with the dominant anthropomorphism traces of an older theriomorphic
view.[44] Even where the gods stand before us in clearly human form, their
kinship with the animals is often expressed in an almost unlimited power
of metamorphosis. Thus the Germanic Odin is the great magician who
changes himself into any desired form: a bird, a fish, a worm. Similarly,
in archaic Greek religion the great gods of the Arcadians were represented
in the form of a horse, a bear, or a wolf—Demeter and Poseidon with the
head of a horse, Pan in the shape of a goat. It was Homeric poetry which
drove this view from Arcadia.[45] And this suggests that perhaps myth would
not by itself have arrived at a sharper division, which essentially conflicts
with its own character, its complex intuition, if other factors and other
spiritual forces had not played a part. It is art which by helping man to
find his own image discovered, as it were, the specific *idea* of man as such.
This development can be followed almost step by step in the plastic representation of the gods. Throughout Egyptian art we find the hybrid forms
which show the god with a human body but the head of a four-legged
animal or a snake, a frog or a sparrow-hawk, while in other works the
body is that of an animal and the face discloses human features.[46] Greek
sculpture, on the other hand, takes a decisive step: in its molding of the
pure form of man it arrives at a new form of the divine itself and a new
relationship between god and man. And in this process of humanization

---

which instead of splitting life from the outset into varieties and classes regards it as a unitary
force, as a whole prior to all divisions. And animal worship as such is a far more universal
phenomenon than true totemism, which seems to have developed out of it only under special
conditions. Thus, e.g., in Egypt, the classical land of animal worship, a totemistic basis of the
animal cult is not demonstrable. Cf. Foucart's critique from the standpoint of egyptology and
comparative religious history of the alleged universality of the "totemistic codex," *Histoire
des religions et méthode comparative* (2d ed.), pp. lii ff., 116 ff.

44. Cf. Oldenberg, *Religion des Veda* (2d ed.), pp. 67 ff.

45. Cf. Wilamowitz-Moellendorff, 2, 227 ff.

46. Cf. the illustrations in Erman, *Ägyptische Religion*, pp. 10 ff.

and individualization poetry plays a role almost equal to that of art. Here again, it is true, poetic and mythical formation do not stand to one another as simple cause and effect; here again one does not simply precede the other. The two are merely different exponents of the same cultural development. "The liberation which came to consciousness through the differentiation of the representations of the gods," writes Schelling,

> gave the Hellenes their first poets, and conversely, the epoch which gave them poets brought with it the first fully developed history of the gods. Poetry did not come first, not real poetry at least, and poetry did not actually produce the explicit history of the gods; neither one precedes the other; both are rather the common and simultaneous culmination of an earlier state, a state of development and silence. . . . The crisis through which the world and the history of the gods develop is not outside of the poets; it takes place in the poets themselves, it *makes* their poems . . . it is not their persons . . . it is the crisis of the mythological consciousness which in entering into them makes the history of the gods.[47]

However, poetry does not merely reflect this crisis; it intensifies it and carries it to completion and decision. Once again we see confirmed the fundamental rule which governs all spiritual development, namely that the spirit arrives at its true and complete inwardness only by expressing itself. The form taken by the inner life reacts upon and determines its essence and meaning. In this sense the Greek epic intervenes in the development of Greek religion. Here it is not the technical form of the epic that is decisive, for its individualization may be no more than a light allegorical cloak over a universal mythical content. The Babylonian epic of Gilgamesh, for example, still bears an evident universal-astral character: beneath the image of the deeds and sufferings of the hero Gilgamesh we recognize a solar myth, a representation of the annual path of the sun, of its reversal at two turning points, etc. The twelve episodes of the epic are related to the twelve signs of the zodiac, through which the sun passes in the course of a year.[48] But though often attempted, an astral interpretation of the Homeric epics is doomed to failure. Here we are dealing no longer

---

47. Schelling, *Philosophie der Mythologie,* pp. 18 ff.

48. Cf. *Das Gilgamesch-Epos,* German trans. by Arthur Ungnad and Hugo Gressman (Göttingen, 1911); Peter Jensen, *Das Gilgamesch-Epos in der Weltliteratur* (Strassburg, 1906), especially pp. 77 ff.

with the destinies of the sun and the moon; here, rather, the *hero* is discovered, and in him the individual man as an active and suffering subject.
And with this discovery a last barrier between god and man falls away;
the hero takes his place between them as an intermediary. Now the hero,
the human personality, is raised to the divine sphere and the gods for their
part are closely interwoven with human destiny, not as mere observers but
as fellow warriors. It is through their relation to the hero that the gods are
fully drawn into the sphere of personal existence and action, in which they
now take on a new form and a new determinacy. And the process begun in
the Greek epic finds its conclusion and completion in the drama. The Greek
tragedy also grows out of a primordial stratum of the mythical-religious
consciousness and never breaks wholly away from this substratum. It arises
directly from a cult ritual, from the Dionysian festival and chorus. But it
does not remain confined within the orgiastic, Dionysiac mood in which it
is rooted; in opposition to this mood there arises, in the course of its development, an entirely new figure of man, an entirely new feeling of the I
and the self. Like all great vegetation cults, that of Dionysus feels the I
only as a violent rending away from the primal source of life, and what it
strives for is a return to that source, the "ecstasy" by which the soul bursts
the fetters of the body and of individuality, to become united once more
with universal life. Here all that is apprehended of individuality is the *one*
factor, the factor of tragic isolation, as directly represented in the myth of
Dionysius-Zagreus, who is torn to pieces and devoured by the Titans. The
artistic view, however, sees in individual existence not so much isolation
as separation—concentration into a self-contained personage. For this view
a definite plastic outline becomes the first guarantee of perfection. And
perfection demands the finite; it calls for fixed determination and delimitation. This striving is realized in the Greek tragedy as in the epic and in art:
first the person of the *coryphaeus* steps out of the chorus as a whole and is
set off from the rest as an independent individual. But the drama cannot
stop here: what it demands is not so much a person as persons, the relation
of the "I" to the "thou," and the conflict between the two. So the next thing,
in Aeschylus, is the introduction of the second actor and then, in Sophocles,
of the third. And to this dramatic progress corresponds, step by step, a
progressive deepening of the feeling and consciousness of personality—and,
indeed, the word "person," which serves us as an expression of this consciousness, meant at first nothing other than the actor's mask. Even in the
epic the figure of the hero, the human subject, is set off from the sphere of

objective events; but although the hero is thus marked out, he is more passive than active in his relation to it. He is involved in these events, but they do not grow directly out of him and are not necessarily conditioned by him; he remains the plaything of friendly and hostile, divine and demonic powers; it is they and not he who determine and guide the course of events. In this respect the Homeric epic, and particularly the *Odyssey,* still borders upon myth and the mythical tale. The guile, the strength, the wisdom of the hero, through which he seems to guide his destiny, are themselves demonic-divine gifts bestowed on him from outside. It is Greek tragedy which for the first time opposes to this passive view a new source of the I by taking man as an independent agent, responsible for his acts, thus making him into a true ethical-dramatic subject. "What man shall testify your hands are clean of this murder?" the chorus replies to Clytemnaestra in the *Agamemnon* of Aeschylus, when she seeks to shift the guilt for her husband's murder from herself to the demonic curse on the family. Here we have a dramatic representation of the same drama that in Greek philosophy found its purest expression in Heraclitus' saying, ἦθος ἀνθρώπῳ δαίμων, and in the development of this principle in Socrates and Plato.[49] The gods are also drawn into this development, for they, too, are subject to the sentence of Dike, the supreme godhead of tragedy. In the *Eumenides* of Aeschylus the Erinyes themselves, the ancient goddesses of vengeance, ultimately bow to the verdict of justice. In contrast to the epic, tragedy shifts the center of events from the outside in, and thus there arises a new form of ethical self-consciousness, through which the gods take on a new nature and form.

But this crisis of the religious consciousness that we find reflected in the forms of the individual gods points at the same time to a crisis in the social consciousness. Just as there is no sharp distinction between the human species and the animal and plant varieties in the thought and feeling of primitive religion—of totemism, for example—so there is no clear delimitation between the human group as a whole and the individual belonging to it. The individual consciousness remains confined within the tribe consciousness and dissolves into it. The god himself is primarily the god of the tribe, not of the individual. The individual who leaves the tribe or is expelled by it has thereby lost his god: "Go, serve other gods"[50] are the

49. Cf. above, p. 172.

50. I Samuel 26:19. Cf. William R. Smith, *Lectures on the Religion of the Semites* (Edinburgh, 1889). German trans. by Stübe, *Die Religion der Semiten* (Freiburg, 1899), pp. 19 ff.

words spoken to the outcast. In all his thoughts and feelings, in all his actions and sufferings, the individual knows himself bound to the community, just as the community feels itself attached to its individuals. Every taint with which an individual is afflicted, every crime he commits, passes by immediate physical contagion to the whole of the group. For the vengeance of the murdered man's soul does not stop at the murderer but extends to all who are in direct or indirect contact with him.

However, as soon as religious consciousness rises to the idea and configuration of personal gods, this involvement of the individual takes on a personal stamp, a personal face, as it were, as opposed to the life of the tribe. And with this trend toward the individual is bound up a new tendency toward the universal—which is only seemingly in conflict with it and in truth is correlative to it. For above the restricted unity of the tribe or the group there now arise more comprehensive social units. Homer's personal gods are also the first national gods of the Greeks, and as such they may be called the creators of the universal Hellenic consciousness. For they are the Olympians, the universal gods of heaven, bound to no particular locality or countryside or cult site. Thus, personal consciousness and national consciousness are achieved in one and the same fundamental act of religious formation. Herein it is once again demonstrated that the mythical and religious imagination does not merely reflect certain facts of the social structure, but is itself one of the factors in the making of all living social consciousness. The same process of differentiation by which man defines the limits of his species leads him subsequently to draw sharper boundaries within the species and so arrive at the specific consciousness of his I.

2. The Concept of Personality and the Personal Gods.
   The Phases of the Mythical Concept of the I.

In the foregoing remarks I have attempted to show how man can discover and determine the universe inside him only by thinking it in mythical concepts and viewing it in mythical images. But this describes only a single direction in the development of the mythical-religious consciousness. Here again the inward path is completed only in conjunction with the seemingly opposite path, from the inside outward. For the most important factor in the growth of the consciousness of personality is and remains the factor of *action*. But here the law that every action must provoke an equal reaction applies in a purely spiritual as well as a physical sense.

The import of man's action on the outside world is not simply that the I, as a finished thing, as a self-contained "substance," draws outside things into its sphere and takes possession of them. Rather, all true action is *formative* in a twofold sense: the I does not simply impress its own form, a form given to it from the very outset, upon objects; on the contrary, it acquires this form only in the totality of the actions which it exerts upon objects and which it receives back from them. Accordingly, the limits of the inner world can only be determined, its ideal formation can only become visible, if the sphere of being is circumscribed in action. The larger the circle becomes which the self fills with its activity, the more clearly the character of objective reality and also the significance and function of the I are manifested.

When we seek to understand this process as it is reflected in the mythical-religious consciousness, we find that at the first stages of this consciousness things only "are" for the I if they affect it emotionally, if they release in it a certain movement of hope or fear, desire or horror, satisfaction or disappointment. Long before nature can become an object of intuition, not to speak of knowledge, it too is given to man only in this way. This fact in itself contradicts all theories which make the personification and worship of certain natural objects and forces the beginning of the mythical consciousness. For things and forces are given in advance to the mythical consciousness no more than they are to theoretical consciousness; they represent, rather, a relatively advanced process of objectivization. Before this objectivization has begun, before the world as a whole has split into determinate, enduring, and unitary forms, there is a phase during which it exists for man only in unformed feeling. In this indeterminacy of feeling certain impressions are set off from the common background by their special intensity and force. To them correspond the first mythological images. They are not products of reflection, which dwells on certain objects in order to ascertain their enduring characteristics, their constant traits, but are the expression of a unique stirring, a momentary tension and release, of the consciousness, which will perhaps never be repeated in similar form. Usener has shown how this peculiar and original productivity of the mythical consciousness asserts itself at far advanced stages and is always at work, how even in a phase characterized by the crystallization of clearly determined "special" gods and distinct personal gods, such momentary gods can always be created anew. If this view is correct, we must conceive of the nature gods and nature demons not as personifications of universal forces or processes of nature but as mythical objectivizations of particular impressions. The more indeterminate and intangible these impressions are—the less they seem to fit into the "natural" process as a whole—the less prepared is consciousness for their incursion and the greater the elemental power they exert on it. Folk beliefs show that this primordial force of the mythical imagination is still alive and active. In it is rooted the belief in the vast throng of nature demons who dwell in field and meadow, thicket and wood. In the rustling of the leaves, the murmuring and roaring of the wind, and the play and sparkle of the sunlight, in a thousand indefinable voices and tones the life of the forest first becomes perceptible to the mythical consciousness as the immediate manifestation of the innumerable elemental spirits who inhabit the woods: the woodsprites and elves, the spirits of tree and wind.

But the development of the wood and field cults shows us step by step how myth gradually grows beyond these figures, how without ever abandoning them entirely it adds other spirits arising from different spheres of thought and feeling. The world of the mere elemental spirits gives way to a new world as the I passes from mere emotional reaction to the stage of action, as it comes to see its relation to nature no longer through the medium of mere impression but through the medium of its own action. It is from the rule of this action, from its cyclical phases, that the reality of nature obtains its true content and fixed formation. The transition to agriculture, to a regulated tilling of the fields, represents a crucial turning point in the development of the vegetation myths and cults. Here again, it is true, man does not at once confront nature as a free subject but feels himself inwardly enmeshed in it, at one with its destinies. Its growth and passing away, its flowering and fading, are intimately bound up with his own living and dying. All great vegetation rites rest on the feeling of this bond, which they express not only in mythical images but also in immediate action: The withering and revival of the plant world is represented as a drama, a δρώμενον.[51] And this idea of interwoven destinies lives on in other beliefs. The family and the individual have their tree of birth and destiny the thriving or withering of which decides their sickness or health, life or death. But beyond this mere belonging-together, this half-physical, half-mythical bond, a new form of bond arises between man and nature. It is not only in his *condition* that man feels connected with some particular being in nature as a whole; he also draws

51. Cf. above, pp. 188 ff.

nature directly into the sphere of his *work*. Just as man's "demon" gradually becomes his tutelary spirit, his "genius," so in nature the elemental ghosts are transformed into guardian spirits. Folk belief has preserved these figures down to our own day. "The *Holzfräulein* in Thuringia and Franconia," writes Mannhardt, "the *wilde Leute* in Baden, and the *Saligen* in Tyrol help the workers at harvest time. *Holzweiber* and *Waldmännchen, Fanggen, Salinge* . . . are forever serving man, caring for the cattle and conferring their blessings on stable and storeroom." [52] That these ever lifelike figures belong to a typical and fundamental intuition of mythical thought and feeling, that they are a necessary part of a certain phase of it, is shown by a comparison with the "occupational" gods which we can follow from the faith of primitive peoples down to the great religions. Among the Jorubas, where a totemic organization prevails, each clan has a family god from whom it is descended and whose commands regulate the whole course of its life. But side by side with this organization and relatively independent of it there is a kind of caste organization of the gods. The warriors, the smiths, the hunters, the woodworkers, regardless of what totem they may belong to, worship a common god, to whom they offer sacrifices. This technical differentiation, this "division of labor" within the mythical world, is carried through in detail: there is a god of blacksmiths and brassfounders, a god of tinsmiths who is said to have bequeathed a certain type of alloy to men.[53] But this idea of occupational gods, each of whom is assigned and in a manner of speaking confined to a special sphere of activity, was developed with the greatest precision in the religion of the Romans. Here every action and particularly every activity necessary to the cultivation of the fields has its own god and its own organized priesthood. The pontifices see to it that in each of these acts the god who is regarded as its guardian is called by his right name and that the gods as a whole are invoked in their proper order. Without this regulation the activity would itself be unregulated and consequently fruitless.

For all actions and conditions special gods are created and clearly named; and it is not merely the actions and conditions as a whole

52. Mannhardt, *Wald- und Feldkulte* (2d ed.), *1*, 153 ff.

53. See Frobenius, *Und Afrika sprach,* pp. 154 ff., 210 ff. Such occupational gods are found elsewhere as well, among the Haida, e.g. Cf. John R. Swanton, *Contribution to the Ethnology of the Haida,* Memoirs of the American Museum of Natural History, Vol. *8,* No. 1 (New York, 1905).

which are deified in this way, but also any segments, acts, or moments of them that are in any way conspicuous. . . . In the agricultural sacrifice the Flamines had to invoke twelve gods in addition to Tellus and Ceres, and these twelve corresponded to as many actions of the tiller of soil: Veruactor for the first breaking of the fallow field (*veruactum*), Reparator for the second ploughing, Inporcitor for the third and final ploughing in which the furrows (*lirae*) were drawn and the ridges (*porcae*) thrown up, Insitor for the sowing, Oberator for the ploughing over after the sowing, Occator for the harrowing, Saritor for the weeding (*sarire*) with the hoe, Subruncinator for the pulling out of the weeds, Messor for the reaping, Convector for the transportation of the grain from the fields, Conditor for the garnering, Promitor for the giving out of the grain from granary and barn.[54]

This building up of the divine world from the particular impulses and directions of man's activity discloses the same form of objectivization as we found in language. Like the phonetic image the mythical image serves not solely to designate already existing differences but also to fixate them for consciousness, to make them visible as such: it does not merely reproduce existing distinctions but in the strict sense of the word *evokes* distinctions.[55] Consciousness arrives at a clear division between the different spheres of activity and between their divergent objective and subjective conditions only by referring each of these spheres to a fixed center, to one particular mythical figure. It is true that this invocation of a special god as guardian or helper presiding over each particular activity suggests a failure to recognize any "spontaneity" of action; all action seems to be regarded as a mere "manifestation" of the god, hence as something coming from without rather than from within. Yet, on the other hand, it is through this medium of the occupational god that action, which might otherwise be forgotten in favor of its mere product, is apprehended in its pure spirituality. Through its various mythical exponents it gradually comes to be known and understood. In the multiplicity of his gods man does not merely behold the outward diversity of natural objects and forces but also perceives himself in the concrete diversity and distinction of his functions. The countless gods he makes for himself guide him not only through the sphere of objective reality and change but above all through the sphere of

54. Usener, *Götternamen*, pp. 75 ff. For the Roman gods of the *indigitamenta* cf. Wissowa, *Religion und Kultus der Römer*, pp. 24 ff.
55. Cf. *1*, 106 ff.

his own will and accomplishment, which they illumine from within. He becomes aware of the trend peculiar to each concrete activity only by viewing it objectively in the image of the special god belonging to it. Action is differentiated into distinct independent functions not through abstract, discursive concept formation but by the contrary process, wherein each of these functions is apprehended as an intuitive whole and embodied in an independent mythical figure.

The content of this process is most clearly shown by the progress of the mythical consciousness from mere nature myths to culture myths. Here the question of origins shifts more and more from the sphere of *things* to the specifically human sphere: the form of mythical causality serves to explain the origin not so much of the world or particular objects in it as of human cultural achievements. True, in accordance with the style of mythical thinking this explanation stops at the view that these benefits were not created through the power and will of man but were given him. They are regarded not as produced by man but as received by him in a state of completion. The use of fire, the ability to fashion certain tools, farming and hunting, the knowledge of certain medicaments, the invention of writing: all these appear as gifts of mythical powers. Here again man understands his activity only by removing it from himself and projecting it outward; and from this projection arises the figure of the god, no longer as a mere power of nature but as a culture-hero, a bringer of light and salvation.[56] These saviors are the first concrete mythical expression of the awakening cultural *self-consciousness*. In this sense the *cult* becomes a vehicle of all cultural development, for it fixates the very factor by which culture differs from all purely technical mastery of nature and by which it evinces its specific, peculiarly spiritual character. Religious worship does not simply follow practice; rather it is this worship which frequently gave man his practical knowledge—as for example in the use of fire.[57] In all probability the domestication of animals developed on a mythical-religious foundation of a very definite kind, that is, chiefly on a totemistic basis. Here the world of mythical images, like that of language or art, serves as one of the basic instruments by which the I "comes to grips" with the world. In this process the figure of the god or culture-hero intervenes, as it were, between the I and the world, at the same time bringing them together and differentiating

56. For the significance and distribution of this idea of the "salvation bringers" cf. Kurt Breysig, *Die Entstehung des Gottesgedankens und der Heilbringer* (Berlin, 1905).

57. Cf. Wilhelm Bousset, *Das Wesen der Religion* (Halle, 1904), pp. 3, 13.

them. For the I, man's true "self," finds itself only through the detour of the divine I. The passing of the god from the form of the mere special god, confined to a narrowly limited sphere of activity, to that of the personal god signifies a new step on the road to the intuition of free subjectivity as such. "From the mass of the special gods," writes Usener,

> personal gods of more inclusive scope arise only when the old concept has frozen into a proper name and has become a fixed nucleus around which mythical intuitions can cluster. . . . Only in the proper name does the fluid intuition solidify into a hard core that can become the vehicle of a personality. This name, like the name of a man, makes it necessary to think of a definite personality to which it exclusively applies. With this the path is opened by which a flood of anthropomorphic intuitions can pour into an almost empty form. Only now does the concept acquire corporeity, flesh and blood as it were. It can act and suffer like a man. The representations which were self-evident predicates for the transparent concept of the special god become myths for the bearer of a proper name.[58]

However, even if we accept its general methodic presupposition—the thoroughgoing reciprocal relation between language formation and myth formation—this theory contains an unsolved difficulty and a peculiar paradox. For Usener, myth rises from the mere "special gods" to personal gods by the same path which language takes in its progress from the designation of the particular to that of the universal. In both cases, he holds, the same process of "abstraction," the same progress from particular perceptions to generic concepts, takes place. But how are we to account for the fact that precisely this turn to the universal, this trend toward generalizing abstraction, should give us the individualization, the determination, of a "personal god"? How can a process which is objectively manifested in a progressive turning away from spatial and temporal particulars lead subjectively to the particularity and uniqueness of the person? There must be another factor which operates in a direction opposed to that of generalizing concept formation. And indeed the progress from the particular to the general in the world of action and in the structure of inner experience is something different from what it is in the structure of outward reality, in the formation of the world of things. As the sphere of action apprehended and designated in the form of a special god broadens and takes in

58. Usener, Götternamen, pp. 323, 331 ff.

an ever greater diversity of objects, an increased emphasis is given to the pure energy of action as such, to the consciousness of the active subject. This consciousness, it is true, still manifests itself in particular modes and forms of action, but it is no longer confined to them and no longer exhausts itself in them. Thus the feeling of the determinacy of the *personality* does not vanish with the gradual detachment from the particularity of the activity but rather is intensified by it. The I now knows and apprehends itself—not as a mere abstraction, not as something impersonal and universal that stands above and behind all particular activities, but as a concrete unity, identical with itself, which links and binds together all the different trends of action. Over against this identical entity as the constant foundation of action the particular creation seems merely "accidental," because it is never more than a partial fulfillment of the I. Now we can understand that as the "specialized god" rises above his original narrow sphere he becomes a medium through which the personality takes on clearer form and evolves more freely. According to traditional logic, any increase in the extension of a concept implies in the mere intuition of things an impoverishment of its intension: the more particular representations the concept embraces, the more it loses in concrete determinacy. Here, however, extension to a larger field signifies an increase in the intensity and consciousness of the action itself. For the unity of the personality can be intuited only through its opposite, through the manner in which it manifests and asserts itself in a concrete multiplicity of forms of action. The further mythical feeling and thinking progress in this direction, the more distinctly the figure of a supreme *creator god* is singled out from among the mere specialized gods and from the throng of individual polytheistic gods. In him all the diversity of action seems, as it were, concentrated in a single summit: the mythical-religious consciousness is now oriented not toward an aggregate, an infinite number of particular creative powers, but toward the pure act of creation itself, which like the creator is apprehended as one. And this new intuition drives the religious consciousness toward the idea of a unitary *subject* of creation.

The idea of a creator, it is true, is one of those fundamental motifs of myth, which as such would seem to require and allow of no further derivation or explanation. We sometimes seem to encounter surprisingly clear expressions of this conception in very primitive stages of religious thinking, particularly in the totemistic sphere. Here we often encounter the idea of a supreme being above and distinct from the totemic ancestors to which the clan traces its origin. This being is viewed as the original source of the things of nature and also of the sacred rites, the cult ceremonies and dances. He himself, however, has usually ceased to be an object of the cult; and man no longer enters into a direct magic relationship with him as with the various demonic powers which fill the world as a whole.[59] Thus, amid the affective and voluntative motifs which dominate all primitive religion and give it its characteristic imprint, we would seem, even in the earliest stages, to find a purely logical, theoretical motif. On closer scrutiny, however, we find that the seemingly abstract conception of "creation" and the "creator" is here never apprehended in true universality but that creation can be conceived, if at all, only as some particular and concrete variety of formation. Thus the Australian Baiame (Bäjämi), who is often cited as a typical example of the "creator idea" among primitive peoples, is thought of as the carver of things: he produces particular objects as one might fashion a figure from bark or a shoe from the skin of an animal.[60] The idea of creation is based wholly on the activity of the artisan, the builder—and even philosophy, even Plato, can apprehend the supreme creator god only through the mythical image of the demiurge. In Egypt the god Ptah was worshiped as the great god of the primal beginning, as the first god; yet in his actions he seems comparable to the human artist and is looked upon as the protector of artists and artisans. His attribute is the potter's wheel, with which as creator god he fashioned both god and man.[61] But through these concrete specialized actions mythical-religious thinking gradually advanced toward its universal conception of action. At an early period of the Vedic religion we find side by side with the pure nature gods other deities which represent special spheres and types of action. Beside Agni as god of fire and Indra as the storm god there is, for example, an "instigator god" (Savitar) who awakens all motion in nature and human life, a "gatherer god" who helps in the harvest, a "retriever god" (Nivarta, Nivartana) who provides for the return of lost cattle, etc. Concerning such gods Oldenberg remarks,

59. For the distribution of the belief in a creator in the primitive religions, see the compilation of material in Schmidt, *Der Ursprung der Gottesidee.* See also the excellent summary in Söderblom, *Das Werden des Gottesglaubens,* pp. 114 ff. For the American religions see Preuss, "Die höchste Gottheit bei den kulturarmen Völkern," *Psychologische Forschung,* 2 (1922), 161–208.

60. Cf. Brinton, pp. 74, 123.

61. Cf. Brugsch, *Religion und Mythologie,* p. 113; Erman, *Ägyptische religion,* p. 20.

In every epoch of the history of language we find side by side with elements of word formation which are no longer effective and which have been preserved only in finished forms inherited from the past others which are in full vitality and which can be used by every speaker to create new words; similarly, from the standpoint of religious history, we must, for the Vedic period and that immediately preceding it, impute extreme vitality to the method of creating gods by means of the suffix *tar*. There is a god Tratar ("Protector"), a Dhatar ("Maker"), a Netar ("Leader"); and there are corresponding feminine forms, the goddesses Varutrit ("Female Guardians") etc.[62])

To be sure, the freedom with which this suffix connoting the central idea of action and agent is used to create new names of gods involves the risk of an almost unlimited fragmentation in the intuition of action itself; but on the other hand, formations of this kind point, through their common linguistic form, to a universal function of action itself, independent of any particular aim and object of action. Thus in the Vedic religion those formations, analogous to the above group, which designate a particular god as the "lord" over a certain sphere—i.e. "Lord of Progeny" (Prajapati), "Lord of the Field," "Lord of the Dwelling," "Lord of Thinking," or of truth, etc.—serve ultimately to subordinate all these different spheres of domination to a single supreme ruler. In the Brahmana period the "Lord of Progeny," Prajapati, who at first was a specialized god like the others, became the true world creator. Now he is the "God in all the spaces of the world." At one stroke he has transformed earth and heaven, transformed the worlds, the poles, and the realm of light; he has dissolved the mesh of the world order: "He beheld it and became it, for he was it." [63]

And in other respects as well the Vedic texts enable us to see the diverse mediations which mythical-religious thinking requires before it can arrive at the conception of the creation and creator of the world. To place being as a whole under the category of creation is at first impossible for myth. Wherever it speaks of the origin of things, the birth of the cosmos, it interprets this birth as a mere transformation. It always presupposes a definite substratum, usually of

62. Oldenberg, *Religion des Veda* (2d ed.), pp. 60 ff.

63. Cf. Paul Deussen, *Die Geheimnisse des Veda, ausgewählte Texte der Upanishad's* (Leipzig, 1907), pp. 14 ff. On the history of the Prajapati see Deussen, "Allgemeine Einleitung und Philosophie des Veda," pp. 181 ff.

a wholly sensuous nature, from which change starts and in which it takes place. It is the cosmic egg or the tree of the worlds or the lotus blossom or the organs of a human or animal body from which the different parts of the cosmos are produced and formed. In Egypt an egg first issues from Nun, the primordial water; from the egg in turn emerges the god of light, Ra, the sun god. He came into being before there were any heavens or living creatures; no one was with him in the place where he was, and he found no place on which he could stand.[64] This shows, on the one hand, that in order to take determinate form the mythical idea of creation must cling to some concrete substratum, but that, on the other hand, it seeks more and more to negate this substratum, to tear itself away from it. We find a progressive series of such negations in the famous hymn of the Rigveda.

> The non-existent was not, the existent was not then; air was not, nor the firmament that is beyond. What stirred? Where? Under whose shelter? Was the deep abyss water?
>
> Death was not, immortality was not then; no distinction was there of night and day. That One breathed, windless, self-dependent. Other than That there was nought beyond.[65]

An attempt is made here to find the origin of being in a pure ἄπειρον, an indeterminate "That." And yet, cosmogonic speculation cannot refrain from determining this "That" more closely in some respect and from inquiring after the concrete substructure, the "scaffolding" on which the cosmos arose. Over and over again it was asked what the foundation was on which the creator stood and which served him as a support.

> What was the resting place, what and how constituted was the point of support from which Vishvakarman, the all-beholder, in creating the earth, revealed the heavens by his power? What kind of wood was it, what kind of tree, from which they carved heaven and earth? Inquire, ye wise men, in your minds whereon he supported himself when he held heaven and earth.[66]

The later philosophical doctrine of the Upanishads attempted to solve the question of the *prima materia,* the πράτη ὕλη of creation, by eliminat-

64. Erman, *Ägyptische Religion* (2d ed.), pp. 20, 32.
65. Rigveda, x, 129. Eng. trans. by Thomas, p. 127.
66. Rigveda, x, 81.

ing its logical presuppositions. In the idea of Brahma as the one-and-all the opposition of matter and form vanishes along with all other oppositions. But where the religious development takes a different path, where in place of this pantheistic dissolution of oppositions we find the idea of a creator worked out purely and clearly as such, the striving becomes more and more pronounced to transfer this idea to another dimension, as it were, to free it from the taint of the physical-material world and give it a purely spiritual imprint. This progress can be followed through the notions of the means by which the creator called the world into existence. At first the description of these means is limited to certain sensuous-material analogies. The oldest Egyptian texts tell us that Tum-Ra, the creator god, formed the gods, who are the original ancestors of all living creatures, in a human manner by an emission of sperm, or that he spat the first pair of gods from his mouth. But very early another more "spiritual" view emerges in the Pyramid Texts. The act of creation is no longer designated by a single material image; now the creator uses no instrument other than the power of his will, which is concentrated in that of his voice and his *word*. The word forms the power which produces the gods themselves, which produces heaven and earth.[67] Once language and word are thus conceived as instruments of world creation, the act of creation itself acquires a new, purely spiritual significance. Between the world as the aggregate of physical-material things and the divine power contained in the creator's word an immediate transition is no longer possible: the two belong to separate regions of being. The relation which religious thinking nevertheless demands between the two must accordingly be

67. Cf. Moret, *Mystères Égyptiens*, pp. 114 ff., 138 ff.: "A Héliopolis on enseignait, aux plus anciennes époques, que Torum-Râ avait procréé les dieux, ancêtres de tous les êtres vivants, à la façon humaine, par une émission de sémence; ou qu'il s'était levé sur le site du temple du Phénix à Héliopolis et qu'il y avait craché le premier couple divin. D'autres dieux, qualifiés aussi démiurges, avaient employé ailleurs d'autres procédés: Phtah à Memphis, Hnoum à Eléphantine modelaient sur un tour les dieux et les hommes: Thot-Ibis couvait un oeuf à Hermopolis; Neith, la grande déesse de Saïs, était le vautour, ou la vache, qui enfanta le Soleil Râ alors que rien n'existait. Ce sont là sans doute les explications les plus anciennes et les plus populaires de la création. Mais une façon plus subtile et moins matérielle d'énoncer que le monde est une émanation divine, apparaît dès les textes des Pyramides: la Voix du Démiurge y devient un des agents de la création des êtres et des choses. . . . Il résulte de cela que pour les Egyptiens cultivés de l'epoque pharaonique et des milliers d'années avant l'ère chrétienne, le Dieu était *conçu comme une Intelligence et comme instrument de création.* . . . Par la théorie du Verbe créateur et révélateur les écrits hermétiques n'ont fait que rajeunir une idée ancienne en Egypte, et qui fasait partie essentielle du vieux fonds de la culture intellectuelle, religieuse et morale." Cf. also my study, *Sprache und Mythos*, pp. 38 ff.

an indirect relation, dependent on definite mediating links and leading through them. In order to create and express this relation a new dividing line must be drawn through being as a whole; the physical existence of things must be given as its foundation a new purely ideal form of being. This motif attained its truly spiritual development only in the field of philosophy, in the creation myth of Plato's *Timaeus*. But it also developed independently of philosophy purely from the sources and problems of religion, and of this the history of religion provides a striking and characteristic example. Apart from Jewish monotheism, it was the Persian religion which gave the category of creation its most determinate form and which developed the purest conception of the creator as a spiritual and ethical personality. The creed of the Iranian religion begins with an invocation of the supreme ruler, Ahura Mazda, who brought forth all being and all order, who brought forth heaven and earth by virtue of his "holy spirit" and his "good thinking." But the creation which here arises from the primal source of thought and spirit remains at first wholly confined within it. The material cosmos does not issue directly from the divine will; what is first created is its purely spiritual *form*. Ahura Mazda's first creative act calls forth not the sensuous but the "intelligible" world. During the first great period of three thousand years the world remains in this immaterial, luminous, spiritual state, and only then, on the basis of its already existing forms, is it remade in sensuous and perceptible shape.[68]

If we survey the whole series of mythical-religious conceptions leading from the diverse "specialized gods," all of whom are limited to a closely circumscribed sphere of action, down to the spiritual and absolute activity of the one creator god, we find once again that the usual view of the anthropomorphic character of this process is inadequate—that it demands a reversal in its decisive point. For man does not simply transfer his own finished personality to the god or simply lend him his own feeling and consciousness of himself: it is rather through the figure of his gods that man first *finds* this self-consciousness. Through the medium of his intuition of god he succeeds in detaching himself as an active subject from the mere content and material product of action. The idea of "creation from nothing," to which pure monotheism ultimately rises and in which the category of creation first acquires its truly fundamental formulation may from the standpoint of theoretical thinking represent a paradox, even an antinomy; but from the religious point of view it nevertheless signifies

68. Cf. Junker, pp. 127 ff.; Darmesteter, pp. 19 ff., 117 ff.

an ultimate and supreme achievement, because in it the stupendous abstracting power of the religious spirit, which must negate and destroy the being of things in order to arrive at the being of pure will and pure action, comes to full and unlimited expression.

And in yet another direction we can see how the consciousness of action demands that the mere objective product of action recede, as it were, into the distance, that it more and more lose its sensuous immediacy. In the first stages of the magical world view scarcely any tension is felt to exist between the simple desire and the object toward which it is directed. Here an immediate power inheres in the wish itself, a power which suffices to intensify its expression in the extreme in order to release an efficacy which of itself leads to the attainment of the desired goal. All magic is permeated with this belief in the practical power of human wishes, this faith in the "omnipotence of thought." [69] And this belief constantly gains new nourishment from man's experience in the field of action that is closest to him: in the influence he exerts on his own body, on the movements of his limbs. For the theoretical analysis of the concept of causality this influence—which would seem to be directly experienced and felt—will itself become a problem. That my will moves my arm (declares Hume) is in no way more comprehensible than if it could stop the moon in its course. But the magical view reverses this relation: because my will moves my arm, there is an equally certain and equally understandable connection between it and all other happenings in "outward" nature. For the mythical view, which is characterized precisely by the fact that it makes no sharp division between objective spheres and is not impelled toward a causal analysis of the elements of reality, [70] this inference has compelling force. Here are needed no middle links which lead from the beginning to the end of the process of causality in a definitely ordered sequence; in the beginning, in the mere act of will, consciousness immediately apprehends the end, the result and product of the willing, and links the two together. Only as the two factors gradually move apart does a separating medium intervene between wish and fulfillment, and with it awakens the consciousness of a necessary "means" which the desired purpose requires for its realization.

But even where such intermediation is actually present in considerable

69. Cf. above, p. 194.
70. Cf. above, pp. 40 ff.

measure, it is not at once recognized as such by consciousness. Even after man has passed from a magical to a technical relation to nature, even after he has learned the necessity and the use of certain primitive implements, for a while these implements retain for him a magical character and efficacy. To the simplest tools man attributes an independent form of efficacy peculiar to them, a certain inherent demonic power. The Pangwe of Spanish Guinea believe that part of man's vital force enters into the implement he has fashioned and that this force can now continue to operate independently.[71] This belief in the magic inherent in certain tools or weapons is found all over the world. The activity performed by means of these implements requires certain magic supports without which it cannot wholly succeed. When the Zuñi women kneel beside their stone baking trough to prepare bread, they intone a song which contains many little imitations of the sound made by the milling stone; they believe that when this is done the implement will do its work better.[72] Thus the veneration and cult of certain favored tools and implements forms an important factor in the development of both religious consciousness and technical culture. At the annual ewe festival of the yam harvest sacrifices are still offered to all sorts of tools and instruments, to the axe, the plane, the saw, and the bell.[73] Although from a purely genetic standpoint magic and technology cannot be differentiated, although it is not possible to indicate a definite moment in the development of mankind when the change took place from the magical to the technical mastery of nature, nevertheless the use of the implement as such constitutes a decisive turning point in the progress of the spiritual self-consciousness. The opposition between "inner" and "outward" world now begins to be more strongly accentuated: the limits between the world of desire and the world of reality begin to stand out more clearly. The one no longer intervenes directly in the other; the two worlds have ceased to merge; through the intuition of the mediating object that is given in the implement there gradually develops a consciousness of mediated action. In his *Philosophie der Religion* Hegel characterizes the most general antithesis between magical and technical

71. See Günther Tessmann, "Religionsformen der Pangwe," *Zeitschrift für Ethnologie, 41* (1909), 876.

72. Otis T. Mason, *Woman's Share in Primitive Culture* (London, 1895), p. 176, quoted in Karl Bücher, *Arbeit und Rhythmus* (2d ed. Leipzig, 1899), pp. 343 ff.

73. Spieth, *Die Religion der Eweer in Süd-Togo,* p. 8.

action. "The very first form of religion, which we call magic is this," he
writes:

> the spiritual is the power over nature, but this spiritual does not yet
> exist as spirit, it does not yet exist in its universality, but is only the
> particular, accidental, empirical self-consciousness of man, who in his
> self-consciousness, although it is mere yearning, knows himself to be
> higher than nature—who knows that it is a power over nature. . . .
> This power is a *direct* power over nature in general and not com-
> parable with the indirect power which we exert through tools on
> natural objects in particular. The power which the educated man ex-
> erts on particular natural things presupposes that he has stepped back
> from this world, that the world has acquired outwardness with respect
> to him, to which outwardness he accords an *independence* and qualita-
> tive determinations and laws of its own, that these things are relative
> to one another in their qualitative determinacy and stand to one an-
> other in diverse relationships. . . . For this it is necessary that man be
> *free in himself;* only when he himself is free does he allow the outside
> world, other men and the things of nature, to be independent.[74]

But this standing off of man from objects, which forms the presupposition
of his own inner freedom, does not take place only in the "educated," purely
theoretical consciousness; the first germinal beginning of it is disclosed
even in the mythical world view. For as soon as man seeks to influence
things not by mere image magic or name magic but through implements,
he has undergone an inner crisis—even if, for the present, this influence
still operates through the customary channels of magic. The omnipotence
of the mere desire is ended: action is now subject to certain objective
conditions from which it cannot deviate. It is in the differentiation of these
conditions that the outward world first takes on a determinate existence
and articulation. Originally the world consists for him solely of what
in some way touches his desire and his action. But now that a barrier is
erected between the inward and outward worlds, a barrier that prevents
any immediate leap from the sensory urge to its fulfillment, now that
more and more intermediary steps are interpolated between the drive and
its goal, a true distance between subject and object is for the first time
achieved. Man now differentiates a set sphere of objects which are desig-

74. Hegel, "Die Naturreligion," Pt. I of *Vorlesungen über die Philosophie der Religion,*
in *Sämtliche Werke* (26 vols. Stuttgart, F. Frommans, 1927–40), *15,* 283 ff.

nated precisely by the fact that they have a content peculiar to themselves, by which they resist man's immediate desire. It is the consciousness of the means indispensable for the attainment of a certain purpose that first teaches man to apprehend "inner" and "outward" as links in a *chain of causality* and to assign to each of them its own inalienable place within this chain—and from this consciousness gradually grows the empirical-concrete intuition of a material world with objective attributes and states. It is only from the intermediation of action that there results the articulation of being, by virtue of which it is divided into separate, mutually related and dependent elements.

Thus we see that even if we regard the implement purely in its technical aspect as the fundamental means of building material culture, this achievement, if it is to be truly understood and evaluated in its profoundest meaning, may not be considered in isolation. To its mechanical function there corresponds here again a purely spiritual function which not only develops from the former, but conditions it from the very first and is indissolubly correlated with it. Never does the implement serve simply for the mastery of an outside world which can be regarded as finished, simply given "matter"; rather, it is through the use of the implement that the image, the spiritual, ideal form of this outside world, is created for man. The formation of this image and the articulation of its elements does not depend on mere passive sense impression or mere "receptivity" of intuition; it issues rather from the mode and trend of the effect which man exerts on objects. In his *Philosophie der Technik* Ernest Kapp coined the term "organ projection" to characterize this process. He refers to the fact that all primitive tools are primarily an extension of the action which man exerts on things with his own organs or limbs. It is in particular the natural implement of the hand—according to Aristotle the ὄργανον τῶν ὀργάνων —which becomes a model for most artificial implements. Primitive hand tools—hammer, hatchet, ax, knife, chisel, drill, saw, and tongs—are in form and function mere continuations of the hand, whose strength they increase, and hence another manifestation of what the organ as such accomplishes and signifies. But from these primitive implements the concept rises to the implements of the specialized trades, to the machines of industry, to weapons, to the instruments and apparatus of art and science, in short to all the artifacts which serve any need belonging to the realm of mechanical technics. In all of them the technical analysis of their structure and the historical study of their origin can disclose definite factors by which they are connected with the natural articulation of the human body. And now this mechanism, which in the beginning was built quite unconsciously after the organic model, can in turn serve, by a reversal of the process, as a means of explaining and understanding the human organism. Through the implements and artifacts which he builds man learns to understand the nature and structure of his own body. He understands his own physiology only in the reflection of what he has fashioned; the type of intermediary tools which he has made opens up to him a knowledge of the laws which govern the structure of his body and the physiological achievement of his organs. But this does not yet exhaust the central and most profound significance of organ projection, a fact which becomes evident only when we consider that here again a spiritual process runs parallel to man's increasing knowledge of his own physical organization, that man arrives at himself, at his self-consciousness, only through this knowledge. Each new implement that man finds signifies a new step, not only toward the formation of the outside world but toward the formation of his self-consciousness. For

> on the one hand every tool in the wider sense of the word is a means of increasing man's sensory activity and as such his only possibility of passing beyond the immediate superficial perception of things, while on the other hand, as a product of the activity of brain and hand, it is so essentially and intimately related to man himself that in the creation of his hand he perceives something of his own being, his world of ideas embodied in matter, a reflection and copy of his inwardness, in short, a part of himself. . . . Such a survey of this outward field, which encompasses the totality of man's instruments of culture, is a self-confession of human nature, and through the act of retrieving the copy from outside us and restoring it to our inwardness, it becomes self-knowledge.[75]

The fundamental argument of the philosophy of Symbolic Forms has shown that the concept which Kapp designates as "organ projection" holds a meaning which extends far beyond the technical mastery and knowledge of nature. While the philosophy of technology deals with the immediate and mediated bodily organs by which man gives the out-

---

75. Ernest Kapp, *Grundlinien einer Philosophie der Technik* (Braunschweig, G. Westermann, 1877), pp. 25 ff., 29 ff., 40 ff. Cf. Ludwig Noiré, *Das Werkzeug und seine Bedeutung für die Entwicklungsgeschichte der Menschheit* (Mainz, 1880), pp. 53 ff.

side world its determinate form and imprint, the philosophy of Symbolic Forms is concerned with the totality of spiritual expressive functions. It regards them not as copies of being but as trends and modes of formation, as "organs" less of mastery than of signification. And here again the operation of these organs takes at first a wholly unconscious form. Language, myth, art—each produces from itself its own world of forms which can be understood only as expressions of the spontaneity of the spirit. But because this spontaneous activity is not carried out in the form of free reflection, it is hidden from itself. In creating its mythical, artistic forms the spirit does not recognize itself in them as a creative principle. Each of these spheres becomes for it an independent "outward" world. Here it is not so much the case that the I is reflected in things, the microcosm in the macrocosm, as that the I creates for itself a kind of opposite in its own products which seem to it wholly objective. And it can contemplate itself only in this kind of projection. In this sense the mythical gods signify nothing other than successive self-revelations of the mythical consciousness. Where this consciousness is still wholly confined to and dominated by the moment, where it simply succumbs to every momentary impulse and stimulus, the gods, too, are enclosed in this merely sensuous present, this *one* dimension of the moment. And only very gradually, as the spheres of action broaden, as the drive ceases to exhaust itself in a single moment and a single object but prospectively and retrospectively embraces a number of different motives and different actions, does the sphere of divine action acquire diversity, breadth, and depth. It is first of all the objects of nature which in this way move apart—which are sharply differentiated for consciousness by virtue of the fact that each of them is taken as an expression of a special divine power, the self-revelation of a god or demon. But although the array of particular gods that can arise in this way may be extended indefinitely, it contains the germ of a limitation in content; for all the diversity, all the differentiation and fragmentation, of divine action ceases as soon as the mythical consciousness considers this action no longer from the standpoint of the objects to which it extends but from the standpoint of its origin. The diversity of mere action now becomes a unity of creation, in which the unity of the creative principle becomes more and more clearly discernible.[76] And to this concept of the transforma-

76. How this tendency is gradually realized even in the polytheistic religions can be seen in that of the Egyptians. In the midst of the deifications of natural powers, which people the Egyptian pantheon, we find at an early period a trend toward the idea of the One God,

tion of the god corresponds a new view of man and his spiritual-ethical personality. Over and over again we thus find confirmation of the fact that man can apprehend and know his own being only insofar as he can make it visible in the image of his gods. Just as he learns to understand the structure of his body and limbs only by becoming a creator of tools and products, so he draws from his spiritual creations—language, myth, and art—the objective standards by which to measure himself and learn to understand himself as an independent cosmos with its peculiar structural laws.

---

who "was from the beginning" and who encompasses everything that is and that will be. (Cf. Renouf, *Lectures on the Origin and Growth of Religion,* pp. 89 ff.; Brugsch, *Religion und Mythologie,* p. 99.) A conscious turn to the fundamental ideas of religious unity is found in the well-known reform of King Amenophis IV (*ca.* 1500 B.C.), which to be sure represents only an episode in the history of Egyptian religion. Here all other gods are suppressed and the cult is restricted to the various sun gods, who are all conceived and worshiped merely as different representations of the One Sun God, Aton. In the inscriptions on the tombs at Tel el-Amarna, the old sun gods Horus, Ra, and Tum appear accordingly as parts of the One godhead. Side by side with the old image of the sun god with the hawk's head, there appears another, representing the sun itself as a disk, sending out rays in all directions, with each ray ending in a hand which holds out the symbol of life. And in this symbolism of a new religious universalism the expression of a new ethical universalism, of a new idea of "humanity," can once again be discerned. If one compares the new hymn to the sun that arose in the cult of Aton with the hymns to the old sun god, says Erman, "one cannot fail to note the fundamental difference. Both praise the god as the creator and preserver of the world and of all life. But the new hymn knows nothing of the old names of the sun god, of his crowns, scepters, holy cities. It knows nothing of his ships and sailors and of the dragon Apophis, nothing of the journey through the realm of the dead and the joy of its inhabitants. It is a song which a Syrian or Ethiopian might equally well sing in praise of the sun. And indeed these lands and their inhabitants are mentioned in the hymn as though to put an end to the arrogance of the Egyptians toward the *wretched barbarians.* All men are children of the god; he gave them different colors and languages and placed them in different lands, but he cares for them all alike." Erman, *Ägyptische Religion,* p. 81. Cf. Wiedemann, *Religion der alten Ägypter,* pp. 20 ff.

Chapter 3

Cult and Sacrifice

THE reciprocal relation between man and god that is established in the progress of the mythical and religious consciousness has thus far been regarded essentially in the form which it assumes in the mythical-religious world of ideas. But now we shall seek to broaden this sphere of inquiry; for the religious spirit has its true and deepest root not in the world of ideas but in the world of feeling and will. Every new relationship to reality which man gains expresses itself not solely in his ideas and beliefs but also in his will and action. And herein man's attitude toward the supernatural powers which he worships must inevitably be more clearly manifested than in the figures and images of mythical fantasy. Consequently, we find the true objectivization of the fundamental mythical religious feeling not in the bare image of the gods but in the cult devoted to them. For the cult is man's active relation to his gods. In the cult the divine is not represented and portrayed indirectly; rather, a direct influence is exerted upon it. It is therefore in the forms of this influence, in the forms of ritual, that the immanent progress of the religious consciousness will, in general, be most clearly expressed. The mythical tale is itself for the most part only a reflection of this immediate relationship. It can be clearly shown that a vast number of mythical motifs had their origin in the intuition of a cultic rather than natural process. They go back not to any physical thing or event but to an activity of man, and it is this activity that is explicitly represented in them. A particular process that is repeated over and over in the cult is mythically interpreted and understood by being linked to a unique temporal event and viewed as its reflection. But actually this reflection takes an opposite direction. The action is the beginning; the mythical explanation, the ἱερὸς λόγος, comes later. This explanation merely represents in the form of a narrative what is present as immediate reality in the sacred action. Consequently, the narrative offers no key to an understanding of the cult; it is rather the cult which forms the preliminary stage and objective foundation of myth.[1]

In establishing this relationship through the study of numerous individual cases, modern empirical mythology has merely confirmed an idea which was first formulated in general speculative terms in Hegel's *Philosophie der Religion*. For Hegel the cult and the particular cult form are always the central point for the interpretation of the religious process. In the cult he finds direct confirmation of his view regarding the universal aim and meaning of this process. For if this aim consists in overcoming the separation of the I from the absolute, in a recognition that this attitude is not the truth but is one which knows itself to be invalid, it is precisely the cult which progressively accomplishes this recognition. "To realize this unity, the reconciliation, restoration of the subject, and his self-consciousness, to bring about a positive feeling of participation in that absolute and a unity with it—this transcendence of the separation constitutes the sphere of the cult." [2] Thus, according to Hegel, the cult is to be taken not merely in the restricted sense of a purely outward action but rather as an activity which embraces the inwardness as well as the outward appearance. The cult is, "in general, the eternal process of the subject making itself identical with the essence of its being." For though in cult, to be sure, God appears on the one side and the I, the religious subject, on the other, still its meaning is at once the concrete unity of both, through which the I becomes conscious in God and God in me. Thus, Hegel sees the dialectical order, according to which he develops the various historical religions, confirmed above all in the unfolding of the universal essence of the cult and of its particular forms; the spiritual meaning of every particular religion and what it signifies as a necessary factor in the religious

1. Cf. above, pp. 37 ff. The idea of the "primacy" of cult over myth has been advocated, among modern historians and philosophers of religion, primarily by Smith, *Lectures on the Religion of the Semites*. German trans. by Stübe, pp. 19 ff. Since then, modern ethnological studies have essentially confirmed the view at which Smith arrived through a study of the Semitic religions. Marett goes so far as to call the theory that rite precedes dogma a cardinal truth of ethnology and social anthropology. "The Birth of Humility," in *The Threshold of Religion* (3d ed.), p. 181. Cf. James, *Primitive Ritual and Belief*, p. 215: "Generally speaking, ritual is evolved long before belief, since primitive man is wont to 'dance out his religion.' The savage does not find it easy to express his thoughts in words, and so he resorts to *visual language*. He thinks with his eyes rather than by articulate sounds, and therefore the root feeling of primitive religion is arrived at through an investigation of ritual."

2. Hegel, *Vorlesungen über die Philosophie der Religion, Werke, 15*, 67.

process as a whole are completely represented only in its cult forms, in which this meaning finds its outward manifestation.[3]

If this reasoning is sound, the relationship which Hegel seeks to establish on the basis of dialectical construction must also be demonstrable from the opposite angle, namely through purely phenomenological inquiry. A unitary spiritual tendency, a trend toward progressive "inwardness," will be found in the external, sensuous forms of the cult itself, even if for the present we merely view them in their empirical diversity. Here again, we shall be justified in expecting confirmation of that relation between inward and outward which provides the guiding line for the understanding of all spiritual forms of expression, namely that the I finds and learns to know itself through its seeming externalization. We can gain a clear idea of this relation through a fundamental motif which we encounter wherever cult and religious ritual have developed to a certain level. The more determinate the form they assume, the more clearly the *sacrifice* appears at their center. It may take the most diverse forms, it may appear as a gift offering or a purification offering, as an offering of intercession, thanks, or atonement; but in all these forms it constitutes a solid core around which the cult action clusters. Here religious faith attains its true visible guise; here it is transposed directly into action. The sacrificial service is fixed by very definite objective rules, a set sequence of words and acts which must be carefully observed if the sacrifice is not to fail in its purpose. But in the formation and transformation of these purely outward regulations we can observe something else, namely the gradual growth and unfolding of religious subjectivity. In this point the constancy and progress of the language of religious forms are expressed with equal clarity, for here we have a universal, typical, and original form of religious action which can always be filled with new content and which in this way can adapt itself to and express all transformations of religious feeling.

Fundamentally, every sacrifice implies a negative factor: a limitation of sensory desire, a renunciation which the I imposes on itself. Here lies an essential trait of sacrifice, which raises it from the very outset above the level of the magical world view. For originally there is no such self-limitation in the magical world view, which is based on belief in the omnipotence of human desires. In its basic form magic is nothing more than a primitive "technique" of wish fulfillment. In magic the I believes it

3. *Ibid.*, pp. 204 ff.

has an instrument by which to subject all outward being and draw it into its own sphere. Here objects have no independent being; the lower and higher spiritual powers, the demons and gods, have no will of their own which man cannot make subservient to himself by the use of the proper magical means. The magic spell is lord over nature, which it can divert from the fixed rule of its being and its course: "Carmina vel caelo possunt deducere lunam." And it also exerts an unlimited power over the gods, bending them and forcing their will.[4] Thus the power of man in this sphere of feeling and thinking is subject to an empirical limit but in principle is unlimited; the I knows no barrier that it does not strive to leap—sometimes successfully. But in the very first stages of sacrifice we find a different trend of human will and action. For the power imputed to the sacrifice is rooted in the self-renunciation of sacrifice, as can be shown even for very elementary stages of religious development. The asceticism which usually comprises a fundamental part of primitive religious faith and activity is grounded in the intuition that any extension and intensification of the powers of the I involves a corresponding limitation. Every important undertaking must be preceded by abstinence from the satisfaction of certain natural drives. Even today the belief prevails among almost all primitive peoples that no military campaign or hunting or fishing expedition can succeed unless preceded by such ascetic measures as protracted fasting, sleeplessness, or sexual continence. And every crucial change, every crisis, in man's physical-spiritual life requires such safeguards. Anyone about to undergo initiation, particularly into manhood, must previously undergo painful privations and trials.[5] Yet all these forms of renunciation and sacrifice have at first a purely egocentric purpose: by submitting to certain physical privations a man aims merely to strengthen his mana, his physical-magical power and efficacy. Thus we are still entirely within the world of magical thought and feeling; but in the midst of this world a new motif makes its appearance. A man's sensory wishes and desires do not flow equally in all directions; he no longer seeks to transpose them immediately and unrestrictedly into reality; rather he limits them at certain points in order to make the withheld and, one might say, stored-up power free for other purposes. Through this

---

4. Regarding the "compelling names" (ἐπάναγκοι) of the gods in Greek-Egyptian magic cf. Hopfner, *Griechisch-ägyptischer Offenbarungszauber*, pp. 176 ff.

5. See the compilation of ethnological material in Lévy-Bruhl, *Das Denken der Naturvölker*, pp. 200 ff., 312 ff.; Frazer, "The Dying God," *Golden Bough*, Vol. 4, Pt. III, pp. 422 ff.

narrowing of the scope of desire, expressed in the negative acts of asceticism and sacrifice, the content of the desire is raised to its highest concentration and thus to a new form of consciousness. A power opposed to the seeming omnipotence of the I makes itself felt. But this power, by being apprehended as such and by imposing its first limit upon the I, begins for the first time to give it a determinate form. For only when the barrier is felt and known as such is the road opened by which it can progressively be surmounted; only when man recognizes the divine as a power superior to him, which cannot be compelled by magical means but must be propitiated by prayer and sacrifice, does he gradually gain a free feeling of self in confronting it. Here again the self finds and constitutes itself only by projecting itself outward: the growing independence of the gods is the condition for man's discovery in himself of a fixed center, a unity of will, over against the dispersal and diversity of his sensory drives.

This typical trend can be followed in all forms of sacrifice.[6] A new and freer relation of man to the godhead is already revealed in the gift offering, since it is given freely. Here again man withdraws, as it were, from the objects of immediate desire. They cease to be objects of immediate enjoyment and become a kind of religious *means of expression,* the instrumentality of a bond which he creates between himself and the divine. The physical objects themselves thus enter into a new light, for behind what they are in their immediate manifestation as object of perception or as means of immediate sensual satisfaction a universal efficacy is now discernible. Thus in the vegetation rites, for example, the last ear of grain in the field is not harvested like the others but is spared, because in it the power of growth as such, the spirit of the future harvest, is revered.[7] On the other hand, it is true, the gift offering can be followed back to a

6. Here we consider these different forms only according to their ideal significance, as diverse expressions and factors of the unitary "idea" underlying sacrifice. The genetic question as to whether there is an original form of sacrifice from which all others have developed can be disregarded in this formulation of the problem. Very different answers have been given to this question. While Spencer and Tylor regard the "gift offering" as this basic form, others like Jevons and Smith have stressed communion between god and man as the original and decisive factor. The most recent penetrating investigation of the question is that of E. Washburn Hopkins (1923), who comes to the conclusion that a definitive decision in favor of one or the other theory is not possible on the basis of the available empirical material, that we must rather content ourselves with recognizing different, equally fundamental motives of sacrifice. *Origin and Evolution of Religion,* pp. 151 ff. In any case the spiritual "stratification" of these motives here attempted has nothing to do with the question of their empirical-historical origin, their temporal "earlier" or "later."

7. Cf. Mannhardt, *Wald- und Feldkulte* (2d ed.), especially *1,* 212 ff.

stage in which it is still closely interwoven with the magical world view and cannot as an empirical phenomenon be separated from it. Thus, for example, in the sacrifice of horses, which appears in the Vedas as the supreme sacral expression of royal power, the primeval magical elements that enter into it are still unmistakable. Only little by little does this magic sacrifice seem to take on new traits which carry it into the sphere of the gift offering.[8] But even where the form of the gift offering attains its pure development no decisive spiritual transformation seems at first to have taken place, since the magical-sensuous idea of *compulsion* now seems to have been replaced merely by the no less sensuous idea of *exchange*. "Give me, I give to thee; lay down for me, I lay down for thee. Offer me sacrifice, I offer thee sacrifice." Thus does the sacrificer speak to the god in a Vedic formula.[9] In this act of giving and taking it is only a mutual need that links god and man together in equal measure and in the same sense. For just as man here becomes dependent on the god, so does the god become dependent on the man. He is in man's power, his very existence depends on the sacrificial gift. In the Hindu religion the drink offering of soma is the life-giving source from which springs the power of gods as well as men.[10] But here, precisely, we discern the transformation which will lend the gift offering a totally new significance and depth. This transformation occurs as soon as religious contemplation ceases to limit itself exclusively to the *content* of the gift and concentrates instead on the *form of giving,* in which it sees the heart of sacrifice. Man's thinking now progresses from the mere material performance of the sacrifice to its inner motive and determinant. It is only this motive of "veneration" (*upanishad*) that can give the sacrifice its meaning and value. It is above all through this fundamental idea that the speculation of the Upanishads and of Buddhism differs from the ritual-liturgical literature of the earlier Vedas. It is not merely that the gift now becomes inward—it is man's inwardness which now appears as the only valuable and significant religious gift. The vast sacrifices of horses, goats, cattle, and sheep cannot be fruitful: the desired sacrifice—as we read in a Buddhist text—is not that in which all sorts of living creatures are destroyed but one which consists of continuous giving:

8. See the account of this Vedic sacrifice in Oldenberg, *Religion Des Veda* (2d ed.), pp. 317 ff.; and E. Washburn Hopkins, *The Religions of India* (London and Boston, 1895), p. 191.

9. Cf. Oldenberg, p. 314; Hopkins, *Origin and Evolution of Religion*, p. 176.

10. Cf. Oldenberg, *Die Lehre der Upanishaden*, pp. 37, 155 ff.; Hopkins, *Religions of India*, pp. 217 ff.

"Worthy of gifts from those that sacrifice
In this world are the learner and the adept.
They walk upright in body, speech and mind,
A field of merit unto them that give:
And great the fruit of offerings unto them." [11]

In Buddhism, however, this total concentration of the religious mind upon a single point—the salvation of the human soul—has a noteworthy consequence. This radical turning back from outward to inward causes not only the external being and action but even the spiritual-religious counterpole of the I—the gods themselves—to vanish from the center of religious consciousness. Buddhism retains the gods, but with regard to one essential question, that of salvation, they have lost all significance and use. And thus they have been excluded from the truly decisive religious process. Only pure immersion, which does not so much magnify the I into a godhead as extinguish it in nothingness, brings true salvation. Though speculative thought does not shrink from its ultimate conclusion, namely that of destroying the *form* of the self in order to arrive at its *essence,* still it is the basic disposition of the ethical-monotheistic religions to take the opposite path. In them both the human I and the personality of God are developed in full sharpness. But the more clearly the two poles are designated and distinguished, the more evident becomes the opposition and the tension between them. True monotheism does not seek to resolve this tension, for it is the expression and condition of that peculiar dynamic in which monotheism sees the essence of religious life and consciousness. The Prophetic religion also becomes what it is through the same turning inward of the concept of sacrifice that is effected in the Upanishads and in Buddhism. But here this turning inward has a different aim. "To what purpose is the multitude of your sacrifices unto me?" says God in Isaiah. "I am full of the burnt offerings of rams and the fat of fed beasts. . . . Learn to do well, seek judgment, relieve the oppressed, judge the fatherless, plead for the widow" (Isaiah 1:11 ff.). This ethical-social pathos of the Prophetic religion preserves the I through the emphatic opposition of its counterpart, the "thou," through which alone the I truly finds and asserts itself. A purely ethical correlation is established between I and thou, and an equally strict reciprocal bond

11. Anguttara-Nikaya, II, 4. Eng. trans. by F. L. Woodward, *The Book of the Gradual Sayings,* Pali Text Society, Translation Series, Vol. 22 (London, Oxford Univ. Press, 1932), p. 58. Cf. Udana, I, 9. Eng. trans. by Woodward.

between man and God. In characterizing the basic idea of the Prophetic religion Hermann Cohen writes: "It is not before the sacrifice or before the priest that man stands to obtain purity. . . . The correlation is ordained and concluded between man and God, and no other link may be interpolated in it. . . . Any participation by another destroys the uniqueness of God, which is more necessary for redemption than for Creation." [12]

But thus, in its highest religious transfiguration, the gift offering merges with another fundamental aspect of sacrifice. For mediation between the divine and the human may well be called the universal meaning of sacrifice, which is somehow present in all its different forms. Some writers have gone so far as to say that a general concept of sacrifice can be abstracted from a survey of its empirical-historical manifestations and that all sacrifice aims to create a bond between the worlds of the sacred and profane through the middle link of a consecrated thing that is destroyed in the course of the sacred action. [13] But although sacrifice is always characterized by the striving for a connection of this sort, the synthesis effected in it is itself capable of the most diverse gradations. It can pass through all stages and degrees from mere material assimilation up to the highest forms of pure ideal community. And every new means here changes the conception of the goal that stands at its end, since for the religious consciousness it is always the means which determines and forms man's view of the end. In the most elementary view the tension between God and man and the restoration of the common bond between them are interpreted according to the analogy of certain basic *physical* relations. And it is not enough to call this mere analogy; in line with a basic trait of mythical thinking this analogy shifts everywhere into real identity. What originally connects man with the god is a physical bond of common blood. Between the tribe and its god there is an immediate blood relationship: the god is the common ancestor from whom the tribe has sprung. This fundamental intuition extends far beyond the strictly totemistic sphere. [14] Through it the true meaning of sacrifice is determined. And here a definite gradation

12. Cohen, *Die Religion der Vernunft*, p. 236.

13. Cf. Hubert and Mauss, *Mélanges*, p. 124.

14. For the Semitic sphere this has been shown, e.g., by Baudissin. While the principal female deity (Ishtar, Astarte) has a definite natural foundation and while she represents the idea of the *life* that is continuously propagated and reborn from death, the Baalim—according to Baudissin—though they also represent the power of fertility, are above all the fathers and hence the rulers of the tribe that is derived from them through a physical reproductive chain. *Adonis und Esmun*, pp. 25, 39 ff.

seems to lead from the basic forms of totemism up to the animal sacrifices in the highly developed religions. In totemism the totem animal must in general be spared; but there are also cases where, though not eaten by individuals, it is consumed by the clan as a whole at a sacral feast in which definite rites and usages must be observed. This common eating of the totem animal is looked upon as a means of confirming and renewing the blood kinship which unites the individual members of the clan with one another and with their totem. Particularly in times of distress, when the community is endangered and its existence seems threatened, this renewal of its primordial physical-religious power is necessary. But the true accent of the sacral act is on performance by the community as a *whole*. In the eating of the flesh of the totem animal the unity of the clan, its relationship with its totemic ancestor, is restored as a sensuous and corporeal unity; we may say that in this feast it is restored forever anew. The investigations of Robertson Smith seem to have demonstrated that this idea of reinforcing the community of the clan, the idea of man's "communion" with the god who passes as the father of the clan, is one of the fundamental factors in animal sacrifice, particularly among the Semitic peoples.[15] At first this communion can be represented only as purely material; it can only be effected through eating and drinking in common, through the physical enjoyment of one and the same thing. But this very act raises the aim toward which it is directed into a new ideal sphere. The sacrifice is the point not only at which the profane and the sacred touch, but at which they permeate one another indissolubly. Anything that is present in it, in a purely physical sense, and fulfills any function in it has thereby entered the sphere of the sacred, the consecrated. But on the other hand this means that sacrifice is not originally a particular action, sharply distinguished from man's common and profane actions; any action at all, however sensuous and practical its mere content, can become a sacrifice as soon as it enters into the specifically religious "perspective" and is determined by it. In addition to the acts of eating and drinking, the sexual act, particularly, can take on a sacral significance; and even in very advanced stages of religious development we find prostitution as a "sacrifice" in the service of the god. The power of religious feeling is here shown

15. Cf. particularly Smith, *Religion of the Semites*. Trans. by Stübe, pp. 212 ff., 249 ff. The view of sacrifice here set forth is confirmed and amplified by Julius Wellhausen, with special reference to the sources of Arabic religion, in *Reste arabischen Heidentums* (2d ed. Berlin, 1897), pp. 112 ff.

precisely by the fact that it embraces the still undivided *totality* of being and action, that it excludes no sphere of physical-natural existence but rather pervades this existence down to its basic and original elements. Hegel sees in this reciprocal relationship a fundamental characteristic of the pagan cult,[16] but on the other hand research in the history of religion has taught us how this mutual involvement and interweaving of sensuous and spiritual motifs in the notion of sacrifice asserts itself more and more strongly throughout the development of Christianity as of other cults.[17] And while religion gains its concrete and historical efficacy only in such an interweaving of the sensuous and the spiritual, it also encounters a limitation here. For man and God, if there is to be any true unity between them, must in the last analysis be of the same flesh and blood. Thus the spiritualization of the sensuous world through the act of sacrifice results directly in a sensualization of the spiritual world. The sensuous world is destroyed as far as its physical existence is concerned—and only in this annihilation is its religious function fulfilled. Only by being slain and eaten is the sacrificial animal enabled to serve as an intermediary between the individual and his clan and between the clan and its god. But this power is bound up with the practice of the sacramental act in its full sensuous concretion and with all the details and particularities that the ritual prescribes—the slightest deviation and omission therein depriving the sacrifice of its meaning and efficacy.

16. Cf. Hegel *Vorlesungen über die Philosophie der Religion, Werke, 15,* pp. 225 ff.: [In the pagan cult] the cult is already what man conceives as ordinary life; he lives in this substantial unity; cult and life are not differentiated and an absolutely finite world has not yet set itself over against a world of infinity. Thus among the pagans there prevails a consciousness of their happiness, the consciousness that God is close to them as the god of the nation, the city—a feeling that the gods are friendly to them and give them the enjoyment of the best. . . . Here, then, the cult is essentially characterized by the idea that it constitutes not something *peculiar* and separate from the rest of life, but an eternal life in the luminous realm of the good. This *temporal, insufficient* life, this *immediate* life, is itself *cult* and the subject has not yet differentiated his essential life from the maintenance of his temporal life and from the actions he performs for immediate, finite existence. At this stage there must presumably be an express consciousness of his god as such, a rising to the idea of an absolute being and a worshiping of this being. But at first this is an abstract self-contained relationship into which concrete life does not enter. As soon as the cult relationship becomes more *concrete,* it takes the entire *outward reality* of the individual into itself; the entire scope of his common everyday life, eating, drinking, sleeping and all actions for the satisfaction of natural needs, enter into a relation to the cult, and the process of all these actions forms a sacred life.

17. Instead of giving a number of different examples for this I merely refer the reader to the excellent compilation and discussion given by Hermann Usener, "Mythologie," *Archiv für Religionswissenschaft,* 7 (1904), 15 ff.

This is also evident in another important element of the cult, which almost everywhere accompanies sacrifice and which in conjunction with it represents the complete cult action. *Prayer,* like sacrifice, aims to bridge the gulf between God and man. But in prayer the means is not merely physical but symbolic and ideal: the power of the word. And yet, here again, the early mythical-religious consciousness draws no sharp dividing line between the sphere of sensuous *existence* and that of pure *meaning.* The power that resides in prayer is of magical origin and kind: the will of the godhead is compelled by the magical force of the word. This character of prayer is evident in the beginnings and early development of the Vedic religion. Here sacrifice and prayer, when correctly executed, are always endowed with an infallible and irresistible power.[18] The sacred hymns and sayings and the songs and meters mold and govern the objective world; the world process depends on their use, their correct or false application. The priest who sacrifices before sunrise causes the sun god to appear, to be born. All things and all powers are woven into the *one* power of the *brahman,* the word of prayer, which not only surpasses the barriers between man and god but actually tears them down. The Vedic texts expressly state that in the act of sacrifice and prayer the priest himself becomes a god.[19] And again, this fundamental view can be followed down to the beginnings of Christianity: with the Church Fathers the purpose of prayer still appears as the immediate union and fusion of man with God (τὸ ἀνακραθῆναι τῷ πνεύματι).[20] But in its later development prayer gradually passes beyond this magical sphere. Taken in its purely religious sense, prayer now rises above mere human desire. It is directed no longer toward relative and particular *goods,* but toward an objective good that is equated with the will of God. The "philosophical" prayer of Epictetus—who prays the gods to grant him only what is in their own will, who abjures man's arbitrary desire, which he looks upon as futile beside the will of the godhead—has its characteristic parallels in the history of religion.[21] In all this, both sacrifice and prayer prove to be characteristic forms of religious expression. They do not provide a passage

18. Richard Pischel and Karl F. Geldner, *Vedische Studien* (3 vols. Stuttgart, 1889–1901), *I*, 144 ff.

19. Cf. Archibald E. Gough, *The Philosophy of the Upanishads* (London, 1882); Oldenberg, *Die Lehre der Upanishaden,* especially pp. 10 ff.

20. Origen, περὶ εὐχῆς, ch. 10, sec. 2, quoted in Farnell, *The Evolution of Religion* (New York, 1905), p. 228.

21. Cf. Marett, "From Spell to Prayer," *The Threshold of Religion* (3d ed.), pp. 29 ff.; Farnell, pp. 163 ff.

from a previously determined and strictly delimited sphere of the I to the sphere of the divine but rather determine both these spheres and draw progressively new limits between them. In what the religious process designates as the spheres of the divine and the human we have to do not with two provinces of being, rigidly separated at the outset by spatial and qualitative barriers, but with an original form of the movement of the religious spirit, of the permanent attraction and repulsion of its opposite poles. Thus the essential factor in the development of prayer and sacrifice would seem to be not that they are mere media communicating between the extremes of the divine and the human but that they establish the meaning of these two extremes and teach man to find it. Each new form of sacrifice and prayer opens up a new meaning of the divine and the human and a new relation between them. It is the tension that arises between the human and the divine that gives to each of them its actual character and meaning. Thus, prayer and sacrifice do not merely bridge a gulf that existed for the religious consciousness from the beginning; rather, the religious consciousness *creates* this gulf in order to close it: it progressively intensifies the opposition between God and man in order to find in this opposition the means by which to surpass it.

This is made apparent by the reversible character of the movement that here occurs: to its thesis there almost always corresponds a definite and generally equivalent antithesis. The union, the ἕνωσις, between God and man, which forms the aim of prayer and sacrifice, can from the outset be seen and described in two ways: man becomes a god and the god becomes man. In the language of sacrifice this relationship is expressed in a motif which can be followed from the most primitive mythical conceptions and usages to the fundamental forms of our great religions. The meaning of sacrifice is not exhausted by the sacrifice *to* the god: rather, it seems to stand out fully and reveal itself in its true religious and speculative depth where *the god himself* is sacrificed or sacrifices himself. Through the suffering and death of the god, through his entrance into physical finite existence in which he is dedicated to death, this existence is raised to the level of the divine and freed from death. All the great mystery cults revolve around the primordial mystery of this liberation and rebirth, brought about by the death of the god.[22]

This motif of the god's sacrificial death is among the truly elementary

22. Cf. above, pp. 188 ff. For the ethnological material and that drawn from the history of religions cf. the compilation in Frazer, *Golden Bough*, Vol. 4, Pt. III.

mythical-religious ideas of mankind: on the discovery of the New World it was found in the American Indian religions in a form closely resembling that prevailing in Christianity. And the Spanish missionaries could explain the phenomenon only by saying that the sacrificial beliefs of the Aztecs were a diabolical mockery and parody of the Christian mystery of the Eucharist.[23] Indeed, what here distinguishes Christianity from the other religions is not so much the content of the motif as the new, purely spiritual meaning that is gained from it. Yet on the other hand, even the abstract speculations of the medieval Christian doctrine of justification move for the most part in the realm of the traditional old mythical ideas. The doctrine of satisfaction which St. Anselm, for example, develops in his treatise *Cur Deus homo* seeks to give these ideas a purely conceptual, rational-scholastic form by starting from the supposition that man's infinite guilt can be "satisfied" only by an infinite sacrifice, that of God himself. But here medieval mysticism goes one step further. For the mystics the question is no longer how the gulf between God and man can be bridged, for they recognize no such gulf; the whole conception is contrary to their fundamental religious attitude. For them man and God are not mere separate entities; they exist together and for each other. Here God is just as necessarily and immediately dependent on man as man on God. In this respect the mystics of all nations and all times—for example, Jalal ad-din Rumi and Angelus Silesius—speak the same language. "Between us," writes the former, "the thou and the I have ceased. I am not I, thou art not thou, nor art thou I. I am at once I and thou, thou art at once thou and I." [24] Here the religious movement that expressed itself in the transformation and progressive spiritualization of the concept of sacrifice has arrived at its conclusion: what previously seemed a purely physical or ideal *mediation* has now been raised to a pure *correlation,* in which for the first time the specific meaning of both the divine and the human is defined.

23. Cf. Brinton, pp. 190 ff. A "substitute penitential sacrifice" is also found in the Babylonian inscriptions. See Heinrich Zimmern, *Keilschriften und Bibel* (Berlin, 1903), pp. 27 ff.

24. Jalal ad-din Rumi, quatrain. German trans. by Ignác Goldziher, *Vorlesungen über Islam* (Heidelberg, C. Winter, 1910), p. 156.

PART IV

The Dialectic of the Mythical Consciousness

The Dialectic of the Mythical Consciousness

THUS FAR we have attempted, in line with the general task of the philosophy of Symbolic Forms, to represent myth as a unitary energy of the human spirit: as a self-contained form of interpretation which asserts itself amid all the diversity of the objective material it presents. From this standpoint we have attempted to disclose the objective categories of mythical thinking —not as though we were dealing with rigid schemata of the spirit, fixed once and for all, but with a view to finding definite original *trends* of formation. Behind the vast abundance of mythical forms we have thus sought to lay bare a unitary formative power and the law according to which this power operates. But myth would be no truly spiritual form if its unity signified merely a simplicity without contradictions. Its basic form does not unfold and imprint itself on new motifs and figures in the manner of a simple natural process; its development is not the tranquil growth of a seed which was present and ready made from the very first, which merely requires certain definite outward conditions in order to unfold and make itself manifest. The separate stages of its development do not simply follow but rather confront one another, often in sharp opposition. The progress of myth does not mean merely that certain basic traits, certain spiritual determinations of earlier stages are developed and completed, but also that they are negated and totally eradicated. And this dialectic can be shown not only in the transformation of the contents of the mythical consciousness but in its dominant "inner form." It seizes upon the function of mythical formation as such and transforms it from within. This function can operate only by continuously producing new forms—objective expressions of the inner and outward universe as it presents itself to the eye of myth. But in advancing along this road it reaches a turning point at which the law that governs it becomes a problem. This may seem strange at first glance, for we do not usually give the naive mythical consciousness credit for such a change of attitude. And indeed we have not to do with an act of conscious theoretical reflection, in which myth apprehends itself and in which it turns against its own foundations and presuppositions. Even in this turn the mythical consciousness remains within itself. It does not move out of its sphere or pass into a totally different "principle," but in completing its own cycle it ends by breaking through it. This fulfillment which is at the same time a transcendence results from the relation of myth toward its own image world. Myth can manifest itself only in this image world; as the mythical consciousness advances it comes to see this manifestation as something "outside" which is not wholly adequate to its own drive for expression. Here lies the basis of the conflict, which becomes gradually sharper and sharper, which creates a cleavage within the mythical consciousness and yet in this very cleavage discloses the ultimate depths of myth.

The positivistic philosophy of history and culture, as formulated especially by Comte, assumes a hierarchy of cultural development, by which mankind gradually rises from the primitive phases of consciousness up to theoretical knowledge and complete spiritual domination of reality. From the fictions, phantasms, and beliefs of those first phases the road leads more and more definitely to the scientific view of reality as a reality of pure facts. Here the merely subjective activity of the spirit is supposed to fall away; here man confronts empirical reality, which gives itself to him for what it is, while previously he saw it only through the deceptive medium of his own feelings and desires, images and ideas. According to Comte this progress falls essentially into three stages: the "theological," the "metaphysical," and the "positive." In the first, man transforms his subjective desires and ideas into demons and gods; in the second he transforms them into abstract concepts; it is only in the last phase that he differentiates clearly between "inside" and "outside" and limits himself to the given facts of inner and outer experience. Here then the mythical-religious consciousness is gradually overcome by a power alien to it. Once the higher stage has been reached the earlier one, according to the positivistic schema, is no longer needed; its content can and must die away. Comte himself, as we know, did not draw this consequence: his philosophy culminates not only in a system of positive *knowledge,* but also in a positivist *religion,* and indeed a positivist cult. This belated recognition of religion and cult is not only significant and characteristic of Comte's own intellectual development but, what is more important, it constitutes an indirect admission of an objective deficiency in the positivist construction of history. Comte's law of the "trois états" does not permit a purely immanent evaluation of the achievement of the mythical-religious consciousness. The goal of myth and religion must here be sought outside themselves in a fundamentally different sphere. But then it becomes impossible to apprehend the true nature and the purely inward dynamic of the mythical-religious spirit. This dynamic is truly disclosed only if it can be shown that myth and religion have within them their own source of motion, that from their beginnings down to their supreme productions they are determined by their own motives and fed from their own wellsprings. Even where they pass far beyond these first beginnings they do not abandon their native spiritual soil. Their positions do not suddenly and immediately shift into negations; rather, it can be shown that every step they take, even in their own sphere, bears, as it were, a twofold omen. To the continuous building up of the mythical world there corresponds a continuous drive to surpass it, but in such a way that both the position and the negation belong to the form of the mythical-religious consciousness itself and in it join to constitute a single indivisible act. The process of destruction proves on closer scrutiny to be a process of self-assertion; conversely, the latter can only be effected on the basis of the former, and it is only in their permanent cooperation that the two together produce the true essence and meaning of the mythical-religious form.

In the development of *linguistic forms* we differentiated three stages which we designated as those of mimetic, analogical, and symbolic expression. In the first stage we found that there is still no true tension between the linguistic "sign" and the intuitive content to which it refers, that the two tend rather to dissolve in one another and achieve a mutual coincidence. The sign, as mimetic sign, strives in its form toward an immediate rendering of the content; it strives, one might say, to absorb it. Only gradually do we find a distance, an increasing differentiation, between sign and content; and it is then that the characteristic and fundamental phenomenon of language, the separation of sound and signification, is achieved.[1] Only when this separation occurs is the sphere of linguistic meaning constituted as such. In its first beginnings the word still belongs to the sphere of mere existence: what is apprehended in it is not a signification but rather a substantial being and power of its own. It does not point to an objective content but sets itself in the place of this content; it becomes a kind of *Ur-sache* ["cause" or, literally, "original thing"—tr.], a power which intervenes in empirical events and their causal concatenation.[2] Consciousness must turn away from this first view if it is to gain an insight into the

1. See *1*, 186 ff.
2. Cf. my *Sprache und Mythos*, pp. 38 ff.; above, pp. 40 ff.

symbolic function and hence into the pure ideality of the word. And what is true of the linguistic sign is true in the same sense of the written sign. The written sign is not at once *apprehended* as such but is viewed as a part of the objective world, one might say, as an extract of all the forces that are contained in it. All writing begins as a mimetic sign, an image, and at first the image has no significatory, communicative character. It rather replaces and "stands for" the object. In its beginnings writing also belongs to the magical sphere. It is a magical instrument by which to gain possession of certain things and ward off hostile powers: the sign that a man impresses on an object draws it into the sphere of his own efficacy and removes foreign influences. The more the writing *resembles* what it is intended to represent—the more purely objective it is—the better it fulfills this purpose. Long before the written sign is understood as an expression of an object it is feared as the substantial embodiment, as it were, of the forces that emanate from it, as a kind of demonic double of the object.[3] Only when this magical feeling pales does man's attention turn from the empirical to the ideal, the material to the functional. From pure picture writing there develops a syllabic and ultimately a phonetic system in which the initial ideogram, the pictorial sign, has become a pure significatory sign, or symbol.

And we see the same relationship in the image world of myth. Where it first appears the mythical image is by no means taken as an image, as spiritual expression. Rather, it is so deeply embedded in man's intuition of the world of things, of "objective" reality and the objective process, as to appear an integral part of it. Here again there is originally no division between the real and the ideal, between the sphere of "existence" and that of "meaning," but there is rather a continuous flux between the two spheres, both in man's thought and belief and in his action.[4] At the beginning of mythical action stands the mime again; and nowhere does he have a merely "aesthetic," a merely representative, significance. The dancer who appears in the mask of the god or demon does not merely imitate the god or demon but assumes his nature; he is transformed into him and fuses with him. Here there is never a mere image, an empty representation; nothing is thought, represented, "supposed" that is not at the same time real and effective. But in the gradual progress of the mythical world view a separation now begins; and it is this separation that constitutes the actual begin-

---

3. For documentation see Theodor W. Danzel, *Die Anfänge der Schrift* (Leipzig, 1912).

4. On this and the following cf. above, pp. 36 ff.

ning of the specifically religious consciousness. The further back we follow it toward its origins, the less the content of religious consciousness can be distinguished from that of mythical consciousness. The two are so interwoven that they can nowhere be definitely separated and set off from each other. If we attempt to isolate and remove the basic mythical components from religious belief, we no longer have religion in its real, objectively historical manifestation; all that remains is a shadow of it, an empty abstraction. And yet, although the contents of myth and religion are inextricably interwoven, their form is not the same. And the particularity of the religious form is disclosed in the changed attitude which consciousness here assumes toward the mythical image world. It cannot do without this world, it cannot immediately reject it; but seen through the medium of the religious attitude this world gradually takes on a new meaning. The new ideality, the new spiritual dimension, that is opened up through religion not only lends myth a new signification but actually introduces the opposition between "meaning" and "existence" into the realm of myth. Religion takes the decisive step that is essentially alien to myth: in its use of sensuous images and signs it recognizes them as such—a means of expression which, though they reveal a determinate meaning, must necessarily remain inadequate to it, which "point" to this meaning but never wholly exhaust it.

In the course of its development every religion comes to a point at which it must withstand this "crisis" and break loose from its mythical foundations. But the different religions do not do this in the same way, and it is precisely in this process that each one reveals its historical and spiritual particularity. Again and again we find that in assuming a new relation to the mythical image world religion enters at the same time into a new relation to the whole of "reality," the whole of empirical existence. It cannot complete its peculiar critique of this image world without drawing real existence into it. Precisely because at this stage there is still no detached objective reality in the sense understood by analytical theoretical cognition—because the intuition of reality remains, as it were, fused with the world of mythical imagination, feeling, and faith—every new attitude of consciousness toward the mythical world must react upon man's general view of existence. Thus, the ideality of religion not merely degrades the totality of mythical configurations and powers to a lower order of being but also applies this form of negation to the elements of sensuous-natural existence itself.

In order to clarify this relationship let us examine a few examples of typical orientations arrived at by religious thinking in this struggle against its own mythical foundations and beginnings. The classical example of this great transformation will always be the form of religious consciousness in the Prophetic books of the Old Testament. The entire ethical-religious pathos of the Prophets is concentrated in this one point. It rests on the power and certainty of the religious will that lives in the Prophets—of a will which drives them beyond all intuition of the given, the merely existent. This existence must vanish if the new world, the world of the Messianic future is to arise. The Prophetic world is visible only in the religious idea and can be encompassed in no mere image which is oriented solely toward the sensuous present and remains confined within it. Accordingly, the prohibition of idolatry, the injunction to make no graven image or likeness "of any thing that is in heaven above or that is on the earth beneath, or that is in the water under the earth" takes on an entirely new meaning and power in the Prophetic consciousness; it becomes indeed the constituent factor in this consciousness. It is as though a chasm unknown to the unreflecting, naive mythical consciousness had suddenly been opened. The polytheistic world, the "pagan" view combated by the Prophets, was not guilty of worshiping a mere "image" of the divine, since for this view there was no difference between the archetype and image as such. In its images of the divine the polytheistic world still held immediate possession of the divine itself—precisely because it took these images never as mere signs but always as concrete-sensuous revelations. In a purely formal sense the Prophetic critique of this intuition therefore rests on a kind of *petitio principii,* for it imputes to this view a conception which is not inherent in it but is brought to it only through the new perspective in which it is placed. With passionate zeal Isaiah assails the folly of man worshiping his own creation and venerating as divine something which he knows to be his own product.

> Who hath formed a god, or molten a graven image that is profitable for nothing? . . . The smith with the tongs both worketh it in the coals, and fashioneth it with hammers. . . . The carpenter stretcheth out his rule; he marketh it out with a line; he fitteth it with planes, and he marketh it out with the compass. . . . He burneth part thereof in the fire. . . . And the residue thereof he maketh a god, even his graven image: he falleth down unto it, and worshippeth it, and prayeth unto

it, and saith, Deliver me; for thou art my god. They have not known
nor understood; for he hath shut their eyes that they cannot see; and
their hearts, that they cannot understand. And none considereth in his
heart, neither is there knowledge or understanding to say, I have burned
part of it in the fire . . . and shall I make the residue thereof an abomi-
nation? shall I fall down to the stock of a tree? [5]

Here, as we see, the Prophet must inject into the mythical consciousness an
alien tension, an opposition it does not know as such, in order to disinte-
grate and destroy it from within. Yet the truly positive factor consists not
in this disintegration itself but rather in the spiritual motif from which it
grows, in a turning back to the heart of religious feeling, which now causes
the image world of myth to be recognized as something merely outward
and material. Since in the basic Prophetic view there can be no relation between man and God other than the spiritual-ethical relation between the I
and the Thou, everything that does not belong to this fundamental relation
now loses its religious value. In the moment when the religious function,
having discovered the world of pure inwardness, withdraws from the world
of outward, natural existence, this existence loses its soul, as it were, and
is degraded to the level of a dead "thing." Thus the images taken from this
sphere cease to be an expression of the spiritual and divine and turn into
its antithesis pure and simple. The sensuous image and the whole sensuous
phenomenal world must be divested of their symbolic meaning, for this
alone makes possible the new deepening of pure religious subjectivity
which can no longer be expressed in any material image.

Another path from the sphere of material existence to the true religious
sphere of meaning, from the image to the imageless, is taken by the Persian-
Iranian religion. In his account of the Persian faith Herodotus notes that
the Persians did not erect statues and temples but rather called it folly to
do so, since they did not, like the Hellenes, believe that their gods resembled
men.[6] Here, as among the Prophets, the same ethical-religious tendency is
at work, for like the God of the Prophets, Ahura Mazda, the Persian
creator god, has no predicates other than those of pure being and ethical
goodness. And yet, on the basis of this fundamental tendency, there arises
a different attitude toward nature and all concrete, objective existence. The
veneration of various elements in nature in the religion of Zoroaster is well

5. Isaiah 44:10 ff.
6. Herodotus, Bk. I, 131; cf. Bk. III, 29.

known. The care devoted to fire and water and the awe with which they are preserved from all taint—contamination of them being punished as severely as the gravest ethical transgression—prove that the bond between nature and religion has by no means been severed. But if, instead of considering the mere dogmatic and ritual facts, we turn our attention to the religious motives underlying them, this seeming nature worship points to a very different relationship. It is not for their own sake that the elements of nature are venerated in the Persian religion; what gives them their actual significance is the position assigned them in the great religious-ethical decision, in the battle between the spirits of good and evil for world domination. In this struggle every natural substance has its appointed place and task. Just as man must decide between the two basic powers, so also the various forces of nature stand on one side or the other, serving the work of either preservation or destruction and annihilation. It is this function and not their mere physical form and power that gives them their religious sanction. Thus nature need not be unhallowed, for, although it may never be interpreted as a direct image of divine being, it does stand in an immediate relation to the divine will and its ultimate goal. It may be either hostile to the divine will, and so descend to the merely demonic, or in alliance with it. Nature in itself is neither good nor evil, divine nor demonic, but religious thinking makes it so, since it looks upon its contents not as mere elements and factors of material existence but as cultural factors, and so draws them into the sphere of the ethical-religious world view. They belong to the "heavenly hosts" which Ormazd employs in his struggle against Ahriman and as such are worthy of veneration. This realm of entities worthy of veneration (the Yazata) includes fire and water as conditions of all culture and human order. The changing over from a purely physical meaning to a distinctly teleological one is clearly shown in the way the elaborate Persian system of theology went about on the one hand denying the indifference to good and evil that seems characteristic of all merely natural things, while on the other hand teaching that the harmful or fatal effects arising from fire and water should not be imputed to these elements directly but at most come from them indirectly.[7] Here again we can clearly see how the purely mythical elements which originally underlie the Persian religion as they do every other religion are not simply suppressed but are progressively transformed in their significance. This gives rise to a characteristic involvement, a peculiar coordina-

7. Cf. Henry, *Le Parsisme*, p. 63.

tion and correlation of natural and spiritual potencies, of material-concrete existence and abstract forces. In certain passages of the Avesta, Fire and Good Thought (Vohu Manah) appear side by side as salvation-bringing powers. When the evil spirit fell upon the creation of the good spirit—it is taught here—Vohu Manah and Fire intervened and overcame the evil spirit so that it could no longer obstruct the waters in their course and the plants in their growth.[8] This involvement and merging of abstraction and image constitute an essential and specific trait of Persian religious doctrine. The conception of the supreme god is indeed fundamentally monotheistic—since ultimately he will overcome and destroy his adversaries—but on the other hand he is only the summit of a hierarchy to which belong natural as well as purely spiritual powers. Next to him stand the six "immortal saints" (Amesha Spenta), whose names (Good Thought and Best Righteousness, etc.) show a distinct abstract-ethical imprint. These are followed by the Yazatas, the angels of the Mazdean religion, who on the one hand personify ethical powers, such as truth, uprightness, or obedience, and on the other hand natural elements, such as fire and water. Thus nature itself takes on a twofold and in a religious sense contradictory meaning through the mediating concept of human culture, through the view of the cultural order as a religious order of salvation. For within a certain sphere it is preserved; but in order to be preserved it must at the same time be destroyed, i.e. divested of its mere material determinacy and through its relation to the basic opposition of good and evil assigned to an entirely different dimension of thought.

In order to express such fine and fluid transitions in the religious consciousness of reality the language of religion possesses a peculiar instrument that is denied to the conceptual language of logic and pure theoretical cognition. For the latter there is no middle term between "reality" and "appearance," between "being" and "nonbeing." Here the alternative of Parmenides applies: ἔστιν ἢ οὐκ ἔστιν. But in the religious sphere, particularly at the point where it begins to be delimited from the sphere of mere myth, this alternative is not necessarily valid and binding. The negation and rejection of certain mythical figures by which consciousness was previously dominated does not mean that they are simply relegated to nothingness. Even after they have been transcended, the productions of myth have by no means lost all meaning and force. Rather, they remain

8. Yasht, XIII, 22. Eng. trans. by Darmesteter.

in existence as lower demonic powers, which appear insignificant beside the divine and yet which, even after they have been recognized as "illusion" in this sense, are still feared as a substantial and, in a sense, essential illusion. The development of the religious language gives characteristic indications of this process in the religious consciousness. In the language of the Avesta, for example, the old name for the Aryan gods of light and the heavens has undergone a decisive change in meaning: the *deivos* or *devas* have become the *daeva,* which designate the evil powers, the demons in Ahriman's train. Here we see how, when religious thought rises above the elementary stratum of the mythical deification of nature, everything belonging to this stratum undergoes, as it were, a reversal of meaning.[9] Yet, with its changed meaning it survives. The demonic world, the world of Ahriman, is a world of deception, illusion, error. Just as the Asha, truth and justice, stand beside Ormazd in his battle, so Ahriman is ruler in the realm of the lie and in some passages he is even identified with it. However, this does not mean merely that he employs lie and deception as his weapons; it means also that he himself remains objectively banished into the sphere of illusion and untruth. He is blind, and it is this blindness, this nonknowledge, which causes him to take up the struggle with Ormazd in which, as Ormazd knows in advance, he, Ahriman, will meet his doom. Thus he succumbs in the end to his own untruth. And yet, Ahriman is not destroyed at once but only "at the end of the eras"; in the time of human history and human cultural development, in the "era of battle," he preserves his power beside and in opposition to Ormazd. Here again, it is true, the religious consciousness of the Jewish Prophets goes a step farther; it seeks to unmask the lower demonic world as an absolute nothing—a nothingness to which no reality, however mediated—no reality of thought or belief or fear—should be attributed. "For the customs of the people are vain," says Jeremiah. "Be not afraid of them; for they cannot do evil, neither also is it in them to do good . . . his molten image is falsehood, and there is no breath in them. They are vanity, and the work of errors" (Jeremiah 10:3 ff.). The new divine life that is here proclaimed cannot express itself without declaring everything opposed to it to be absolutely unreal, delusion. And yet here, too, only the religious geniuses,

9. With regard to this change in linguistic-religious signification see Schröder, *Arische Religion, 1,* 273 ff.; Jackson, in *Grundriss der iranischen Philologie, 2,* 646. In opposition to Darmesteter, Henry, *Le Parsisme,* pp. 12 ff., stresses that this is something more than a "linguistic accident."

the great individuals, draw the line radically; the general religious development takes a different direction. Here the images of the mythical fantasy keep rising to the surface even after they have lost their actual life, even after they have become mere dreams and shadows. Just as in mythical belief the dead still live and act as shades, so the mythical image world long continues to demonstrate its old power, even when its existence is denied in the name of religious truth.[10] Here again, as in the development of all symbolic forms, light and shadow go together. The light manifests itself only in the shadow it casts: the purely "intelligible" has the sensuous as its antithesis, but this antithesis is at the same time its necessary correlate.

A third great example of how, in the progress of religious thought and speculation, the mythical world gradually sinks into nothingness and how this process spreads from the figures of myth to those of empirical existence may be found in the doctrine of the Upanishads. It too achieves its highest aim through negation, from which it may be said to make its basic religious category. The only name, the only designation, remaining for the absolute is negation itself. That which is, the atman, is called "No, No," and above this "thus it is not" there is nothing.[11] It is a final step along this same road when Buddhism extends the negation from object to subject. In the Prophetic-monotheistic religion, as religious thought and feeling are freed from the sphere of mere things, the reciprocal relation between the I and God becomes purer and more energetic. Liberation from the image and its objectivity has no other aim than to place this relation in the sharpest relief. Here the negation ultimately finds a fixed limit: it leaves untouched the center of the religious relationship, the individual and his self-consciousness. As the objective world recedes, a new mode of formation comes more and more distinctly to the fore: the formation of will and action. But Buddhism passes beyond this last bar-

10. This peculiar vacillating, intermediary condition of the religious consciousness is often strikingly evident in the linguistic designation for the mythical, the "lower" demonic world. Ahriman, e.g., is designated in the Avesta as the Lord of the lie (*druj*). The Indo-Germanic root (Sanskrit *druh*) contained in this word recurs in the Germanic root *drug*, which in modern German has developed into *Trug* and *Traum*. It recurs also in the Germanic designations for demons and ghosts (Old Norse, *draugr*-ghost, OHG *troc, gitroc*, etc.). Cf. Golther, *Handbuch der germanischen Mythologie*, p. 85; F. Kluge, *Etymologisches Wörterbuch der deutschen Sprache* (5th ed. Strassburg, 1894), *s.v.* "Traum" and "Trug."

11. Cf. Oldenberg, *Lehre der Upanishaden*, pp. 63 ff.; Paul Deussen, "Die Philosophie der Upanishad's," *Allgemeine Geschichte der Philosophie*, Vol. *1*, Pt. II (1899), pp. 117 ff., 206 ff. Eng. trans. by A. S. Geden, *The Philosophy of the Upanishads* (Edinburgh, 1906).

rier; for Buddhism the form of the I becomes just as accidental and external as any mere material form. The religious "truth" of Buddhism strives
to surpass not only the world of things but the world of will and action
as well. For it is precisely action and will that confine man to the cycle of
becoming, that chain him to the "wheel of births." It is the act (*karman*)
which determines man's road in the unceasing sequence of births and so
becomes for him an inexhaustible source of suffering. Thus, true liberation lies not only beyond the world of things but above all beyond action
and desire. For him who achieves it, it is not only the opposition between
the I and the world which vanishes; so also does the opposition between
I and thou. For him the personality is no longer the kernel but the husk,
the last remnant of the sphere of finiteness and images. It possesses no
permanence, no substantiality of its own, but lives and *is* only in its immediate actuality—that is to say, in the coming and going, the genesis and
passing away, of diverse and forever new elements of existence. Thus the
I, even the spiritual I, also belongs to the world of dispersing configurations, the Samkhara, whose ultimate cause is to be sought in nonknowledge.[12] "Like an ape in the forest who prowls around a thicket, who
seizes a branch, lets it go, and seizes another, so does that which is called
spirit or thought or knowledge come into being and pass away, alternately
day and night." Thus the individual, the self, is no more than a name
which we give to a complex of perishable contents of existence, just as the
word "wagon" designates only the totality of yoke and frame, shafts and
wheels, but not, over and above these, a definite something existing for
itself. "Here there is no *essence*." This inference in turn reveals with particular clarity a general trend of religious thinking. It is characteristic of
this thinking that all being, the being of things as well as the I, and of
inward things as well as outward, has content and significance only insofar as it is related to the religious process and its center. This center is
essentially the sole reality: everything else is either without being or, as a
factor in this process, possesses a derived, a secondary, being. According
to the diverse views of the religious process in the various historical religions, according to their shifting value accents, different elements are
singled out and, to speak in Platonic terms, "endowed with the seal of
being." A religion of action must therefore proceed differently from a

12. On the position of the concept of Samkhara in Buddhist doctrine cf. Richard Pischel,
Leben und Lehre des Buddha (Leipzig, 1906), pp. 65 ff.; Oldenberg, *Buddha* (4th ed.), pp.
279 ff.

religion of suffering, a culture religion differently from a pure nature religion. Fundamentally, the religious intuition imputes "being" only to those contents which receive light from the religious center, while everything else, everything that is indifferent from the standpoint of the central religious decision, is an ἀδιάφορον that sinks back into the darkness of night. For Buddhism the I, the individual, and the individual soul must be assigned to this sphere of nothingness because they do not enter into the Buddhist formulation of the basic religious problem. For even though Buddhism in its essential meaning and goal is a religion of redemption, the redemption it seeks is not that *of* the individual I but *from* it. What we call soul, what we call personality, is itself not real but only the ultimate illusion, the illusion that is hardest to see through and overcome, the illusion in which we are involved by empirical thinking, the thinking that clings to "form and name." For him who has left this realm of form and name totally behind him the illusion of an independent individuality has lost its power. And along with the substantial soul its religious correlate and counterpart, the substantial godhead, must also vanish. Buddha did not deny the gods of the popular religion, but for him they were merely individual beings which, like everything individual, are subject to the law of perishability. From them no help can come, no release from suffering, for they themselves are confined within the cycle of change and hence of suffering. In this respect Buddhism becomes a type of atheistic religion, not in the sense of denying the existence of the gods but in the far more deep-seated and radical sense that this existence is irrelevant and meaningless in the light of its central problem. Nevertheless, those who say for this reason that it is no religion but merely a body of practical ethical doctrine are arbitrarily narrowing the concept of religion. For it is not the content of a doctrine, but solely its form, that can serve as a criterion for its classification as a religion: what stamps a doctrine as religion is its affirmation not of any being, but of a specific "order" and meaning. Any element of existence—and for this Buddhism is one of the most significant examples—can be negated, provided the universal function of religious symbolism is maintained. Here the basic act of religious synthesis is such that only the process itself is ultimately apprehended and subjected to a definite interpretation, while every supposed substratum of this process dissolves and finally sinks into nothingness.

In its whole development Christianity also fights this battle for its own peculiar definition of religious "reality." Here release from the world of mythical images seems all the more difficult because certain mythical intuitions are so deeply embedded in the fundamental doctrines, the dogmatic substance of Christianity, that they cannot be removed without endangering this substance itself. Schelling observed this historical relationship and drew the inference that "natural religion" is and remains the necessary presupposition even for every "revealed religion."

> It [revealed religion] does not create the matter in which it develops; it finds it independently present. The formal achievement of revealed religion is to surpass mere natural, unfree religion; but for this very reason it has the natural religion in itself, for the surpasser contains the surpassed. . . . If it was permissible to find distortions of revealed truths in paganism, then, conversely, it cannot possibly be forbidden to see in Christianity a corrected paganism. . . . For the kinship between the two [mythology and revelation] has been shown in their common outward destiny: in the attempt to rationalize them both by the identical differentiation of form and content, of essentials and mere timely dress, i.e. to reduce them to a rational, or at least to the most seemingly rational, meaning. But if the pagan element were banished, precisely then would all reality be removed from Christianity.[13]

Subsquent research in the history of religions has confirmed this statement to an extent which Schelling himself could scarcely have foreseen. Today, on the basis of this research, it can be said that there is scarcely a single feature in the world of Christian faith and ideas, scarcely a symbol, for which mythical-pagan parallels might not be shown.[14] The entire history of dogmas, from the earliest beginnings down to Luther and Zwingli, indicates a constant struggle between the original historical significance of symbols, sacraments, and mysteries and their derived, purely spiritual meaning. Here again the ideal develops only very gradually from the sphere of material, empirical reality. Particularly, baptism and the Eucharist are at first evaluated entirely in this empirical sense, according to their immediate efficacy. "For that epoch," Harnack remarks, speaking of the early Christian period, "the symbolic is not to be conceived as the antithesis of the objective, the empirical; it is rather the mysterious, the God-wrought

---

13. Schelling, *Philosophie der Mythologie*, p. 248.

14. Here I content myself with referring to a recent investigation in which this relationship has been illuminated from all sides: Eduard Norden, *Die Geburt des Kindes. Geschichte einer religiösen Idee*, Studien der Bibliothek Warburg, Vol. 3 (Leipzig, 1924).

(μυστήριον), as opposed to the natural, profanely clear." [15] Here a distinction is expressed which goes back to the ultimate roots of mythical thinking.[16] And precisely in this barrier of Christianity lies much of its historical power. It might, in late antiquity, have succumbed in the contest with the oriental religions if it had not possessed this mythical indigenousness which it asserted over and over again despite all attempts at reform. This factor can be followed in detail in the elements of the Christian liturgy.[17] Thus, the new religious tendency that characterizes Christianity, the new attitude expressed in its call for μετάνοια, could not be directly stated and could not grow directly; this new form could only be expressed and could only mature through the mythical substance which played, as it were, the role of a psychological-historical datum. The development of dogma was at every step determined by these two sets of conditions, for dogma is nothing more than the form assumed by pure religious meaning when men seek to express it in terms of objective representation.

But here again it is mysticism which attempts to arrive at the pure meaning of religion as such, free from all encumbrance with the "otherness" of empirical-sensuous existence and of sensuous images and representations. In mysticism the pure dynamic of religious feeling strives to slough off and negate all rigid outward data. The relation of the human soul to God finds adequate expression neither in the image language of empirical or mythical intuition nor in the sphere of "actual" existence and events. Only when the I withdraws entirely from this sphere, only when it dwells in its essence and foundation, can the simple essence of God touch it without the mediation of an image; then alone do the pure truth and inwardness of this relation open up to it. Accordingly, mysticism rejects both the mythical and the historical elements of faith. It strives to overcome dogma because in dogma, even when expressed in purely intellectual terms, the factor of imagery is still predominant. For all dogma isolates and limits: it seeks to transfer what is meaningful only in the dynamic of religious life to the determinacy of representation and its static productions. Thus, from the standpoint of mysticism, image and dogma—the concrete and abstract expression of religion—amount to the same thing. The incarnation

15. Adolf von Harnack(*Lehrbuch der Dogmengeschichte* (3d ed. 3 vols. Leipzig, Mohr, 1894–97), *1*, 198.

16. Cf. above, pp. 73 ff.

17. Here again I shall not go into detail. It suffices to recall the penetrating analysis of the various liturgical images given by Dietrich in the second part of *Eine Mithrasliturgie*, pp. 92 ff.

of the God must no longer be taken as a mythical or historical fact but rather as a process which operates continuously in human consciousness. Here two independent antithetical "natures" are not united; rather, it is from the unity of the religious relation, which for mysticism is the only known and original datum, that the duality of the elements of this relation bursts forth. "The Father," writes Meister Eckhart, "bears the son unceasingly, and I say more: he does not bear me alone, his son; but more: he bears me for himself and himself for me." [18] This fundamental idea of a polarity which strives to dissolve into a pure correlation and which must nevertheless be preserved as a polarity, determines the character and course of Christian mysticism. It is also characterized by the method of negative theology, which is carried consistently through all the categories of intuition and thought. In order to apprehend the divine we must first cast off all the conditions of finite, empirical being, the "where," the "when," and the "what." God, according to Eckhart and Suso, has no "where": He is "a circular ring; the center of the ring is everywhere and its circumference nowhere"; and likewise all difference and contrast of time—past, present, and future—are extinguished in Him: His eternity is a present now, that knows nothing of time. Thus for Him there remains only "nameless nothingness," the form of formlessness. Christian mysticism, like other mysticisms, is threatened by the constant danger that this nothingness and meaninglessness will seize not only upon being but upon the I as well. And yet there remains a barrier beyond which, unlike Buddhist speculation, it does not go. For the problem of the individual I, of the individual soul, remains at the center of Christianity; and consequently liberation from the I can only be conceived as also signifying liberation *for* the I. Even where Eckhart and Tauler seem to approach the edge of the Buddhist Nirvana, even where they extinguish the self in God, they seek, as it were, to preserve the individual form of this extinction: there remains a point, a "little spark," with which the I *knows* this dissolution of itself.

Here again the dialectic that runs through the whole development of the mythical-religious consciousness stands out with particular sharpness. As we have seen, it is a fundamental trait in mythical thinking that wherever it posits a definite relation between two members it transforms this relation into an identity. An attempted synthesis leads here necessarily to

18. Meister Eckhart, in Franz Pfeiffer, ed., *Deutsche Mystiker des Vierzehnten Jahrhunderts* (2 vols. Leipzig, G. J. Göschen, 1845–57), 2, 205.

a coincidence, an immediate concrescence of the elements that were to be linked.[19] And even where religious feeling and thought grow beyond their initial mythical contingency there remains an echo of this form of striving for unity. Only when the difference between God and man has vanished, when God has become man and man God, does the goal of redemption seem achieved. Even the Gnostics saw the true and supreme goal in immediate deification, apotheosis: τοῦτό ἐστι τὸ ἀγαθὸν τέλος τοῖς γνῶσιν ἐσχηκόσι θεωθῆναι (Poimandres, Bk. I, 22, 2). Here we stand at the line which divides the mythical-religious view from the philosophy of religion in the narrower and stricter sense. The philosophy of religion sees the unity between God and man less as a substantial than as a synthetic unity: a unity of different entities. For it, therefore, differentiation remains a necessary factor, a condition for the achievement of the unity itself. This is expressed with classical force in Plato. In Diotima's speech in the *Symposium* the bond between God and man is provided by Eros, who as the great intermediary has the task of conveying and interpreting to the gods what comes from men, and to men what comes from the gods. Standing half way between the two, he fills the gap between them; it is he who connects the parts of the universe. "For God mingles not with man; but through love all the intercourse and converse of god with man, whether awake or asleep, is carried on." [20] In this rejection of "mixture" between God and man, Plato as a dialectician draws the sharp dividing line which can be drawn neither by myth nor mysticism. Apotheosis, the identity between God and man, is now replaced by the demand for ὁμοίωσις τῷ θεῷ which can be fulfilled only in man's action, in his steady progress toward the good, while the good itself remains "beyond being" (ἐπέκεινα τῆς οὐσίας). Here, though Plato is far from rejecting the mythical image as such and though from the standpoint of content he seems very close to certain fundamental mythical ideas, he announces a new form of thought which points beyond myth. Synopsis no longer leads to συμπτῶσις: it becomes the unity of the ideal vision which is constituted precisely by the reciprocal relation, the insuperable correlation between combination and separation.

In the religious consciousness, on the other hand, the conflict between

19. Reitzenstein, *Die hellenistischen Mysterienreligionen* (2d ed. 1920), pp. 38 ff.; Norden, *Agnostos theos*, pp. 97 ff.

20. Θεὸς δὲ ἀνθρώπῳ οὐ μίγνυται, ἀλλὰ διὰ τούτου πᾶσά ἐστιν ἡ ὁμιλία καὶ ὁ διάλεκτος Θεοῖς πρὸς ἀνθρώπους, καὶ ἐγρεγορόσι καὶ καθεύδουσι. *Symposium*, 203A, Eng. trans. by Benjamin Jowett (New York, Random House, 1937).

the pure meaning it embraces and the image in which it is expressed is never resolved but bursts forth anew in every phase of development. A reconciliation between these two extremes is continuously sought but never fully achieved. The striving beyond the mythical image world and an indissoluble attachment to this same world constitute a basic factor of the religious process itself. Even the highest spiritual sublimation of religion does not cause this opposition to disappear but only makes it increasingly clear and understands it in its immanent necessity. At this point a comparison between religion and language once again suggests itself. And this comparison is no mere subjective reflection seeking to establish an artificial bond between two spheres far removed from each other in their inner meaning; it springs rather from a relationship to which religious speculation was frequently drawn in its own development and which it repeatedly sought to define with its own conceptual instruments. What appears to the common, profane world view as the immediately given reality of "things" is transformed by the religious view into a world of "signs." The specifically religious point of view is indeed determined by this reversal. All physical and material things, every substance and every action, now become metaphoric, the corporeal, imaged expression of a spiritual meaning. The naive indifference of image and thing, the immanence of both as we find it in mythical thinking,[21] begins to give way: in its place there develops more and more clearly that form of transcendence—to speak in ontological terms—in which is expressed the new division which the religious consciousness has now experienced in itself. Things and events do not now simply signify themselves but have become an indication of something "other," something "transcendent." In this strict distinction of copy and prototype the religious consciousness achieves its intrinsic and peculiar ideality, and at the same time it approaches a fundamental idea which philosophical thinking progressively works out by entirely different methods and on the basis of other presuppositions. Here, in their historical workings, the two forms of the ideal can act directly upon each other. When Plato teaches that the idea of the good is "beyond being" and accordingly compares it with the sun, which the the human eye cannot view directly but can contemplate only in its reflection in the water, he has provided the language of religion with a typical and enduring means of expression. In the history of Christianity

21. See above, pp. 36 ff.

the development and deepening of this means of expression can be followed from the books of the New Testament down to the dogmatic and mystical speculations of the Middle Ages and thence to the eighteenth- and nineteenth-century philosophy of religion. From St. Paul to Eckhart and Tauler and thence to Hamann and Jacobi there runs an unbroken chain of religious thought. And here the problem of religion merges again and again with the problem of language through the decisive mediating concept of the sign. "To speak to you from the bottom of my soul," writes Hamann to Lavater,

> my whole Christianity is a taste for signs and for the elements of water, bread, and wine. Here there is abundance for hunger and thirst —an abundance which does not, like the law, merely cast a shadow of *future* benefit but rather gives αὐτὴν τὴν εἰκόνα τῶν πραγμάτων insofar as it can be represented and actualized through a glass darkly; for the τέλειον lies beyond.[22]

Just as in Eckhart's mystical view, where all creatures are nothing other than the "speech of God," [23] here all creation, all natural as well as spiritual and historical events, become a continuous speaking of the creator to the creature through the creature. "For one day says it to another and one night reveals it to another. Their watchword runs through every climate to the end of the world and in every language their voice is heard." [24] In Jacobi, who in his thinking seeks to fuse the basic elements of Hamann's metaphysical-symbolic world view with Kantian principles, the objective relationship here disclosed takes a subjective psychological-transcendental turn. Here language and religion are closely related through their derivation from one and the same spiritual root; they are simply different abilities of the mind to see the sensuous in the suprasensory, and the suprasensory in the sensuous. All man's reason, since it is a passive perception,

22. Johann G. Hamann to Lavater (1778), in *Hamann's Schriften*, ed. Friedrich Roth (9 vols. Berlin, G. Reimer, 1821–43), 5, 278. For Hamann's symbolic view of the world and of language see the excellent works of Rudolf Unger: *Hamanns Sprachtheorie im Zusammenhang seines Denkens* (Munich, 1905) and *Hamann und die Aufklärung* (Jena, 1911).

23. Cf. e.g., Eckhart, ed. Pfeiffer, 2, 92, and elsewhere.

24. Hamann, "Aesthetica in nuce," in *Hamann's Schriften*, 2, 261. How powerful this view originating in mysticism remains even in modern epistemology is made particularly evident by the example of Berkeley, whose psychological and epistemological theories culminate in the idea that the whole world of sense perception is merely a system of sensuous signs, in which the infinite spirit of God communicates itself to finite spirits. Cf. *1*, 139 ff.

requires the help of the sensuous. The world of images and signs is always and necessarily interpolated as an intermediary between the human spirit and the essence of things.

> Always there is something between us and the true essence: feeling, image, and word. Everywhere we see only something that is hidden; but that hidden thing we see and sense. For what is seen and surmised we set the word, the living word, as a sign. There lies the dignity of the word. It does not itself reveal, but it shows revelation, consolidates it, and helps to disseminate it. . . . Without this gift of immediate revelation and interpretation the use of speech would never have arisen among men. *With* this gift the whole human species invented speech all together, at the very beginning. . . . Each race fashioned a tongue of its own; none understands the other, but all speak—all speak, because all, in like though not identical degree, received with reason the gift of understanding and recognizing the inward from the outward, the hidden from the revealed, the invisible from the visible.[25]

If the philosophy of religion and the philosophy of language thus tend toward a point of intersection at which language and religion unite to form as it were a single medium, that of spiritual "meaning," it creates a new problem for the philosophy of symbolic forms. This philosophy cannot, of course, strive to dissolve the specific difference of language and religion in any original unity, whether this unity be defined as subjective or objective, as a unity of the divine source of things, of reason, or of the human spirit. For its inquiry is directed not toward a common origin, but toward a common *structure*. It does not seek a common unity of foundation for both language and religion but asks whether in these two absolutely independent and unique forms a unity of function may not be demonstrable. If there is such a unity, it can be sought only in a basic trend of symbolic expression, in an inner rule according to which it develops and unfolds. In our investigation of language we have endeavored to show how the word and the linguistic sound, before realizing their purely symbolic function, pass through a number of intermediary stages in which they hover as it were between the world of "things" and the world of "significations." Here the sound can "designate" the content at which it aims only by assimilating itself to it in some way, by entering into a relation of im-

25. Friedrich H. Jacobi, *Über eine Weissagung Lichtenberg's* (1801), in *Werke* (6 vols. Leipzig, G. Fleischer, 1812–25), *3*, 209 ff.

mediate similarity or mediated correspondence with it. The sign must in some way fuse with the world of things, must become similar to this world, if it is to function as its expression. In its initial form religious expression is also characterized by this immediate proximity to sensuous existence. It could not come into being and endure if it did not thus cling with all its strength to the sensuous, material world. True, there is no manifestation of the religious spirit, however primitive, in which we cannot, as in language, discern a tendency toward the separation, the "crisis," that will take place in it. For even in the most elementary forms of religion a distinction is always made between the worlds of the sacred and the profane. But this division between the two worlds does not exclude a perpetual transition between them, an enduring interaction and mutual assimilation. On the contrary, the sacred reveals its power precisely by its immediate sensuous domination of every single physical thing and physical event—which it is always prepared to seize upon as an instrument for its own purpose. Thus every thing, however particular, accidental, and sensuous, possesses at the same time a magical-religious "significance"; indeed, this very particularity and accidental character becomes the distinguishing mark by which a thing or event is withdrawn from the sphere of the commonplace and transferred to that of the sacred. The technique of magic and sacrifice attempts to draw certain fixed lines through this maze of "accidents," attempts to introduce a definite articulation and a kind of systematic order into them. In observing the flights of birds the augur divides the heavens as a whole into different regions, which he designates in advance as sacred zones, each inhabited and governed by a god. But even outside of such fixed schemata, which show a first impulse toward universality, every particular, however isolated, can at any moment take on the function of an omen. Whatever is and happens belongs to a magical-religious complex, the complex of signification and augury. Thus all sensuous reality, even in its sensuous immediacy, is also "sign" and "wonder," for at this level of thinking the two belong necessarily together and are only different expressions of one and the same relationship. The particular becomes a sign and a wonder as soon as it is regarded not in its mere spatial-temporal existence but as an expression, a manifestation, of a demonic or divine power. Here the sign as a fundamental religious form relates everything to itself and transforms everything into itself—but at the same time the sign itself enters into the whole of sensuous-concrete existence and fuses intimately with it.

Thus the development of language is determined by its tendency to cling to the sensuous and yet strive beyond it, to surpass the narrow limits of the mere mimetic sign. And religion discloses the same characteristic opposition. Here again the transition is not immediate; between the two extremes there lies a kind of intermediary attitude. In religion the sensuous and the spiritual by no means coincide, but nevertheless they point continuously to one another. They stand to one another in a relationship of analogy, by which they are both interrelated and separate. In religious thinking this relation occurs wherever a sharp line divides the world of the sensuous and the suprasensory, the spiritual and the corporeal—but where on the other hand the two worlds undergo their concrete religious formation by reflecting each other. Hence "analogy" always bears the typical features of "allegory": for no religious understanding of reality flows from itself; in it the reality must be related to something else, through which its meaning becomes known. This progressive process of allegoresis is illustrated above all in medieval thought. Here the objective world loses its immediate material significance to the degree in which its is subordinated to a specifically religious interpretation. Its physical content remains only cloak and mask, behind which its spiritual meaning is hidden. It is this meaning which must be interpreted in the fourfold form of exegesis, which the medieval sources differentiate as historical, allegorical, tropological, and analogical. While in the first an event is apprehended in its purely empirical actuality, it is the three others which disclose its true meaning, its ethical-metaphysical significance. Dante still preserved this medieval conception unchanged and his poetics is no less rooted in it than his theology.[26] This form of allegoresis provides a new and characteristic perspective, a

26. Dante, *Convivio,* second treatise, ch. 1: Le scritture si possono intendere e debbonsi sponere massimamente per quattro sensi. L'uno si chiama litterale, e questo è quello che non si distende più oltre che la lettera propia. . . L'altro si chiama allegorico, è questo che si nasconde sotto il manto di queste favole, ed è una verità ascosa sotto bella menzogna. . . Il terzo senso si chiama morale; e questo è quello che li lettori deono intentamente andare appostando per le scritture a utilità di loro e di loro discenti: siccome appostare si può nel Vangelio, quando Cristo saliò lo monte per trasfigurarsi, che delli dodici Apostoli, ne menò seco li tre; in che moralmente si può intendere, che alle secretissime cose noi dovemo avere poca compagnia. Lo quarto senso si chiama anagogico, cioè sovra senso: e quest' è, quando spiritualmente si spone una scrittura, la quale, ancora nel senso litterale, Eziandio per le cose significate, significa delle superne cose dell' eternale gloria; siccome veder si può in quel canto del Profeta, che dice, che nell' uscita del popolo d'Israele d'Egitto, la Giudea è fatta santa e libera. Che avvegna essere vero, secondo la lettera, sie manifesto, non meno è vero quello che spiritualmente s'intende, cioè che nell' uscita dell'anima del peccato, essa si è fatta santa e libera in sua potestade. Eng. trans. by W. W. Jackson, *Dante's Convivio* (Oxford, 1909).

new relation of distance and proximity to reality. The religious spirit can now immerse itself in reality, in the particular and the given, without remaining confined in it, for what it perceives in reality is never its immediacy but the transcendent meaning which finds its mediated representation in this reality. Here the tension between the world to which the sign itself belongs and what is expressed through it has attained an entirely new breadth and intensity, and thus a new and intensified *consciousness* of the sign is also achieved. At the first stage the sign and what it designates belongs as it were to the same plane: one sensuous "thing," one empirical event, points to another and serves as its symptom and token. Here, however, no such direct relation prevails, but only a relation mediated by reflection. The form of tropological thinking transforms all physical reality into a mere trope, a metaphor, but the interpretation of this metaphor requires a special art of religious hermeneutics, which medieval thought seeks to reduce to set rules.

Yet such rules can be drawn up and applied only if there is *one* point at which the world of spiritual, transcendent meaning and that of empirical-temporal reality come into contact, despite their inner divergence and antagonism—and if at this point they directly permeate each other. All allegorical-tropological interpretation relates to the basic problem of redemption, and thus to the historical reality of the redeemer as its fixed center. All temporal change, all natural events and human action, obtain their light from this center; they become an ordered, meaningful cosmos by appearing as necessary links in the religious plan of salvation by taking a significant place in it. And from this one spiritual center the circle of interpretation gradually broadens. The supreme, the "anagogical," sense of a text or event is disclosed when a reference can be found in it to the transcendent or to its immediate historical manifestation, the Church.[27] Here even the most far-reaching spiritualization of natural being is bound up with a contrary motif, the presupposition that the Logos itself descended into the sensuous world and there was incarnated in temporal uniqueness. But to this form of allegory medieval mysticism opposed a new

27. "Allegoria est, quando aliud sonat in littera et aliud in spiritu, ut quando per unum factum aliud intelligitur; quod si illud sit visibile, est simplex ἀλλήγορια, si invisibile et caeleste, tunc dicitur ἀναγωγή, ut cum *Christi praesentia vel Ecclesiae sacramenta* verbis vel mysticis rebus designatur. Anagoge dicitur . . . sensus, qui a visibilibus ad invisibilia ducit . . . ad superiora sive ecclesiam . . . et de praemio futuro et de futura vita disputans." Guilelmus Durandus, *Rationale divinorum officiorum* (1286), proem, fol. 2a, quoted in Sauer, *Symbolik des Kirchengebäudes*, p. 52.

interpretation of the fundamental symbols of Christian doctrine. It dissolved the temporal uniqueness in eternity, divesting the religious process of all mere historical content. The process of redemption is restored to the depths of the I, to the abyss of the soul, where it is enacted free from all outside mediation in an immediate correlation of I and God, God and I.[28] And here it becomes evident that the meaning of all basic religious concepts depends on the character and direction of the symbolism that lives in them; for the new mystical orientation of this symbolism now gives these concepts a new meaning and, as it were, a new mood and coloration. All sensuous things are and remain signs and metaphors—but the sign no longer has a "wonder" or miracle about it if the character of the wonder is seen in its particularity as an individual revelation of the transcendent. True revelation no longer occurs in any particular but only in the whole: the world as a whole and the entirety of the human soul.[29]

This brings us to a fundamental view the full development of which leads beyond the limits of the religious sphere. It is only in the history of modern philosophical idealism that the new view of the "symbol" that emerges in mysticism achieves its full intellectual form. Leibniz starts expressly from Eckhart's saying that all individual being is a "footstep of God": "In our selfhood," he writes in his essay *Von der wahren Theologia mystica*, "there is an infinitude, a footprint, a likeness of God's omniscience and omnipotence." [30] And thence arises his view of a world "harmony" which rests not on any manner of causal influence, not on any interaction of individuals, but on their original reciprocal "correspondence." Each monad is entirely independent and self-contained; but precisely in this particularity and independence it is the living "mirror of the universe" which it expresses, each monad according to its own perspective.

28. Cf. above, p. 249.

29. See Albert Görland, *Religionsphilosophie als Wissenschaft aus dem Systemgeiste des kritischen Idealismus* (Berlin and Leipzig, W. de Gruyter, 1922), pp. 263 ff.: For this religion . . . everything becomes a "footstep of God" toward the I, a footstep of the I toward God. And thus the "world" is nothing other than the path on which "proximity to God" is gained. . . . The religious word "world" signifies this relation. And if the relation of I and God is eternity, the relation of I and the world is temporality; world, as the dead middle point between God and I, signifies the finding of eternity in temporality, of temporality in eternity. . . . All religion—and in the clearest form . . . the German mysticism of an Eckhart—bears witness that the striving for a total sanctification of the world rises from the profoundest source of religious experience.

30. Leibniz, *Von der wahren theologia mystica*, in *Deutsche Schriften*, ed. Gottschalk E. Guhrauer (Berlin, 1838), *1*, 411.

Here arises a kind of symbolism which does not exclude, but rather includes, the idea of the thoroughgoing and unbroken lawfulness of all being and all change, which indeed is essentially based on this idea. The sign has definitively cast off all character of the particular and accidental; it has become the pure expression of a universal order. In the system of universal harmony there are no more "miracles." Rather, the harmony itself is the enduring, universal miracle which negates and thereby absorbs all others in itself.[31] The spirit no longer manifests itself by making a particular copy or analogue of itself in the sensuous world; it is rather in the totality of the sensuous world that the spiritual is revealed. "Toute la nature," writes Leibniz to Bossuet, "est pleine de miracles, mais de miracles de raison."[32] Thus a new and original synthesis is effected between the "symbolic" and the "rational." The meaning of the world opens up to us only when we rise to a standpoint from which we view all being and change as rational and symbolic at once, and even Leibniz's logic—through his idea of a "universal characteristic"—is intimately bound up with his view of symbolism.

Among the modern philosophers of religion it is Schleiermacher who has developed and systematized this fundamental view. His *Reden über Religion* takes up the problem just as it is formulated by Leibniz. And it is precisely this ideal and historical relationship that raises Schleiermacher's religion of the "universe" above the level of a mere naturalistic "pantheism." According to Schleiermacher religion consists in taking all particulars as part of the whole, everything limited as a representation of the infinite. But space and mass do not constitute the world and are therefore not the substance of religion. To seek infinity in them is to think like a child. "What actually speaks to the religious sense in the outward world is not its masses but its laws." And it is precisely in these laws that the true and authentic, the properly religious, meaning of the miracle lies.

> What is then a miracle? Tell me in what language it means anything other than a sign, a token? Hence all these terms signify nothing other than the immediate relation of a phenomenon to the infinite, to the universe. But does this preclude an equally immediate relation to the finite and to nature? Miracle is only the religious name for event; every

31. Leibniz, *Réponses aux réflexions de Bayle,* in *Die Philosophischen Schriften,* ed. C. J. Gerhardt (Berlin, 1880), *4,* 557: "Le merveilleux universel fait cesser et absorbe, pour ainsi dire, le merveilleux particulier, parce qu'il en rend raison."

32. *Oeuvres* (7 vols. Paris, Fouchard de Careil, 1861–75), *1,* 277.

event, even the most natural, provided the religious view of it can be the dominant one, is a miracle.[33]

Here we stand at the opposite pole from the original view in which the symbolic signified something objectively real, the immediate work of God, a mystery.[34] For the religious significance of an event depends no longer on its content but solely on its form: what gives it its character as a symbol is not what it is and whence it immediately comes but the spiritual aspect in which it is seen, the relation to the universe which it obtains in religious feeling and thought. The movement of the religious spirit which constitutes its form, not as a static figure but as a character-istic mode of configuration, consists in a living oscillation between those two fundamental views. Here we find that correlation of meaning and im-age and also that conflict between them which are both deeply rooted in the essence of symbolic expression. On the one hand, the very lowest, most primitive mythical configuration proves to be a vehicle of meaning, for already it stands in the sign of that primordial division which raises the world of the sacred from the world of the profane and delimits the one from the other. But on the other hand, even the highest religious truth remains attached to sensuous existence, to the world of images as well as things. It must continuously immerse and submerge itself in this existence which its intelligible purpose strives to cast off and reject—because only in this existence does religious truth possess its expressive form and hence its concrete reality and efficacy. Speaking of concepts, of the world of theo-retical cognition, Plato said that here the division of the one into the many and the return of the many to the one has neither beginning nor end but always was and is and will be as an "immortal and never-aging element" of our thought and discourse. And similarly, the involvement and opposition of meaning and image are among the essential conditions of religion. If this involvement and opposition were ever replaced by a pure and perfect equilibrium, the inner tension of religion, on which rests its significance as a symbolic form, would be negated. The striving for such an equilibrium points therefore to another sphere. Only when we turn from the mythical image world and the world of religious meaning to the sphere of art and artistic expression does the opposition which domi-

33. Friedrich E. D. Schleiermacher, *Über die Religion. Reden an die Gebildeten unter ihren Verächtern* (1799), ed. Rudolf Otto (Göttingen, 1899), pp. 33, 47, 66. Eng. trans. by John Oman, *On Religion. Speeches to Its Cultural Despisers* (London, 1893).

34. See above, p. 248.

nates the development of the religious consciousness appear to be in a sense appeased, if not negated. For it is characteristic of the aesthetic trend that here the image is recognized purely *as such,* that to fulfill its function it need give up nothing of itself and its content. In the image myth sees a fragment of substantial reality, a part of the material world itself, endowed with equal or higher powers than this world. From this first magical view religion strives toward a progressively purer spiritualization. And yet, again and again, it is carried back to a point at which the question of its truth and meaning content shifts into the question of the reality of its objects, at which it faces the problem of "existence" in all its harshness. It is only the aesthetic consciousness that leaves this problem truly behind it. Since from the outset it gives itself to pure "contemplation," developing the form of vision in contrast to all forms of action, the images fashioned in this frame of consciousness gain for the first time a truly immanent significance. They confess themselves to be illusion as opposed to the empirical reality of things; but this illusion has its own truth because it possesses its own law. In the return to this law there arises a new freedom of consciousness: the image no longer reacts upon the spirit as an independent material thing but becomes for the spirit a pure expression of its own creative power.

General Index

Action, mythical and physical, 38, 39, 49, 53, 105, 184, 185, 199–208, 211–214, 217, 219, 220, 222, 225–228, 238, 261
Alchemy, 66, 67
Algonquins, 58 n., 76 and n., 78 n., 158
Allegoresis, 38, 256
Allegorical interpretation of myths, 2–4, 38, 39
Almacabala, 144
Anatomy, magical, 92
Ancestor cult, 126, 127, 171, 176
Animism, 16, 36, 43, 58, 78, 155, 159, 172, 192
Asclepias, priests of, 58
Asha, 115, 117, 121, 139, 244
Assyria (Assyrian), 113, 145
Astrology, 66, 89, 90, 93, 97, 144
Astronomy, 138, 139, 144
Atharvaveda, 115 and n.
Atman, 173, 245
Australian aborigines, 180, 181; Baiame, 207
Avesta, 115–117, 121, 122, 243, 244, 245 n.
Aztecs, 139, 231

Baalin, 188
Babylonia (Babylonians), 18, 93, 96, 113, 116, 138, 139, 145, 188, 196
Baptism, 248
Bataks, 56, 161 n., 168, 172
Bororos, 65
Brahmin, 54, 55, 91, 122, 229
Buddhism, 123, 224, 225, 245–247; see also Buddha
Bushmen, 179

"Calendar myths," 18
Causal concepts, 14, 37, 43–59, 61, 63, 66, 69, 80, 178–181, 183, 192, 204, 212, 215, 258
Celts, old, 168
Cherokees, 147
Chinese, 87, 114, 124–127, 147, 162, 176

Chinvat, Bridge of, 167
Christ, 102
Christian (Christianity), 102, 145, 147, 148, 191, 228, 229, 231, 247–250, 252, 253, 257, 258
Christian-Germanic, 91
Christmas, 110
"Copernican revolution," 29
Cora Indians, 46, 96, 98 n.
Creation, 54, 96, 97, 100, 113, 116, 117, 120, 170, 206–208, 210, 211, 226
Cross, 102, 147
Cult, 37, 39, 81, 109, 161, 166, 190, 191, 199, 201, 204, 207, 213, 219–221, 228–230, 236

Death, 37, 47, 49, 98, 109, 127, 136, 159–161, 161 nn., 163 and n., 164, 166, 167, 209
Demons (Demonic), 113, 168, 169, 172, 173, 198, 200–202, 213, 217, 222, 236, 238, 242, 244, 255
Dogma, 249

Easter, 110
Edda, 54 n.
Egypt (Egyptian), 41, 56, 96, 114, 127, 128, 160, 162, 163, 166, 167, 191, 195, 207, 209, 210, 217 n.
Eleatic school, 2
Etruscans, 87 n.
Eucharist, 248
Euclidean geometry, 83, 84; space, 83
Euhemeristic interpretation of myths, 4
Ewes, 57

Fates, 132
Finns, 168
Flamines, 203
"Folk ideas." See Bastian
Four, the sacred number, 147
Furies, 134

Geography, mythical, 92, 93
Germanic, 99, 110, 116, 145, 169, 191, 195

Index of Proper Names

266